Dreams
That Blister
Sleep

A Nurse in Vietnam
by Sharon Grant Wildwind

photographs by Sharon Grant Wildwind

Memoirs of a Nurse in Vietnam.

River Books and The Books Collective acknowledge the ongoing support of the Canada Council for the Arts and the Alberta Foundation for the Arts for our publishing program. We also acknowledge the support of the City of Edmonton and the Edmonton Arts Council. We would also like to thank Lindsey Kydd at Convention Graphics.

Editors for Press: Candas J. Dorsey, Larry Pratt

Cover design by Gerry Dotto

Inside layout and design by Dianne J. Cooper at The Books Collective in Times New Roman, I Times Italic, Arial Black, Arial, CS Century Schoolbook and Wingdings in Mac OS, Quark X-Press 4.03.

Printed at Convention Graphics

Published in Canada
by River Books, a member of The Books Collective,
214-21 10405 Jasper Avenue,
Edmonton, Alberta, T5J 3S2.
Telephone (780) 448 0590

Canadian Cataloguing in Publishing Data

Wildwind, Sharon Grant.
Dreams that blister sleep

ISBN 1-895836-70-0

1.Wildwind, Sharon Grant. 2. Vietnamese Conflict, 1961-1975--Women--United States 3. Vietnamese Conflict, 1961-1975--Medical care. 4. Nurses-Vietnam--Biography. 5.Nurses--United States--Biography. 6. Vietnamese conflict, 1961-1975--Personal narratives, American. 1. Title.

DS559.S.W515 1999   959.704'37'092 C99-911171-X

Dreams that Blister Sleep

You try to repress them because you know
In scraps of sleep you want another chance.
You are probably going to come back.

You strip-searched the mama-sans for the man.
You didn't know about sisterhood then. Now
you try to repress them because you know.

You piece shards of friendship to keep Barry
alive. You saw him his last day. You owe him.
You are probably going to come back.

Sudden gunfire in a play. You can't stop
crying. The tears break you ten years late.
You try to repress them because you know.

You take your man's abuse for years. He leaves.
Did Viet Nam cripple you or him?
You are probably going to come back.

Dreaming the guts out of faded pictures.
scratchy tapes, a diary. Devouring them.
You try to repress them because you know.
you are probably going to come back.

Sharon Grant Wildwind

Prologue

My brother took this picture in the New Orleans airport.

That was me in the middle, in the summer green uniform with the forage cap and vinyl folder on my lap. I hardly know the other people in the picture.

My father wore a wide tie, twenty years out of date.

My mother had white-rimmed glasses and a scarf tied around her neck. She sat with her right arm across her chest, protecting herself.

My aunt wasn't looking at he camera. She never did.

My uncle, her husband, looked straight at the camera. He understood machines.

My grandmother protected her purse firmly on her lap. When this picture was taken she was in her eighties. For ten years she had said, "This may be the last time we see each other." Maybe this time she was right. She sent her two sons off to World War II and had lived to see both of them home safely.She and I found that reassuring.

I had visited my family for three weeks, much longer than we could handle.

When my flight was called, we hugged.

I thought of them going home:stopping for lunch on the New Orleans side of the causeway, then the drive home and my aunt and uncle taking my grandmother home to New Iberia.

A tremendous weight lifted.
I was free. I was on my own. I was off to war.

Dedicated

to

Barry H.

"Rest in Peace"

1970 MAY 1970

Thursday, 14 May 1970, California. Today I ride a bus from San Francisco northeast to Travis Air Force Base and watch the San Francisco Bay bridge, fast traffic, orange trees, homes built on the side of steep hills roll past the bus window. I worry that today, now, while I'm here, there will be a huge earthquake and I'll be prevented from going to Viet Nam because I'm killed as California falls into the ocean.

We arrive at Travis Air Force base and the bus stops in front of a large terminal on the runway. I half-carry, half drag my duffel-bag though the door. This is it! Someone will look at my orders and put me on the first plane going west because I am a nurse and I have important work to do. Only it isn't like that at all. The clerks at the desk don't seem to care when or if I leave. They tell me to check in at the Transient Officers' Quarters and come back to check in a couple of times a day. Do they have any idea when I might get a flight? A shrug of the shoulders and, "What's your hurry, lady?"is the only response I get. What's my hurry? Don't they realize I have important work to begin? I am so excited to be on my way that I don't know how I can stand the waiting, especially with the uncertainty of not knowing how long that wait will be.

I find Sue in the Transient Officers Quarters. We decide as long as we have to wait, we might as well enjoy ourselves. As we go in search of the Base Exchange to do a little shopping, we cross a grassy area. An Air Policeman on the other side of the road yells, "Stop." We look around and see no one else but decide he can't be talking to us. We start walking again. He pulls his side arm and yells, "I said to stop. Lie down on the ground. Now." Sue and I look at each other and lie down against the concrete side walk. "What is going on here?" I ask Sue. The policeman yells, "No talking." I am really frightened. Kent State happened only a few weeks before. When I saw the newscasts I began to cry because they were shooting women my own age. Now I am lying on ground, under the gun. I can't imagine what horrible transgression we have committed. It is a green and peaceful lawn, without "Restricted" signs. I turn my head a little until I see the road in front of me. In a moment two men come out carrying a heavy canvas bag: probably a payroll or a large amount of cash. They cross the street beside the policeman who is holding the gun on us and enter the back door of a building. The policeman holsters his gun, turns and walks after them.

That's it. No "Sorry." No "You can get up now." He just leaves us there. Sue and I look at each other and laugh. "Think we can get up now?" she asks. "I think so." We both laugh nervously and brush ourselves off. He did that to us because he could. If we'd any sense, we would go straight away to the Air Police Detachment and report him. But we don't. We feel like we did something wrong, even if it was just being in the wrong place at the wrong time. It doesn't seem as if we have any right to complain.

We go to dinner at the Officers' Club and play billiards afterwards with some men who are also waiting for planes to Viet Nam. Neither Sue nor I talk about what happened to us this afternoon. We don't think the men are interested in it.

Friday, May 15, 1970. Travis Air Force Base, California. Waiting is so hard. The terminal building is a large grey warehouse of corrugated iron; combat boots make hollow sounds on the concrete floor. Inside men in fatigues or summer uniforms wait everywhere, sleep on grey wooden benches, read paperback books with the cover folded back, or wander and smoke cigarettes. I've been down here three times only to be told I'm not yet manifested on a plane.

Sue and I are afraid. We have heard stories that the Viet Cong rape women prisoners, that they never take women prisoners alive, that in Tet of '68 nurses were issued a suicide capsule. Since no U.S. servicewoman has ever been captured, our imaginations, fed by boredom and anxiety, are overworked. We are afraid of being captured, raped, tortured. We are afraid of our plane crashing and never getting there. Most of all, we are afraid of somehow not measuring up.

A lot of the Army is like this, proving you are as tough or tougher than the guys. It is the kind of thing that worried us about going to basic. We had seen movies and heard stories about being awakened at 0430 and having to run 5 miles and do physical calisthenics for any infractions of rules. In the end it wasn't like that at all. It was "Yes, Ma'am" and "No, Ma'am" from the enlisted men and the sergeants. Sometimes we were a little disappointed, as if they didn't think we could pass the rigorous tests, so they never gave them to us. We wanted to be tested. We still want to be tested.

After supper, we take a walk along the fence that protects the airstrip. The sun is going down. A med-evac plane has just landed and casualties are being loaded from the plane onto a bus. We stand with our fingers interlocked with the mesh fence, our faces pressed up against the metal links. I wonder where the casualties have been, who they are, if I know the nurses are who cared for them. I am so tired of waiting, so keyed up that I want to jump the fence and do something, adjust I.V.s, check dressings, take vital signs, anything to be a part of what is happening. I look at Sue's face and know she feels the same way. We have been preparing for this for a long time. We want to be a part of this war.

About 9 p.m. I make one more visit to the manifest desk. The rather bored

Specialist verifies my name and serial number on a clipboard. "Two a.m. Saturday morning." My mouth goes dry. I'm really going to Viet Nam! I go back to the Officers' Quarters and say goodbye to Sue. I wish we could travel together, but she still isn't manifested on a plane. We know we will probably never see each other again.

I try to sleep, but am too excited. Finally I get up, dress and fuel myself with several cans of Coke. I call a military taxi to take me and my duffel bag over to the terminal about midnight. My duffel bag contains everything I can cram into one long green cloth tube; what's in there has to last me a year. Six sets of fatigues, two pairs of combat boots, a couple of summer dresses, underclothes, tennis shoes, a robe, extra shampoo and toothpaste, my diary, a small camera, a tape recorder, my address book and some stationery. The bag has my name stenciled on the side and it's locked with a padlock. I wear the key around my neck beside my dog tags.

The night is dark and warm. A hot breeze blows across the runways and large orange lights illuminate the terminal. I hear a ghetto blaster from the barracks down the road from the terminal; the building is just too far away to make out the song. Inside the terminal, I'm the only woman in the building except for a black specialist checking names at the embarkation desk and a woman in a Red Cross uniform on the far side of the terminal who's serving coffee, juice and cookies.

When it comes down to this hot California night, when my duffel bag disappears along the sterile aluminum chute, when I have a ticket in my hand and my name on a manifest list, I am terrified. I should be working in a hospital in New Orleans or Atlanta, surrounded by civilians and peace. Why have I gotten myself into this twilight zone of barn-like terminals, blaring intercoms, people with drawn and scared faces? I don't belong here.

Yes, I do. When I saw those men carried off the plane yesterday, I knew I had to be here, to do what I am about to do. I can't let them go to this war alone. It wouldn't be honourable. When I was in high school I read *Starship Trooper*s by Robert Heinlein. In that world people who had done a tour of voluntary service could vote and people who hadn't, couldn't. I think that's the way it should be. We have to do something to earn the right to be citizens.

It's more than that, a lot more personal. Viet Nam has been so much with me for the past five years. I saw the fear of this war on the faces of the boys in university every time an exam paper was handed back, felt it on the Hallowe'en night when I was at a party and Johnson announced the mining of Haiphong harbour. This war had run through the past decade of our lives. My brother Ward can be drafted. I don't want him to be here in this terminal. I can't let those boys from university, from that Hallowe'en party do this alone. And yet, it is only discipline that brings me to the ramp of the plane where a black sergeant looks over his clipboard.

"Name, rank and serial number?"

"Grant, Sharon M., First Lieutenant." I have memorized my serial number so I can rattle it off in short bursts: three numbers, two numbers, four numbers. He salutes and I board the plane.

Sunday, May 17, 1970. Over the Pacific. Either someone with the airline has a perverse sense of humour or it is an incredible coincidence that *M*A*S*H* is the movie shown on my flight to Viet Nam. I lose interest when the football sequence starts, remove my earphones and watch the water, grey and smooth, pass beneath the plane. I nap. The stewardess, the only other woman I've seen for hours, serves a meal. I've lost track of what meal I am eating. The stewardess clears away remains of sliced beef, cottage fries and glazed carrots. I pull my black leather purse from under the seat and walk the gauntlet of male eyes to the front of the plane. A tall man with a wide, country face comes out of the bathroom marked "Women." Why not? There are certainly more men than women on the plane. I can afford to share.

Inside the toilet, I pull down my panty hose and massage my stomach and thighs, envying the men who travel in trousers. My hair is long and thin, constantly escaping from the bobby pins meant to hold it in a tight roll at the back of my head. I take my hair down and, leaning over, brush it from the underside until it stands out in this large auburn halo around my head. I've just done a colour job before leaving home so that even the roots are auburn and the tips dry from the added colour. I wondered where, if anywhere, I can get a haircut in Viet Nam. My uniform is wrinkled and travel-stained, one of the silver bars on my shoulder smudged. I polish it with a piece of toilet paper, then for good measure, polish the other bar, my caduceus, my U.S. pin and the black plastic name tab with white letters saying "Grant" over my right breast. Then I stand with my hand on the door, take a deep breath, and prepare to run the gauntlet of stares back to my seat.

Even though I've been in a mostly male environment for almost nine months, this plane-load of all men is intimidating. Most of them ignore me. I have a double seat to myself, as if the men want to put some space between me and them. Many of them are sleeping, some are drunk. The ones that are awake stare at me all the way up the aisle to the washroom and back again.

We land in Hawaii at 0600. The airport has just been renovated and none of the concessions are open. I've come all the way to Hawaii and can't even buy a postcard. From Hawaii we fly to Wake Island, Guam, Okinawa. I look at these tiny, tropical islands—Wake is little more than a runway built into a coral atoll—and think how many American lives have been lost here. I wonder when we are going to stop spending our lives in the Pacific?

After twenty-two hours the plane descends into Bien Hoa Air Base. In the monotone usually reserved to wish visitors a pleasant stay, the stewardess announces our arrival. As soon as the plane stops, a sergeant with a clipboard comes on board. In the same monotone the stewardess used he tells us to leave the plane quickly, keep low and run for the terminal. It looks really peaceful outside and I think, "Right, he just wants to get us to think in the terms of reference about being in a war zone." Still there could be something out there. . . .

"Couriers, women and senior officers disembark first," he announces over the plane's P.A. system.

I grab my purse and run down the steps between two colonels, stopping only when I am inside the building. The heat hits me like a wall. The terminal is hot and dust blows across the concrete floor from the backwash of the planes and from large fans in the terminal. A thin black man in fatigues with a ghetto blaster glued to his left ear jive-walks past me. He lets out a coarse whistle and says, "All right, mama," moving his hips in time with the music.

I put my purse strap over my shoulder and walk with eyes straight ahead as I've been taught at Ft. Sam Houston. I am an officer and a gentleman by an Act of Congress and I mean to act like one. Besides, I know my short, overweight body is nothing to whistle at.

Two small men in camouflage fatigues, iron helmets and field packs pass me, speaking in a fast, musical language, gesturing with their hands. They look like obscene Barbie dolls. I stare at the A.R.V.N. (Army of the Republic of Viet Nam) soldiers until they round a concrete post and disappear.

My duffel bag has gone missing. No one seems particularly concerned. The airman at the desk shrugs his shoulders and says it will probably show up eventually. He directs me to a grey bus waiting in the hot afternoon sun. I am the only woman on the bus. Some of the men throw their duffel bags into a corner, curl up on the seats and go to sleep. Others, like me, stare out one window, then the other. I take in the coils of barbed wire around each compound, the hot smell of diesel fuel, the green vehicles on the streets, and think, "So this is Viet Nam."

I am taken with the twenty men to a briefing room in a Quonset hut. Grey benches fill the cool, blue room. On the front wall a map of Viet Nam, an orange, green and yellow curve, which reaches like an arthritic finger along the side of Indochina. A staff sergeant in pressed khakis and polished boots stands in front of the group.

"Good afternoon, gentlemen. I am Sergeant Gonzalez and for the next hour I will be your principal instructor for your in-country briefing."

He hands out little booklets with a colour map like the one behind him on the cover. He reminds us that we are guests of the Viet Namese and must not criticize unfamiliar customs. We are not to give the Viet Namese American money or Military Payment Certificates, not to eat any local food or drink the water, not to smoke at night because of snipers. He reminds everyone to take their malaria pills. I can tell which of the men are on their second tour of Nam: they sleep through the lecture. Then the sergeant asks me to leave and several of the men titter. I walk out, knowing he is going to discuss B-girls and the clap.

It is almost 6 p.m. and the sun is going down into a brilliant salmon colour, covered by grey clouds. It has rained while I was in the briefing and there are large puddles in the parking lot of the in-processing station. A driver takes me to a warehouse, where I am issued a bag containing a flak jacket and helmet. "When do I put these on?" I ask the clerk. He laughs. "Never, if you can help it. Most nurses put them under their bunk and forget about them." He makes it sound like we nurses aren't real soldiers.

We are taken to a mess for supper and afterwards a Spec-4, who says he's from Jersey and has 62 days left in-country, takes me around to the depot to look for my lost duffel bag. On the way there, he says, "Don't worry, ma'am. If we can't find it, we'll lend you some of our fatigues." I am absolutely humiliated at the idea. I think, I'm 4'11", overweight and have really tiny feet. If they try to fit me with any of their fatigues, they either won't button over my stomach or they will be miles too big and I'll have to roll them up. I will look like a cartoon character and I want to look so sharp and professional. But I realize the man is only trying to be kind. Fortunately, my duffel bag sits almost alone in a corner of the depot, a rather small green lump, flanked by several other small and forgotten pieces of luggage.

At the entrance to the Women's Quarters there is an armed sentry. He salutes me and I return the salute, wondering: is he there to keep me in or the men out? Beside the sentry is a wooden sign, black and red letters painted on white board. It gives the safety rules:

NO VISITORS ALLOWED.
DON'T LEAVE THE COMPOUND WITHOUT AN ESCORT.
BE READY WHEN THE BUS COMES TO PICK YOU UP.
IN CASE OF ATTACK, GO TO THE NEAREST BUNKER.

The quarters are a wooden building: single storey, unpainted, dirty, smelling of hot, unwashed bodies. There is a bunker next door and the specialist from New Jersey says with a parting wave, "If anything happens tonight, Ma'am, go to the bunker." I want to ask him how I am supposed to know what "anything" is, but he reverses the jeep and shoots away, his tires spraying gravel.

I am the only person here tonight and have the whole place to myself. There is a lounge area with unfinished plywood walls and a black-and-white television with aluminum foil crimped around the antennae. Nothing is being broadcast. My room is eight feet by six feet, with one screened window, but no door, furnished with a cot and a straight-back chair. I console myself with the thought I've been in worse Girl Scout camps. I unlock my duffel bag and take out the robe and toilet case I've packed on the top so I can get at it first. Just like packing for camp, I think, and that strikes me as a pretty silly idea.

The latrine is connected to the hooch by a plank sidewalk, listing at a crazy angle into sticky, black mud. I turn on the water to wash my face. One of the faucets moves when I touch it. I scream and stare at the lime green frog I've mistaken for a faucet in the dim light. I quickly run my hand under cold water, hoping the frog isn't poisonous. The shower floor is slick. One of the nurses at Ft. Riley warned me to bring flip-flops, so at least my feet are out of the slime. I shower, wash my hair and brush my teeth. My mouth keeps the first aftertaste of metallic, treated water.

I hang my uniform jacket carefully on the chair, knowing a night's airing won't remove the body odour under the arms. I wonder when I can stop wearing the class A uniform and change into fatigues. I was taught alway to travel in the class A, so I'd better wait until someone tells me to change clothes. The sagging mattress and heavy pillow smell like hundreds of people have slept there before me. The night is hot and there is no breeze through the screened window. A flare goes off outside—a red dot, then a white light as it falls to the ground. I lay very still, wondering if the flare signals the "anything" the driver mentioned. Nothing happens.

So this is it, I am really, finally here. I think of the hospitals all over the country, of the nurses on night duty, of the wards that should be, by this time of night, quieting as the patients settle for the night. The last thing I hear before I sleep is an automatic rifle, far away.

A man knocks on the door frame. His voice in the darkness says the bus for the airport leaves in ten minutes. I lie uncovered, sweating in the heat, as he stares at my naked body. After he leaves, I look at my watch. 4 a.m. I dress in the green summer uniform and the jacket sticks to my body. My skin and hair are sticky with sweat and I roll the damp hair ends into the roll at the back of my neck.

The half dozen men on the bus are also drugged to silence by fatigue and heat. The glass in the grey school bus windows has been replaced by wire to keep out flying objects. An armed guard, naked from the waist up except for a flak jacket, boards the bus. I wonder what his name is and how long he has been in country. After all, my life might depend on this stranger.

As the bus moves through Long Bien, we encounter a barricade of boxes and tins that blocks the street. The shacks of scrap lumber and cardboard press dangerously close to the bus. The guard yells for us to lie on the floor. On someone's command, I lie on my stomach for the second time in less than a week, press my cheek into the grey metal floor and focus my eyes on a line of rivets. I imagine someone asking me what going to Viet Nam was like and replying "Well, I lay on the floor a lot." I am seized with a desire to giggle.

Maybe this is just harassment. Maybe the barricade is booby-trapped to explode when moved. Maybe a child waits in the shadows to roll a grenade under the bus. I wait for the sound of the grenade, like a stone rolling on concrete, but hear only my own heartbeat loud in my ears. I feel as if I am about to vomit.

The bus door creaks open and the guard's footsteps go down the stairs. In a couple of minutes I hear boxes being thrown to the side of the street. This is when the sniper will fire. He'll go for the guard first, then the driver. If there is gunfire, the driver will try to run the barricade. I am absolutely furious: it's not fair to come all this way and be killed on the first day in an ambush that won't make the six o'clock news. I am lying on top of the gas tank. I am the only officer and the only medical personnel on the bus.

All right then, one of the noncommissioned officers will have to take command. I'll have to handle the first aid. My mind goes back to a hot August afternoon at Camp Bullis, Texas. My basic class sits sweating in bleachers while Maj. Jimmy W. lectures about the long row of Army vehicles parked behind him. I close my eyes, remembering his droning voice with the slight southern accent. "The first aid kit in a bus is located behind the driver's seat." I look and there it is. Okay then, when the shooting starts, make a dive for the first aid kit. Find the natural leader, the one who automatically takes command and stick to him. We'll make a good team, him and me.

The street is dead as the guard removes the last of the barricade. He climbs back into the bus, muttering, "Fucking gook kids." The driver guns the motor. In ten minutes we are at the terminal. I wait in line to board a plane to Da Nang. I feel as if I left home a hundred years ago.

Tuesday, May 19, 1970. Da Nang, Viet Nam. I spent yesterday in-processing and meeting the Chief Nurse here, who I remembered fondly from basic at Ft. Sam Houston. My assignment is the 71st Evacuation Hospital in Pleiku. I've heard about the 71st from nurses at Ft. Riley. It's in the mountains of the Central Highlands, near the Cambodian border. It even has a swimming pool. This assignment sounds too easy and I am disap-pointed. I want something along the Demilitarized Zone, some place where there is a lot of action. At least it isn't the 3rd Field in Saigon, where the nurses wear white uniforms and trip over colonels and generals. I guess Pleiku is a compromise. Another nurse, Alice D., is also going to Pleiku. She's been trained as an operating room nurse, so I don't guess we'll get a chance to work together.

When we were processing through Da Nang, Alice and I had to make our wills. Make my will. What do I have to leave? Some clothes. My books from nursing school. A cookie jar shaped like a house. A radio I bought with my first paycheck. Nothing of any real value except a car, which my brother would prob-ably want. Leave it all to my family, I suppose.

Last Will and Testament

I, First Lieutenant Sharon Marie Grant,
Army Nurse Corps,
do hereby leave all my possessions
to my mother, to do with as she sees fit.
I ask that all my debts be paid
and that any remaining money
be divided:

one quarter to St. John's Catholic Church,
one quarter to the College of Nursing,
University of Southwestern Louisiana,
one quarter to each of my brothers

Drawn and quartered, signed and sealed, this day in
Da Nang, R.V.N.

A Spec-4 set up his office outside on a card table, which I thought was pretty smart, considering the heat in un-air-conditioned buildings. The heat here is oppressive.

He pulls a file from the cardboard box on the chair beside him.

"Grant?"

"Here."

"Let me have two copies of your will." I give them to him and he shoves a stack of papers towards me. "Sign at the bottom, all three copies. Do you want your pay to go into a fund if missing?"

"Why would my pay be missing?"

He looks at me, extremely bored, and says patiently, "No, Ma'am. What do you want us to do with your pay if you're missing?"

"Missing? Where am I going that the Army can't keep track of me?"

It's a new fear, something Sue and I didn't think to worry about at Travis.

"Do you want your pay to go into a fund?" The specialist repeats, tapping his ball point pen on the triplicate copies of papers.

"Yes. No. Yes." The clerk checks off "Yes" three times quickly before I can change my mind again, and I sign the papers.

Alice and I won't leave for Pleiku until tomorrow, so we go over to the hospital to find my classmates from basic, Margaret and Marie. The three of us did a lot together during basic.

Marie is from New York. We introduced her to country music at a Johnny

Cash concert and she spent more time watching the audience than the perform-
ers. She couldn't believe so many people actually listened to that kind of music.

Margaret had the room next to mine. We shared a bathroom. We made sure each
other got up by 0430 to go to Camp Bullis. We debated the merits of soaking boots
in the bathtub to break them in versus rubbing them down with mink oil. We checked
each other's shoulder brass and laughed at each other in fatigues. Amid the neat green
lawns and pink-roofed Spanish buildings of Ft. Sam Houston, Texas, we felt at home.

Basic had been a good time. We were away from home, earning money, part
of a group. I had a new car and we would drive around San Antonio seeking out
Mexican restaurants, or go to Dallas or El Paso for the weekend. During the week
we played at being soldiers.

For a week in August we went to Camp Bullis, Texas. We ate our breakfast
from mess kits and learned to wash the kits in garbage cans of boiling water. Our
long, pony-tailed lines marched over the winding Texas hills. In the gas chamber
we whipped off our gas masks and recited our name, rank and serial number, then
ran for the door of the tent without taking a breath. We lay on the ground outside,
choking, with the tears streaming down our faces. We had weapons demonstra-
tions, but never fired the .45 pistols we were authorized to carry because when it
was our day for the range someone had forgotten to request ammunition. They
shot goats for us so we could learn to suture wounds and do emergency
tracheostomies. Afterwards, the Special Forces had a goat barbecue. I don't
remember half of what they told me in basic and now I have to use it.

Margaret and Marie came to Viet Nam straight from basic, while I went to Ft.
Riley, Kansas. It has only been eight months since I saw them, but we all feel as
if it has been a lifetime. We don't talk about Viet Nam when we go to the Navy
Club for supper. I don't have the words yet to ask them questions, they are so far
past the questions they can't tell me what the war is like. Mostly we talk about
basic and San Antonio, about the great Mexican restaurants, about how loud the
music was in our hangout, The Pit.

It's so strange in Da Nang. There is no shooting and movement isn't terribly
restricted. I don't know what I expected of a war zone, but it wasn't this calm-
ness, this routine. I wonder if Pleiku will be this calm?

Wednesday, May 20, 1970. Pleiku. We arrived about 1000 hours this
morning. The air is cool, foggy, wet. Green hills surround the city, which was a
summer resort when the French held the country. From the plane neat rows of
white stucco houses were visible on the outskirts of town. The Air Force Base
and the hospital compounds are adjacent, so I didn't see any of the city. Most of
the hospital buildings are blue-grey tin Quonset huts. There are covered walk-
ways connecting the wards and other buildings, banana and palm trees in the
compound and bright red flowers outside headquarters. The swimming pool is

closed because it needs a new filter. Green scum covers the water. At the back of our compound are two tremendous radio towers called Tropo Towers. They monitor the radio traffic in North Viet Nam. I wonder at the logic that put a hospital compound between two targets for mortar attacks, the Towers and the Air Force Base.

Four wards are open. They are metal Quonset huts, looking like huge tin cans half buried in the earth. Most of the wards have large screened windows that open into the mountain air. The Medical Ward, where they keep the malaria patients, is sealed and air-conditioned. It feels like a dark, cool cave.

The officers' quarters, our hooches, are at the top of a small hill, the hospital and helipad in the middle and the enlisted hooches at the bottom of the hill. The Emergency Room, Intensive Care and Operating Room are all grouped in the same building, called the Surgical-T. I have been assigned to the Recovery Room/Intensive. That scares me because I have only worked in the Emergency Room for the past six months, but the other nurses say I.C.U. is rewarding work because the guys there are so badly hurt.

Rockets hit near here just before we arrived. The Assistant Chief Nurse met us at the airport wearing her helmet and flak jacket and told us to put ours on, too. Everyone is edgy. The nurses make jokes about rockets, but we all carry flak jackets and helmets. I guess the clerk in Long Bien was wrong; nurses don't just put their jackets under their beds and forget them. It's impossible to remember so many names and faces, so many strangers to meet at once. We fall back on the usual questions. When were you at Ft. Sam? Was Maj. Jimmy W. still teaching compass-and-map reading? Did he still call the nurses "pretty ladies?" Where were you stationed before? Oh, did you know so-and-so there? The common introduction litany of all Army posts.

Thursday, May 21, 1970. I live in one of the eight nurses' hooches; mine is next to the Officer's Club. It's a tin and wooden building with screen windows near the roof and sandbags around the lower two-thirds of the wall. There are five bedrooms and a bathroom arranged around a hall that runs the length of the building. The rooms are six feet square. Right now a nurse named Ruth H.

...The sandbags keep the tin roof from blowing away...

and I are the only occupants. Ruth has been here three months. She's engaged to a helicopter pilot, Lt. B., from Camp Holloway. She enlisted so they could come to Viet Nam together.

Our common bathroom has two basins, a toilet and a shower. The floor is concrete, slimy with dirt and green mold. A wooden pallet covers the floor of the shower, but it's slimy, too. Rust stains run down the basins and toilets. Ruth has given up on the wooden pallet and wears sandals in the shower. The water has a heavy metallic odour and taste. It's often lukewarm, rarely hot.

My bed occupies much of my room. It's built three feet off the ground and has two mattresses so I can get under it under a mortar attack. I feel like the princess climbing up to bed, only there is no pea. From the last occupant I inherited an electric blanket and a blue spread. The electric blanket stays on all day to keep the sheets from mildewing. I also inherited a small refrigerator. Apparently Sears and Montgomery Ward will send anything to Viet Nam. There is also a dresser with mirror, a chair and a metal locker in the room. The windows have wooden covers that can be let down. There are screens, but no glass. No curtains either. My view from the window is the side of the Officers' Club.

The Officers' Club is also a tin-topped building, big enough for half a dozen tables. It is air-conditioned and there are no windows. It's cool, dark, smoky. There is a bar at one end and a small kitchen behind the bar. They serve ham sandwiches, steaks and fries. On Friday night they sometimes serve lobsters and

French bread, bought off the local economy. Ruth says there are weevils in the bread. She says, "If it's not moving, eat it. It's a little extra protein."

We toured the hospital today and did more in-processing. About 1000 hours the Chief Nurse told me I had to report to the Commanding Officer immediately. I wondered what trouble I could have gotten into having been here less than 24 hours. I went in and saluted, all proper like. I was shaking in my boots.

"Lieutenant, we have a message for you from the Red Cross."

I think. "Oh, God, someone in my family died." Can they make me turn around and go home for a funeral?

"Yes, sir.

"Your mother asked the Red Cross to trace you because she hasn't gotten any mail from you."

In spite of standing in front of a Colonel, I break out laughing. "Colonel, I left Travis three days ago. I've been traveling ever since. I only got here yesterday morning. With all respect, sir, even if I had written my mother, I don't think the letter would have reached her by now."

He shrugs his shoulders as if to say, "Civilians. What are you going to do with them?" Aloud he says, "I don't know, Lieutenant, but write your mother."

"Yes, sir." I salute and turn and walk out, embarrassed and furious at my mother. I don't need a year of her contacting the Red Cross every time she doesn't hear from me for a few days.

Ruth took me to the club tonight for supper. I met more nurses and some pilots and Special Forces officers at the club. I'm lying on my bed after supper, with the window open, writing this. I have written a letter to my mother, a polite, sane letter, telling her I arrived safely. I didn't tell her how angry I am that she contacted the Red Cross.

It rained again today. I write that like I'm an old hand here. What I mean is it rained when we arrived yesterday and it rained again today. I don't know if that is a pattern or not. The weather and the altitude have made me so tired.

Since 1700 a lot of choppers have been flying in and out. I don't know if this is normal or not, but I seem to remember people who have been here saying they don't ordinarily fly missions at night. Is 1700 considered night? Is something happening? Is the phone at the end of the hall going to ring? Am I going to have to go to work, suddenly, with no orientation? I don't know if I want that to happen or not. I left home eight days ago. It feels like I've been flying, traveling all of that time. I just want time to get my feet on the ground again.

Friday, May 22, 1970. Intensive Care is one big room with a tin roof, plywood walls with small, high windows and a dividing wall five feet high down the centre of the room. The walls are light blue, but everything else—the linens, the towels, the fatigues—are green. Air conditioning, banks of fluorescent lights, hand-cranked iron beds make the room feel cold though the temperature outside is 110° F. The head nurse is named Captain Marie B. She takes me around the ward. Most of the patients today are Viet Namese, two are G.I.s.

The sickest patient is in the bed next to the nurse's desk. He's tall, blond, skinny, about twenty-six, an Infantry Lieutenant with a gunshot wound of the abdomen, a colostomy and a high fever. A sniper got him about a week ago, about the same time I was leaving the States.

Captain B. asks me to give him a bath. It's not like he's really my patient, I don't have to worry about his I.V.s, his tubes, his vital signs, make a judgment if anything goes wrong. All she wants me to do is give him a bath.

I feel like a student again; I remember what it felt like to be all thumbs, but he's not going to know this. Not if I can help it. I walk back to his bed, slowly, very professional. I introduce myself and he snaps back, "How long have you been in-country?"

I think, "Why? Does it show?" Aloud I say, "A week."

"Do you know what you're doing?"

I want to say "I don't have a clue," but instead I don't back down from his pale blue eyes, bright with fever. "Yes."

He breaks off the staring contest first. "Okay." and I think, "I won this one."

A cloth ditty bag with toilet articles, a letter postmarked California, and a stainless steel basin take up very little room in his bedside stand. I take the basin and ditty bag and the closing drawer makes an empty metal sound as I close it.

"This is going to take about an hour. Do you want something for pain before I start?"

He hesitates, then looks down at the bed and picks an imaginary piece of lint off the sheet. "Yes."

This is going to work. That was what they taught me to ask in nursing school and I got the right answer. Maybe I do know enough.

I give him Demerol. His buttocks are covered with needle marks. I shave him and help him brush his teeth, then get fresh water for the bath. The steam rises warm in my face. His arms are covered with bruises from the I.V.s and I have to wash carefully around the I.V. in his neck. His skin is hot under my hands and every rib protrudes.

His name is Jim. He's from San Francisco, has been in-country nine months and wants to be evacuated to the Praesidio so he can be near his family. Talking tires him, so I don't press with questions. His thin abdomen is covered with a large white bandage. I remove his colostomy bag and clean the skin around the stoma. Before I can put another bag in place, brown diarrhea runs down his side and onto the sheet. I feel his body rigid under my hands and he won't look at me as I mop up stool with a towel.

"It's okay, Jim. After a while the accidents stop."

"The doctor said they would get rid of it in a couple of months. Is that true?"

"Yes, as soon as your bowels heal."

I put on a new bag, smoothing the edges of the plastic against his skin to prevent leaks. In the utility room I empty the brown water down the hopper, trying not to gag on the odour of stool and old blood. Then I go back to finish. His legs are sticks, the muscles already flabby from a week in bed. I spread the towel under his feet.

"Ticklish?"

"No."

I wet his feet with a wash cloth, then mix soap and lotion, rubbing the warm mixture over his feet until they are white. Jim actually smiles and I smile back. When I rinse and dry his feet, a layer of tough, calloused skin comes off on the towel. I turn him on his side. His back copies in red lines every wrinkle in the sheet. I wash his back and rub it with lotion until the streaks disappear. The clean sheet goes under him easily and I pull it tight so there are no wrinkles.

"You need to stay on your side for a while."

Grudgingly, he agrees and I put a pillow behind his back and one between his legs.

"Want anything else?"

"Some water."

I pour a cup of water and hold the straw for him. A.F.V.N., the local Armed Forces Radio Station, plays in the background. "If you are going to San Francisco/Be sure to wear some flowers in your hair. . . ." Jim stops drinking and closes his eyes. I stand for a minute with my hand on his shoulder because I can't think of anything else to do. In the utility room my hands shake and water from the basin splashes on the wall.

The rest of the shift is incredibly hard. I am so lost, drowning in the difficulties of a first day. Since I don't have an assignment of my own, I try to help out where ever I can, but I feel I'm an outsider. I don't understand some of the jokes, I don't have people to go to coffee with. Caring for the Viet Namese is so hard. The language barrier makes even simple conversations impossible. By the time I go home my legs ache, my shoulders feel as if they are carrying a ton.

Saturday, May 23, 1970. It doesn't seem like the weekend today; it's just another work day. We got a break today and only had to work eight hours instead of the usual twelve. Lt.-Col. G., the Assistant Chief Nurse, says we are to go to a six-day work week starting Sunday. There was a horrible mortar attack in March. The V.C. hit a mess hall on one of the other compounds just as a meal was being served. There are stories about people working days without a break.

All the patients are more familiar today. The two little Viet Namese boys are so full of energy. I think they will move them out of I.C.U. soon. Jim went back to surgery today to have an abscess drained. Since he came back, green pus has drained constantly from tubes in his abdomen and no amount of bathing can get rid of the sticky, sweet smell. We want him out of here. If we can't get him well enough to make it to Japan, the infection will kill him. He looks at me as I walk by his bed, his eyes asking questions I can't answer. I'm glad to be assigned to the Viet Namese patients at the other end of the room.

...The two littleVietnamese boys are so full of energy...

Monday, May 25, 1970. We're in a high-risk area for malaria. The troops in the field are supposed to take a daily Dapsone pill in addition to the weekly Chloroquin-Primiquin pill that we take. Every Monday there is a big bowl of the C-P pills next to the trays in the mess hall. We're supposed to take one with our lunch. They give us diarrhea and sometimes that's the only thing that keeps us from getting constipated. I worry about putting this stuff in my body. What if someone finds out down the road that it's toxic? But I'd rather not have malaria, so I take the pills.

Tuesday, May 26, 1970. We went on red alert early this morning. I put on my flak jacket and helmet, threw a pillow under the bed, rolled under myself and tried to go to sleep. It was very noisy. The A.R.V.N.s across the street were laughing and talking, our artillery was firing outgoing and the Air Force Base was taking incoming. I was terrified until I realized if the hooch got a direct hit I'd never know it and if it didn't I'd probably survive. So I went to sleep and woke up at dawn, still sleeping under the bed.

Thursday, May 28, 1970. Nuygen Van, the Viet Namese Lieutenant we have been taking care of all week, died this morning just before change of shift. I held his wife to keep her from throwing herself on his body. How can the guys say that the Viet Namese are cold and don't express emotions? We also lost a Montangnard baby from meningitis. There is so much death here.

Friday, May 29, 1970. Jim went to Japan today. The Air Force didn't want to take him because he still has such draining wounds. We pleaded with the doctor to send him and he finally agreed. Ruth says there is a ward in Japan for patients who aren't expected to live. The Army flies families over to be with the men when they die. I wonder if that's where Jim is going? I will never know if he makes it to San Francisco or not.

The doctors had a party this evening and served "punch." Some punch—Everclear mixed with a bit of fruit juice. Lynn is having problems with one of the doctors. He's married and wants Lynn to go to bed with him. She's not sure what she wants to do and he's very persistent.

❀ ฿ ❀

Calgary, Alberta. Over twenty years later, I still don't know if Jim made it to San Francisco or not. The Viet Namese Lieutenant and Jim are the only patients whose names I can remember and, at that, not even Jim's last name. I've heard other nurses say the same thing. We never knew what happened to our patients. For us it left a lot of circles unclosed.

❀ ฿ ❀

Saturday, May 30, 1970. The rain started about 1800 last night. If it rains any harder, we will wash away. It comes down in sheets, rolls off the tin roof, flows in front of the windows like a waterfall. All the dirt has turned to mud. I get soaked running from the hooch to the first covered walks. Now I understand why all the wards are connected by covered walkways.

In Intensive Care we have three burn cases, a man with half his brain shot away and two of our Viet Namese children are dying. A lot of choppers came in with A.R.V.N.s injured in Cambodia. The body chopper brought in eight body bags. They are heavy black plastic with web strap handles at either end. They have thick zippers. The body shed is a small wooden shed outside the Emergency Room. The smell of decomposing bodies has sunk into the wood and I can smell them when I walk past. When he saw the body chopper, one of our corpsmen went around singing under his breath, "I'm going home in a body bag, doo-da, doo-da; I'm going home in a body bag, oh-doo-da-day." My wardmaster says you have to make light of it if you can. Otherwise it will get to you. I still don't think it's the right thing to sing in front of the patients.

I look forward to lunch; a chance to get away from the I.C.U. There are no curtains there, no walls, and we are constantly on stage. All the patients watch us; it's like working in a fish bowl. It's hard to check a penis or give a bedpan or even speak comfortingly to a patient or hold someone's hand in full view of the whole ward. My only escape is half an hour in the mess hall.

The mess hall is painted light green. There are the ever-present screen windows that open to a lovely view of the mountains to the east. The food is served in pale green plastic bowls and cups on metal trays. We eat well here; even all the rolls are freshly baked. Sometimes we have "mystery meat," a big roasted joint of meat, usually over-cooked, covered with thick gravy. We hope it's beef or something close to a cow. The current rumour is that it's horse meat. My lunch today was a piece of meat on a roll and a big bowl of ice cream. I've learned to smell the milk before drinking it because half the time it's spoiled. All the water is flavoured with Kool-aid to mask the treated, metallic taste.

On day shift we work between eight and twelve hours, beginning at 0700. About 1400 Captain B. decides how many of us can go home early. We take turns going off-shift early. It's so hard to find something to do after work. There are a lot of days I come back to the hooch, strip to my underwear and lie down on my bed for a nap. Often I'm too tired in the evening to get dressed again to go to the mess hall for supper. In my fridge I have cheese spread, jelly, M & M's, orange soda in half-rusted cans, potted ham and peanuts. That's my supper, unless I can get the energy and courage up to go to the Officers' Club for a steak and fries.

Except for the nurses who are working night shift, people can dawdle over supper, have longer conversations, go to the club afterwards for a drink. It's that as much as anything that keeps me away from supper. I have a hard time making friends and I still feel like such a newcomer. I wonder if it would be easier if I'd been here in March for the "big push." Sometimes I'll complain about how tired I am at the end of a day and someone will say, "Oh, you think this is something. You should have been here it March when we were really working." I want to yell at them that it's not my fault I wasn't here in March.

I'm not going to have to worry about the singing corpsman or the burn cases much longer. I've been transferred to the Emergency Room, starting tomorrow. At Ft. Riley, I worked in the E.R. and loved it, but now, after just two weeks in I.C.U., I feel a sense of loss at going there. It's as if I had these two weeks to prove myself and have failed. It has been weeks since I've had a group to be part of. I've left family, friends, all that is familiar except the Army. I want to be part of this I.C.U. team, but feel they're rejecting me, that somehow I just haven't proven myself good enough. Ruth says that's crazy. There's no rhyme or reason to what the Army does. Talking to her doesn't comfort me very much.

There is one person who does comfort me. His name is Barry H., a Captain in Special Forces. If I go into the Officers' Club and smell cigar smoke, Barry is there, always in the same chair with his back against the wall, his eyes moving constantly, aware of everyone in the room. I don't think that even when he's deep in a poker game—which is often—he loses track of anything that's happening in the room. When I come in Barry nods just enough that I know he sees me. I sit down at one of the tables while Barry finishes his hand.

The bartender and I have a system. My first drink is always whiskey and coke. After that, if a man orders a round for me, the bartender serves me plain coke; if I order for myself, I get a real drink. Barry is the only one who has ever caught on. We were three drinks down apiece last night when he reached over and tasted my drink.

"So that's how you're keeping up with me. Look, if you don't want a drink, say so. No more Saigon tea when you're drinking with me. I don't like dishonesty."

Barry looks like he is in his thirties. He has a broad forehead, red-brown hair which he combs straight back, and marvelous, square hands with a missing finger-tip on one hand. He's on his second or third tour of Viet Nam. We talk about my feelings of failure, about how I want to do a good job, what looking at patients in the I.C.U. does to me, about my anger at being transferred to the Emergency Room.

"First of all," Barry says, "You have to know what combat is like."

He talks about his own fears, the jungle, the waiting, the attacks and fire fights. He tells me what he felt seeing men he has lived with die and what he wrote to their families. He covered up that they had died in bed with a hooker or that they had been blown in half and still lived for an hour. He tells me about torturing prisoners. We spend a lot of time going over and over questions until I have a feel for what it's like to be in the field.

"I thought you wanted to be in the thick of things? The Emergency Room is your chance to get muddy and bloody with the rest of us." He says it lightly, joking as he relights his cigar and blows a ring of new smoke. Then he lowers his voice. "When you get a casualty in the Emergency Room, just remember what we talked about tonight. One of the hardest things I did in the field was to put my men on a Dustoff chopper and hope the people who took them off gave a damn about what they'd been through. Somebody taught you well; you don't scare easily. I would trust you with my men. You can take that as a compliment and Special Forces doesn't give many compliments. You know soldiers take orders. So they are ordering you to the Emergency Room. You may not like it, but you're going to go and do the best fucking job you can there."

I don't scare easily. I don't, as long as you put me up against some "thing." I've discovered I can fly half-way around the world, lie on the floor of a bus waiting for an ambush, go to sleep during a mortar attack. The worst thing that has happened to me so far is losing my duffel bag because I might have had to borrow clothes that would make me look silly and fatter. People scare me. Jim scared me. Ruth scares me. Captain B. scares me. The doctors scare me. Even the corpsmen scare me. I'm most afraid of not living up to my own expectations. And I will never let anyone see how scared I am. This is a place of courage and that's all I intend to show to the world.

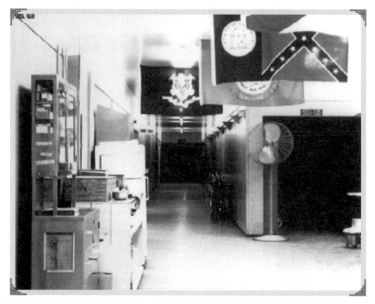

Sunday, May 31, 1970. There is a green bench outside the Emergency Room, where we sat this afternoon because things were slow. Over the door a sign reads, "You are Entering the Finest Facility in Viet Nam" with our hospital motto, "To Serve With Pride." I sit on the bench and look at the sign and think it's true. To serve with pride is what we're all about. So maybe Barry is right. It doesn't matter so much where I'm working as long as I do a good job.

Working in the Emergency Room is like being in a large barn. This barn has bright blue walls, a concrete floor, tin roof, scratched plastic windows, stainless steel, dirt, mud, equipment, instruments, hot surgical lights. The only human touch is flags of different states hung from the ceiling. It made me feel better this morning to come in and see the Louisiana flag there.

Across the hall is the clinic. We do cardiograms there, treat clap and foot infections, do physicals, see out-patients, give immunizations. We are doctor's clinic, public health office, out-patient clinic as well as Emergency Room. The majority of our patients come for the clinics rather than as casualties. On an average day we'll see seventy-five patients and only ten or twelve of them will have been injured as a result of combat. Some days it's absolutely boring and we have to find something to do to keep from going crazy from the inactivity. We have one habit the patients find  devastating. Hidden under the front desk is a little machine that makes loud clapping and laughing sounds. When a patient comes to be treated for V.D. we reach under the desk and turn on the machine. Everyone in the E.R. stops working and gives a series of whistles, claps and cat calls.

X-ray is next to the E.R., the Operating Room and I.C.U. down the hall in the same building. Lab is behind us, out the back door and around the hill by Sterile Central Supply. We are a self-contained world and the whole war spins down into these few rooms and the people I work with.

Our head nurse is a captain, Joan P. There are usually two or three nurses and half a dozen corpsmen on the day shift. Night shift is 1900 to 0700 with one nurse and one corpsman working the whole twelve hours. Most of the corpsmen are nineteen or twenty, and a wardmaster with the rank of Sergeant is in charge of them. Two of the corpsmen are Conscientious Objectors. We also get corpsmen from line units for temporary duty. They come to us for a few months from field units to brush up on their skills.

I learn all of this on the bench outside the Emergency Room door, talking to the corpsmen, sucking on home-made grape popsicles and watching helicopters lazily sweep the Ming Ying pass. We have only a couple of patients, one guy with malaria whom we admit and send off to the medical ward and one with a cut hand. The doctor stitches him up and he goes back to his unit.

Sharon K. and Linda S. had a goodbye party after work. They are the first people to leave since I came here. They are going to try to sneak their dogs onto the airplane, which is strictly against regulations. If they can get them to Da Nang they have friends there who will manifest them on the plane home.

I saw Barry at the club after work. "Well, how was it?"

"Piece of cake. This is what I've been doing for the past six months. I can do it with my eyes closed."

Barry points his hand with the missing finger tip at me. "Don't get cocky. You get cocky, you make mistakes."

1970 JUNE 1970

Monday, June 1, 1970. Some wounded-in-action (W.I.A.s) come in this morning, right after shift change. On the second stretcher in the door is a big, blond soldier with his leg blown off at the hip. The stump is an open mass of muscle and bone fragments about the size of a large platter. Blood pours out, soaks into the green canvas stretcher. I've never seen anything like this. I stand by the medicine cabinet and think something stupid like, "That must really hurt." I am immobile, knowing I should do something, unable to move. One of the corpsmen pushes past me, runs down to surgery and gets the anesthetist. He puts the man to sleep right there in the Emergency Room.

Joan grabs the pneumatic tourniquet from the top of the instrument cabinet. There isn't enough of a leg left to hold the tourniquet. The cuff slips, holds, slips. One of the surgeons reaches in bare-handed and scoops out a double handful of blood clots. He clamps bleeders with surgical clamps. They wheel the man to the operating room with clamps sticking from his stump at angles.

I know how to clean, to wash down the floor, pick up instruments, soak the tourniquet in hydrogen peroxide to remove the blood. The pneumatic tourniquet is in the upper left corner of the instrument cabinet. I won't forget that.

The whole day I am no help. The open mass of bone and muscle, the blood pouring onto the stretcher has been constantly in my mind. Joan says this is as bad as it gets. I console myself by thinking that perhaps I didn't do a thing to help but I didn't pass out or throw up.

I learn from one of the corpsmen who went to the airport to say good-bye to Sharon and Lynn that they didn't get their dogs out. They were caught at the airport and had to have the dogs put down. Damn it, what would it have hurt to let them take them with them? The people at the airport say health regulations forbid exporting animals, but they would have had the vet see to them as soon as they got home. They're nurses, after all. We are all sad for them.

I come home shaking and exhausted. Ruth is somewhere with her fiancé. A new nurse, Terri S., moved into our hooch today. We were in the same basic class together. I can't talk to her; she hasn't been through what I went through today.

So I lock the door of my room and lie exhausted on the bed, staring at the ceiling until I fall asleep. I don't want to talk to anyone about this, even Barry. Most especially Barry. Oh, God, he trusts me. He thinks I know what I'm doing.

Tuesday, June 2, 1970. Today I tried to find out where Al is. He is one of two non-medical officers who lived in our Bachelor Officers' Quarters at Ft. Riley. He and his room mate, Yancy, were either Signal Corps or Ordnance. I can't remember which. We would kid them about being in the real Army. Al's bedroom and mine shared a wall. One day we had to go to a dress supper for the Commander of the Continental U.S., a four-star general. I remember pounding on the bedroom wall and yelling, "Al, you're in the real Army. Which lapel does my caduceus go on?" Six of us in the B.O.Q., including Al, Yancy and myself, received orders for Viet Nam the same weekend. We took Yancy's air pistol out behind the quarters and shot target practice. After all, we were officers on our way to a war. Then we made spaghetti and got roaring drunk on red wine.

I want to talk to him, to tell him I am here. I don't think I can talk to him about the man with his leg blown off. I just want to remind myself that I'm in this with people I know. I want to hear that he's safe because I've seen the kind of injury that could happen to him. I got as far as battalion level; I'll try again tomorrow.

I also tried to make a M.A.R.S. call home this morning, but without much luck. I guess it takes quite a while to get an open line. Maybe I just want to hear my mother's voice, too.

The E.R. ran 22 patients through today but with less hassle than happens in the States. Perhaps having no families here has something to do with it; we don't have to worry about families getting in the way. Two Australians came in to have a child seen. It seems funny to have civilians working here voluntarily. When I think about Viet Nam I never imagine non-military people here. We have to be here, but I wonder: what are they doing here? I feel some kind of demarcation between myself and civilians, as if I've done something to cross the line and will never be a civilian again. Maybe it is coming up against a realization that this war is bigger than I am and that it can hurt me. I have put myself solidly in the Army's camp. The Emergency Room here isn't like the one in the States. I have to worry about soldiers here; I don't have to worry about dependents—civilians, in other words. There are just us soldiers here.

Wednesday, June 3, 1970. More casualties, about six or seven of them, come in today. I am right in there working, doing what I can. One of the patients' Commanding Officer comes in with him. He's a Captain, not much older than I am. He just stands in a corner and watches us work. When he sees that the man is going to live he asks to use our phone to call for transportation to his unit. No planes are available so he's spending the night on our compound. I see him later, eating supper at the club. When I come in he pulls out the chair next to him for me and looks at me with very tired eyes.

"Thank you."

I don't know how to respond to that gratitude.

❀ ♩❀

Calgary, Alberta. I remember my wardmaster angrily telling me a story about a new nurse in the Emergency Room who, he said, went up to a stretcher and introduced herself with, "Hello, I'm so-and-so and I will be your nurse this morning" . . . et cetera. Meanwhile the guy was bleeding to death. The wardmaster had to push her out of the way to get to the guy and stop the bleeding.

I can't remember the sequencing of the story, whether he told it to me before or after the casualty came in with his leg blown off, but I remember learning from that story that it's okay to introduce yourself as long as you're doing something at the same time.

Doing what I could. I learned the routine very quickly by watching what other people did. The first few times I didn't know what I was doing, what I was supposed to be looking for. I just did what I'd seen other people do. We cut their clothes off, one person on either side with a big pair of scissors: started at the cuffs of the sleeves, up to the shoulders, down the sides of the shirt, down the sides of the pants legs and finished up with the boots. I learned a lot by feel. How heavy the clothes were with blood, how wet with sweat. I learned to check the pockets before I tossed the shreds of clothes into a pile in the corner. Sometimes I found pictures or other personal things. Sometimes I found grenades and bullets.

I learned get their attention, get them to look at me. "Hi, my name's Sharon. You're at the 71st Evac in Pleiku. You're going to be okay. I'll tell you what I'm going to do so there won't be any surprises. What's your name?"

Keep their attention. Get them to talk to you. "Are you in pain? Where does it hurt? Can you feel this? Are you allergic to anything? Now this guy is from admitting. He has some questions to ask you for the paperwork. I'll be just across the room. I'll keep an eye on you."

Anybody who was in the Emergency Room would watch us do it. They stood gaping at us, while we hovered like bees around the blood. Sometimes, like the

Captain that day, they would just stand in a corner and watch. We said, "Move!" as we pushed by them.

When he said "Thank you" to me that night, I wanted to say, "Your buddy wasn't in really bad shape. You should see some of the casualties we get in here. You don't have to thank us. This is what we're for." And part of me was very proud of being thanked.

❀ ㄷ❀

Thursday, June 4, 1970. This is my day off. One of the sergeants asks me if I will go to the Catholic orphanage with him. A lot of the nurses and doctors volunteer at the leprosarium or the local hospital. I guess that's expected of us, so I go with him. He tells me that a lot of the kids in the orphanage have American fathers and that their mothers abandon them when they are born and become prostitutes.

The orphanage is in a run-down building. It must have been one of the French villas when the French came to Pleiku for summer holidays, but now the paint is peeling off the walls and the place is very dirty. There are no screens on the windows; flies are everywhere. The children sleep on bare boards laid across cinder blocks. There's no grass in the yard, just brown dirt, and I'm sure all of the children have worms from running through the dirt barefooted. I see over a hundred children, most of them under ten or twelve. It's hard to tell because they are so small. It's easy to tell that some of them have black fathers because they have kinky hair and Negroid features. The nuns speak French and we communicate pretty well, even with my halting college French.

These children don't have anything. The sergeant's wife has organized their church to sent them secondhand clothes. He says before he came they were all dressed in rags.

The nuns are anxious for me to look at a very sick child. He is lying on a pile of old clothes. It is obvious he has a high fever and is dehydrated. He may be in a coma. I advise the nuns to take him to the doctor. He is later brought into the 71st and admitted. We sometimes admit civilians as a humanitarian gesture. The doctors haven't diagnosed his illness yet, but he is in I.C.U. I hope I didn't overstep my boundaries. What right do I have to tell the nuns what they should do?

❀ ㄷ❀

Calgary, Alberta. There were no pictures of this day. I don't even remember if I had my camera with me. Probably not because the small camera I had taken with me died shortly after my arrival and it was a few weeks before I bought a new one. In any case, even if I had a camera, I couldn't have brought myself to photograph those children. The sergeant, whose name I don't remember, seemed to be the only one who was trying to do something for them. I remember him telling me that he had tried to get other doctors and nurses to come out there, but no one was interested. They wanted to go to the leprosarium where "things were more interesting." After all, they could see dirty, malnourished children at home.

I never went back either. It was too much of a shock, I suppose. I was too overwhelmed by their needs and my inability to meet all of those needs. The boy in I.C.U. died the next day from brain malaria and pneumonia.

❀ ♪ ❀

Friday, June 5, 1970. All day we have casualties from one end of the Emergency Room to the other. Plus today is physical exam day. There are about seventy-five Viet Namese and P.A. & E. workers (mostly Filipinos, who work for Pacific Architects and Engineers) to have physicals.

One of the nuns from the orphanage is so grateful that we admitted the boy yesterday that she brings in another child today. The doctor speaks only English, the nun speaks only Viet Namese. One of the P.A. & E. foremen speaks Viet Namese and French. I speak French and English. So we line up: doctor to me to foreman to nun with the question and nun to foreman to me to doctor with the answer. In the middle of this very complicated translation effort, one of the casualties goes into cardiac arrest and dies.

The patients are stacked like wood and I come home covered with blood. The men come in, they go out, we never know from where or to where. The war is just one room with bright blue walls. We strip the patients naked, one person on each side with big scissors, cutting up the uniform and down into the combat boots. The admissions clerk stands with clipboard in hand, asking questions. Men lie there with their skin peppered with shrapnel fragments, shattered femurs protruding through their thighs, belly wounds, arms or legs hanging by a piece of flesh. One patient, lying naked except for a green towel over his genitals, rattles off his Social Security Number, birthday, next of kin, unit and home address, but he can't remember his name. Meanwhile the Viet Namese construction workers file by the stretchers, each carrying his physical papers. At the head of the line one of the corpsmen waves wildly, calling, "Lau day! Lau day!" which means "Come here—this way."

We are a short cut to the rest of the hospital. People wander through, stop to watch us work on casualties. I can never decide if they watch because of the natural fascination for blood and gore or because they want reassurance that if they are hit, we'll work just as hard for them. We call ourselves the best show in Pleiku and think about charging admission, twenty-five cents a head.

It is about fifty feet down to the door of Surgery. That is my responsibility, my war, from the helipad into the Emergency Room and down fifty feet of hall. We start I.V.s with thick, sharp needles, big enough for blood if it is needed. It takes a lot of force to get the needle through weather-beaten skin. Each I.V. is a personal challenge. I stand beside the stretcher, cleaning the skin, applying the tourniquet, explaining what I am doing. All the time the voice inside of me prays, "Just let me hit this one. He needs it so badly." I need it badly, too, to be equal with the rest of the nurses, not to foul up, not to be thought to pull less than my share of the work.

There is Kool-aid in the refrigerator next to the bags of blood. I grab half a dozen bags for one patient, thinking about the six people who donated blood, wishing I could show them how grateful we were to have it so readily available. We run the cold blood through a coil of tubing placed in a bucket of warm water. It seems to take hours for the blood to flow, coil by coil, through the tube until suddenly it spurts out the last few inches, baptizing the patient and me.

When the man has an I.V. going and has had some Morphine, I take a deep breath. He is at least going to make it to surgery. The stretcher goes down the hall trailing I.V. tubes, warming bucket for the blood, shreds of clothing. As soon as the double steel doors closes behind the stretcher I mentally chalk up one more for our side. I don't think about how they will live without legs, blind, burned, half the brain gone. Get them to surgery alive, that is my only job. Today we repeated the same journey down the corridor twenty times, in one door and out the other, like working on a freeway. Our care is not impersonal. Each man I take care of has a name, a unit, a home town. Most of the time that is all I know. I call the patients by their first names. Even when I just stand beside a stretcher, surveying the general confusion and deciding what to do next, I put my hand on the man's arm or shoulder. When a guy asks, "Am I going to die?" we say, "Are you kidding? I'm too busy to make out the paperwork for a death." The ones who are going to die are too far gone to ask anything. Somebody always stays with them until the end.

No One Under 18 Admitted

I kissed a Negro, trying to breathe life into him.
When I was a child—back in the world—
the drinking fountains said, "White Only."
His cold mouth tasted of dirt and marijuana.
He died and I put away the things of a child.
Once upon a time there was a handsome, blond soldier
without enough of a leg left to use a tourniquet.
We grabbed at flesh, combing out
bits of shrapnel and bone with bare fingers.
A virgin undressed men, touched them,
raped them in public.
By the time I bedded a man who didn't smell
like mud and burned flesh,
he made love and I made jokes.

Saturday, June 6, 1970. Some of the Special Forces officers invite me to supper at the home of their Viet Namese counterpart, Colonel N. Going there means being off the hospital compound at night and being in town, both against our Chief Nurse's orders. I go because breaking the rules is an adventure. After all, I have been in-country three weeks and I can take care of myself. I lie in the sign-out book and say I am going to the Officers' Club at the Air Force Base.

When Pleiku was a French vacation area, Colonel N.'s house was a summer resort for tourists. Unlike the orphanage, it's well kept, constructed of wood and pink plaster with a stone fence around it. Barbed wire has been added to the fence.

There is no glass in the windows, only screens. Small, dim bulbs hang from the ceiling, casting a dusky yellow light over the people there. None of the Viet Namese officers are below the rank of Captain, so I know the officer who owns the house is important.

All of the men—Americans and Viet Namese—wear fatigues. There are a few Viet Namese women there in ao-dias, a tight-fitting silk dress worn over black silk pants. They wear heavy makeup and perfume to cover their lack of bathing. When the women talk they mix rising, shrill laughter with scraps of pidgin English and private remarks to each other in Viet Namese. There are two other nurses, all of us guests of the Special Forces officers. We are in dresses and I feel conspicuous. We are such prizes, real round-eyes, which is the G.I. term for American girls. I wonder if this evening is going to be such a great adventure after all.

The whiskey is American. We eat steak for supper, so either Special Forces or the black market is supplying this house. The atmosphere during the meal is strained. The Viet Namese women try to talk to us, but their English is poor and our Viet Namese non-existent. The conversation finally dissolves into them giggling behind their hands and talking among themselves and us smiling painfully at them. The men, after an initial show of great courtesy, pulling out our chairs and serving us wine first, lose themselves in talk about the war and how much can be flown from Okinawa. After dark, I hear scattered rifle fire not far away. Through the windows I see Viet Namese guards walking back and forth on patrol around the house, exchanging greetings in Viet Namese.

At about 2300 I realize if I haven't returned to the hospital to sign in by the time the Air Force Officers' Club closes, I will be absent without leave. The man I am with is drunk, in a nasty, fighting mood. His friends, who are as drunk as he is, barely keep him out of a fight with a Viet Namese major. The other two nurses have disappeared with the men they came with. I am scared and angry at my own impotence to get out of the situation.

Barry walks in, surrounded by a cloud of cigar smoke. I take him to a quiet corner and blurt out how I have to get back before curfew, how the person I had come with is drunk, how scared I am. He takes me home in an open jeep. At night, snipers are a constant danger, as is a grenade ambush with a trip-wire strung across the road to catch in the wheels of the jeep. Barry hands me his loaded rifle.

"If anything happens, I'll be too busy driving to use it."

He doesn't say a word the whole way home, just clamps an unlit cigar between his teeth and looks at the road. Every time we hit a bump his rifle bangs against my leg and I know I will be bruised. I sign in five minutes before curfew.

Barry follows me into the hooch, still silent, his combat boots making heavy thumping sounds on the wooden floor. Once we are indoors, he lights his cigar and blows angry smoke down the hall. He follows me into my room, deliberately throwing the bolt lock.

"Are you mad at me?"

"Hell, yes."

"I can go out with anyone I want."

"You can do anything you damn well please, honey. I don't care if you sleep with every guy you meet, or go to the Colonel's house, or make a killing on the black market. I'm mad at you because you didn't cover your ass."

"Do what?"

"Did you tell anyone where you were really going?"

"No."

"Did you memorize the way to N.'s house, so you could find your way back?"

"No."

"Can you drive a jeep?"

"No."

"Did you know anyone at the party?"

"Only the guy who brought me."

"Who is now drunk, passed out and not going anywhere for hours. The Military Police have been watching that house. Some night soon, maybe tonight, they're going to raid the place. What would you have done if I hadn't come in?"

"I don't know."

I feel terrible, not just the liquor and the fear, but a real sense that I've let Barry down. He finally stops pacing and sits beside me on the bed. He puts his arm around me.

"Go ahead and cry."

"I'm too mad to cry."

He lets go of me and smiles. "Good. Now do something with that anger. I don't care if you're going into a room or a battle, make sure you have a way out. Watch what's going on and don't get so drunk you can't handle yourself. And always have a backup plan. That's what I mean by covering your ass."

"How come I seem to be your special project?"

"Because you don't get upset when I talk about torturing Viet Cong prisoners. Because somewhere you learned to think like a soldier and you don't put me down for what I've done here." He takes the cigar out of his mouth and puts it down, getting rid of his prop. His voice is quiet. "I'm a good soldier. I do my job well, but a lot of people can't understand what that job is like, especially in this war. One day you're going to find out just how much they hate us back in the world for what we're doing here. Besides, the last time I was here I ended up with a six-inch hole in my stomach. If the nurses at Phu-Bi hadn't known what they were doing, I would have died. If I don't take care of you, who's going to take care of guys like me?"

"What do I need to know?"

"The most important thing is nobody can take care of you as well as you can take care of yourself. I know you think I somehow have all the answers, but I don't. I can't make everything better for you. We've talked a lot about war. War is ninety-eight percent boredom and two percent sheer terror and the boredom is a lot harder to handle. You have to learn to like yourself because this next year you're going to be living closer to yourself than you've ever done before. Trust yourself and cover your ass. And don't take everything so seriously. Relax. Enjoy what's going on."

And then I do cry.

Sunday, June 7, 1970. Quite a few of our patients lately are Montagnards. They are the true Viet Namese aboriginal people, pushed into the remote areas like the Central Highlands by the Chinese several hundred years ago. They are a small people. Most of the men are just about five feet and the women smaller. They have very dark skin and wear almost no clothes, except for a nubby black cloth with red and yellow stripes, which they weave for themselves. We call the material 'Yard cloth. Their name in French means Mountain Guards and they live in small farming villages in the deepest parts of the mountains. Barry says all they want is to be left alone to farm and raise their families and pigs and chick-

ens. He likes them, says they are an honourable people. They make really good fighters because Special Forces trains them to fight on their own territory. They are literally fighting in their own back yard. Our general feeling is if the Viet Cong ever take the Central Highlands, they will commit genocide on the Montagnards.

When a 'Yard comes in as a patient everybody comes with him: parents, wife, children. They squat at the edge of the room, fold their arms around their knees and watch us. There is a quiet dignity about everything they do. When the patient is in surgery, they sit for hours outside the operating room, never moving. And when he is successfully out of surgery, they bow to the doctors and shake our hands. We smile and bow back. I guess they think we work a miracle; perhaps sometimes we do.

After surgery we keep some of the more seriously wounded; Ward 5 is for indigenous patients. While they are on the ward their family moves into the tent out behind the mess hall where all of the indigenous families live. It is not easy for them because the Viet Namese hate the 'Yards. Sometimes fights break out in the tent. It isn't the cleanest place to live either. When it rains hard the tent floods and the tent floor turns to mud. The people in the tent are given food from the mess hall and water from the wards. In a country where few people have much, these people have even less. They don't even know how long they will be here; it depends on what happens to their relative in the hospital.

The head nurse from Ward 5 makes rounds in the tent sometimes, looking for people who might be sick. A couple of days ago she brought a child to the Emergency Room with fever and sores all over his body. We called one of the doctors to examine him. The doctor was originally from India and he could tell from across the room that the child had smallpox.

During the day the families help care for the patient. The children play under the bed. The wife nurses her baby and the parents squat outside the ward door and smoke or chew betel nut. They learn how to help with the dressings or the tube feedings and become quite skilled at giving care.

We can't keep all of the 'Yards because of lack of space. The rumour is that it isn't a good idea to send them to the Viet Namese hospital in Pleiku because they are put in a corner and left to die. There is a C.I.D.G. Hospital in Pleiku. C.I.D.G. means Civilian Irregular Defense Group. It is the name given to the Montagnards who fight with Special Forces. Their hospital is

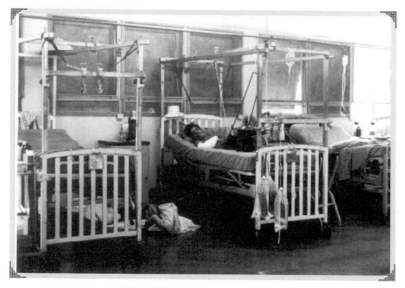

...The children play under the bed...

staffed by ten Special Forces medics, two doctors and an administrator. They also train Montagnards as medics and ward attendants. We try to send the 'Yard patients there if we possibly can.

There is also a hospital that is run by Dr. Pat S. in Kontum, thirty miles north of here. The S.s, a husband-and-wife team of missionaries, started the hospital years ago. In Tet of '68, Dr. S., Pat's husband, was taken away by the Viet Cong. She stayed to run the hospital.

The 71st gives them supplies and medicines whenever we can and Special Forces takes care of them, too. Barry says Special Forces has encouraged Dr. S. to leave for a long time. There is rumoured to be a price on her head; the Viet Cong want to kill her just as they killed her husband, but she refuses to leave. When the time comes for all the troops to pull out of the Central Highlands, there is a general understanding among Special Forces that no matter how much she protests, they are going to take Dr. S. and her missionaries with them.

Monday, June 8, 1970. Fighting started again somewhere today and we receive a steady stream of indigenous casualties, all badly wounded. One of them is a North Viet Namese prisoner. He receives the same care, has the same people working on him that he would have if he was A.R.V.N. or Montagnard. Fortunately, he's just a Lieutenant. He doesn't know enough for anyone to want to kill him. The corpsmen say that last spring they had an North Viet Namese Army general here and Charlie kept shelling the hospital, trying to kill him.

Sometimes a North Viet Namese soldier will Choy Hoy, or come over to our side. We use them for scouts and to question prisoners. Often our guys have them walk point, be the first person in line if they go through areas that might be booby-trapped or mined. A lot of them are killed that way. In any case, they are dead. When we pull out, either the A.R.V.N.s will kill them or the Viet Cong will.

I feel so helpless looking at these people who are helping us, who are trying to defend their homes or lives. We seem to be screwing them all of the time. I wish we could just go home. I wish there wasn't a war here.

I moved across the hall into my new room today. At least this one has intact screens. I won't be kept awake by mosquitoes at night any more. There are three of us in here right now: Ruth, Terry and myself. The other two rooms, one of which I just moved out of, are vacant and will probably stay that way. We are beginning to close down here and they aren't sending us many replacements.

Tuesday, June 9, 1970. About five this afternoon one of the helicopter pilots, Aimee, came to me in the Emergency Room.

"You heard from Barry?"

"No, he was going flying with some Air Force type. He's supposed to call me when he gets back so we can have supper."

I turn around and look at his face and I know. The only thing I ask is, "When?"

"Ground control lost contact with the plane about two o'clock this afternoon. Search and rescue is out looking for them now."

I am numb. I can't believe he is dead, that I will never see him again. I thought I understood. I don't. I can't. All that line he tried to give me about learning to like myself, about taking care of myself is so painful. I want him back. I want him around to take care of me. I want to be able to take care of him.

Wednesday, June 10, 1970. There is still no word about Barry. His friends and I tell each other he is going to walk out of the boonies. I try to rationalize that this is the way he would have wanted to die. None of us want to die. I have this desperate empty feeling of being incapable of doing anything to help him. I have an image of a plane going into the ground, hard, then nothing. No movement, no sound, no fire. Just swallowed up by the jungle. Sometimes wreckage is never found. Barry fills my thoughts during the day and my dreams at night.

There isn't a Catholic chaplain here. Finally I swallow my pride and go to the Protestant chaplain. We pray for Barry. The chaplain asks that wherever he is, God give him peace.

Thursday, June 11, 1970. Weekly casualties come out every Thursday in Stars and Stripes. Barry is listed as Missing in Action, Presumed Dead. I want to cry, but tears will not come. I go to work today and look at a casualty and want it to be Barry. Even burned, wounded, disfigured, I want him alive. I saw him late Monday night. We had a lot of fun, talking and giggling. It was dark when he walked out of the hooch. I remember him standing in the circle of light by the door, lighting a cigar. I was one of the last people to see him alive. He was married, but I don't even know where he was from or where he lived. I want to write to his wife, tell her that one of the last things he ever did was to talk some sense into a very green and scared woman. But I won't write to her. We were never intimate, but I don't know what she would think of a letter from another woman. It must be so hard for her.

❀ ♫ ❀

Calgary, Alberta. "Capt. Barry W. Hilbrich / United States Special Forces 6-9-70 South Viet Nam / Texas." That's what it says on the Missing In Action/Prisoner Of War bracelet I have. Texas. That sounds about right; I knew it was some place in the south. It took me almost twenty years to find that out. In Edmonton a few years ago I joined the group, Viet Nam Veterans of Canada. They had a drive for all of us to get M.I.A./P.O.W. bracelets. They asked me if there was anyone's name I wanted. I told them Barry's name. I was hoping they would come back and tell me they couldn't find his name on the list. I didn't want him missing in action, presumed dead, not after all this time. But his name was on the list and one night at the Army, Navy and Air Force club someone handed me the red bracelet. I put it on and cried all over again.

It doesn't seem right, after all this time, to still not know what happened to him. I don't believe any of these stories about prisoners of war still in Viet Nam.

It would be too crazy politically for the Viet Namese to still be holding any U.S. soldiers. Barry is dead. He's been dead for over twenty years.

It was the swiftness of his death which so affected me. I'd never known death before. The last time anyone in my family had died was my grandmother when I was six. This was my first experience with war being personal and I didn't know what to make of any of it. It took a long time to sink in, a long time before I could get far enough back from it to think about it. Barry would laugh if he knew what I think about sometimes, about how much I respect and revere him. I'm far enough from his death now to know it wasn't a special death. There was nothing heroic about it. He was simply a friend who went away and died. If he had lived we probably would have lost track of each other. I never even knew him long enough to know his really bad habits. Maybe he drank too much. Maybe he was violent and abusive. Maybe he had a lot of flaws. I'll never know.

Maybe we all need one friend who is forever young, forever faithful. Barry is never going to go away from me. He'll always be my friend and I'll be his. A long time ago we liked each other. He was important to me then and he still is today.

❀ ♫ ❀

Friday, June 12, 1970. One of the medics who was with us on temporary duty in the Emergency Room was killed today by our own artillery. A radio operator called in the wrong coordinates. I took a picture today of one of the medics, leaning against the post outside the Emergency Room door. He'd just received the news. I don't know what I'll do with it: taking it seems like an invasion of his privacy. Maybe I'll just keep it until none of this matters any more.

His death is no easier for the medics than Barry's death is for me. We all have just lost close friends, yet I feel a need to comfort the corpsmen. I am an officer and a nurse, quite aware of my roles.

Saturday, June 13, 1970. Our yearly inspection, what we call the I.G., will happen in a few weeks, so the Hospital Commander is conducting his own inspection, the pre-I.G., in two days. We painted the Emergency Room with another coat of blue paint today. Thank heavens for something to take everyone's mind off of the death yesterday. Dave, one of the corpsmen, got zinnia seeds in a care package from home. We made a little flower bed and planted it next to the shed we use to store stretchers. It is a secret act of defiance for the I.G. The flowers won't be up when they come to inspect. All they will see is a pile of dirt. But we know the flowers are underneath.

We are all so short-tempered with the patients today. What we want is a chance to be by ourselves, to think, to work things out, but there is no private place: not at work or in the hooch. I still can't talk to either Terry or Ruth about Barry's crash. I won't go to the club because it reminds me of Barry. After work I go to my room, lock the door and cry.

Sunday, June 14, 1970. A pilot from Camp Holloway went down on Dragon Mountain yesterday. He was out there overnight and everyone was sure he was dead. This morning they find him alive. He is burned and has a broken back, but will live. His best friend finds him on the mountain and stays with him in the Emergency Room. He is in tears.

We can see Dragon Mountain from the E.R., a broad, flat-topped blue hill, often lost in the mist. I borrowed someone's telephoto lens the other morning and brought it in as close as I could to take a look at it. I had so many lens extenders on the camera that the mountain faded into a flat, blue plateau, almost invisible against the sky. It's supposed to be a Viet Cong stronghold. All the pilots say if you go down on Dragon Mountain, you die. This pilot beat the odds. He is an instant local legend. I wonder why he beat the odds and Barry didn't. There isn't any logic here, no pattern, no cause and effect. I can't hope to survive by being good. Barry was good. He hasn't survived. What he told me about taking care of myself now becomes a matter of survival. Barry was right. No one is going to take of me. No good guys and bad guys, no cavalry to arrive at the last minute and save the day. From now on I trust only myself.

When I think back on the few weeks Barry and I knew each other, the one comforting thought is that we never held back from each other. We joked, played poker, got angry, talked, laughed, hugged, gave what we had to give in friendship. Someday, maybe his death will stop hurting and I can enjoy the memories. Right now all there is is pain.

Monday, June 15, 1970. There is a tremendous disproportion of males to females here. Sometimes it feels like the men look at us like animals look at fresh meat. I want to hide, want to turn into something other than a woman just so I won't be on display all the time. The enlisted men are supposed to be off-limits to us and us to them. A lot of our contacts are group activities. We eat in the same mess hall, carry on our usual banter of jokes and teasing when work is slow, go to the Red Cross Recreation Room for a movie or pool game. Our quarters are at opposite ends of the compound and it is hard to find a neutral ground where someone can bring a guitar or where a group can just sit, talk and drink beer. The swimming pool is frequently used as a common ground, though it has been open only one or two days for swimming. Mostly people just sit around looking at the scum-covered water and talk. If an officer and an enlisted man want to date, there is no place for them. He can't come to the Officers' Club, she can't go to the Enlisted Club.

Most nurses prefer to be with other hospital people rather than going out with men from other units. Dating means going to the movie shown once a week or going to the Air Force Club to watch the Philippine floor show. Watching the floor show, as one of four or five women among a hundred men, sends me a very strong message about being a woman.

Rolling on the River

Pink-spangled Manila blowfish
roll on clear water rivers.
Strobe sweat runs down sequined scales.
Suffocated, choked in smoke,
they swim against the semen tide
of "Go, Baby" and flashes aimed up legs.
I drown, too, in sweat
of men, tables wet with spilled drinks,
but more I go down in shame
of being woman.

This sexual pressure, this constant feeling of being on display, up for grabs like goods on a shelf, is horrible. I go to the Officer's Club with an Air Force major. He is what we call a geographic bachelor, married only as long as his wife is around. He wants me to go to bed with him and the more he drinks, the more insistent he becomes. I won't go out with him any more, but sometimes, even among all these men, I become so lonely.

Somehow, my schedule never matches Terri's or Ruth's. By the time I cross the compound from supper, day turns into a quiet, pink sunset. The evening is still: too late for trucks to be on the road, too early for mortar attacks. It's getting easier to go back to the club. Sometimes I stop there for a drink after work, but I leave before a lot of other people arrive. I just find it hard to be with people. I am usually alone in the hooch. I take off my fatigues, dump them in a corner for mama-san to wash, and take a shower. Our hooch is next door to the club. Somehow the voices, music, laughter drifting across to my windows seem either a punishment or a test of strength. Loneliness is the price I expect to pay for being alive. Since Barry's death I'm afraid to get close to anyone. I can't stand another loss right now. I can face mortar attacks and the thought of snipers, but I can't face a room of people who probably would like to be my friends.

Other people must think me stuck up or a non-person. There are a few non-people around. We appear for work and disappear into a hole for the night. I'm sure some of my co-workers don't even know where I live. This is my private war, this constant battle between needing company and hating myself so completely I think no one else can like me. Sometimes a voice in my head says, "Damn it, quit complaining. The only person stopping you from being over there is yourself. If you want to go, go. If you don't, shut up." On really good nights I am so tired I fall asleep by eight o'clock. On bad nights I cry until after midnight.

Tuesday, June 16, 1970. The Civilian Irregular Defense Group (C.I.D.G.) Hospital is operated by Special Forces. It's for the Montagnards because they won't be taken care of in the Viet Namese hospitals. It's on a compound close to the hospital and I went over there today. There are two doctors there and an administrator; the rest of the staff are Special Forces medics and Montagnard ward aides that the medics have trained. The medics want me to help with their rehabilitation ward because I'm interested in orthopaedics and rehabilitation. I don't have a clue where to start. I don't speak either of the two Montagnard dialects, I don't know what would motivate these people to work on their own recovery.

Tonight is my first time on night duty in the Emergency Room. We have a mud puddle out beside the stretcher shed—it's larger right now because we've been watering Dave's zinnia seeds and all the run-off water seeps into this depression. It's customary to dunk someone in the mud puddle the first time they work night duty. I don't know why the medics do this other than that the mud puddle is there. So I get dunked and the corpsmen cover for me while I go back to the hooch to change. Later Dave brings his guitar and we sit around singing folk songs. He plays really well. Ellis, the radio operator from Dust-off, comes over for a while. He leaves tomorrow for thirty days of leave, then he's coming back because he has extended for six more months here.

Night duty is so different. They tell me we hardly ever have patients and that most nights the most interesting thing I will do is clean the Emergency Room. The worst part of night duty is the bugs. I am sitting at the front counter, with the door open because it's so hot, and this tremendous thing flies in. It is as big as a bat and, at first, I think it is a bat. I yell and dive under the counter and Dave comes over and laughs at me. Then he gets a magazine and squashes it. It is some kind of an armoured beetle. Dave says they come in all the time, attracted by our lights.

Wednesday, June 17, 1970. There is an article in *Life* magazine today about conditions in the Veteran's Hospitals in the States, especially on the wards for the men with spinal cord injuries. I knew the hospitals were in bad shape, but not that bad—mice running over the patients, long line-ups for a shower or help going to the bathroom. It makes me angry to see the neglect, the almost primitive conditions. It's so unfair to ask our patients to go back to conditions like that. We pride ourselves on saving 99 out of 100 patients who reach us alive. For what, I wonder?

Thursday, June 18, 1970. There was a fight last night over at Camp Wilson. Just like back at Ft. Riley on a Friday night. So we were really busy last night: sewing up cuts, x-raying skulls, trying to sober people up. Don't we have enough fighting over here without this? Maybe the lack of fighting is the reason this erupted. The area around Pleiku has been very quiet for a while and people need a way to release the tension of always waiting for something to happen.

Well, we flunk the pre-I.G. inspection. The Hospital Commander says the Emergency Room isn't clean enough. Our paper work isn't up to date. Our supplies aren't in order. So we have a party to celebrate flunking. As one of the corpsmen says, "We may have failed the I.G., but we never failed any G.I. that came through that door."

Only the I.G. doesn't go away that easily. The actual inspection is in a few weeks and the Commanding Officer has told us that we will pass that inspection! I see a lot of overtime coming up, but what else is there to do?

Friday, June 19, 1970. I get my first M.A.R.S. call through to home. The connection is very clear. Three minutes is really too short to say much, but at least I get to hear Mama's voice. John is up in Idaho and Ward is working for the Port of New Orleans, the same place that Daddy works. Mama has trouble remembering to say "over" when she is finished speaking and the ham operator keeps reminding her to say it. There are times I miss them and times I don't. I wish I could explain to them more of how I feel about things, about what's happening here, but we are literally in two different worlds.

A new nurse came in today, Anita M. from Fitzsimmons. She and Ruth went to basic together. It's hard to believe it was a month ago that I was arriving. I feel as if I am very well settled here and have met a lot of people. It's hard to remember what my first few days were like.

Saturday, June 20, 1970. One of the corpsmen, Brian, lent me his camera tonight. The little camera I brought with me has broken and I want to order one from the Pacex catalog. They have all of these lovely Japanese-made cameras at ridiculously low prices. I think I want a Pentax and am trying Brian's to see how I like it. There are so many things here I want to photograph. I wish I was really good with a camera; I would do a whole series of pictures, like what people's faces look like when they're working or the really unusual scenery.

Leslie, one of my roommates from college, writes today that she thought I was bored here. I wonder what in my letters gives her that impression. Whatever I am, bored certainly isn't it.

Sunday, June 21, 1970. Some Wounded in Action (W.I.A.s) come in tonight. Being the only nurse in the Emergency Room is really challenging. I want to do everything calmly and orderly, but inside I feel like I'm working in chaos. I want to be a part of every patient's care and I find myself taking over things the corpsmen can do. That's not giving them a chance to do their work and I know they don't like it. Sometimes we disagree about what should be done for a patient or how patients are to be treated. I've only been out of school a year, but I did go to nursing school and they didn't. I don't know where to draw the line, where to get off of their cases. It's not making me very popular. I keep getting dunked in the mud puddle every night and I'm beginning to wonder if it's all in fun.

Monday, June 22, 1970. My last night duty for a while—hurrah! If I can only discipline myself to sleep only five or six hours I'll have time to do something besides work and sleep. But I'm so exhausted after work that I sleep about ten hours. Sometimes I'm just falling asleep and some one will yell outside the window or a truck will backfire and then I'm awake and I have to settle down and try to sleep again. I'm only eating two meals a day: supper and midnight supper. I've found if I eat breakfast between work and trying to sleep I can't fall asleep. I feel like I'm on a treadmill and work is becoming anything but

interesting. I missed a lot of things on the cleaning last night and the Head Nurse wasn't at all pleased about that.

Tuesday, June 23, 1970. There is a mass casualty this evening about 2200 hours. A fully loaded Chinook helicopter crashes. We have fifty-two patients at one time and all of them make it! —Everyone, the Chaplain, the Red Cross workers, the cooks— pitches in to help. It is the first time I've seen triage in action. It works! The G.I.s are terrific. Each one asks that his buddy be taken care of first. They have been in the field for days with little time to sleep or eat. I never believed some sandwiches, milk and a clean bed could make people so happy.

One of the casualties has this large gash in his back—only a surface cut, but really long. The doctors ask those of us that are new if we want to learn to suture. About three of us say yes, so we take turns sewing up this guy's back. He thinks the whole thing is funny and we crack jokes the whole time we are doing it. Among us, the three of us put in about seventy-five stitches. Then when we're finished and he stands up, he almost passes out because of all the local anesthetic we injected into him.

Friday, June 26, 1970. I don't have any mail again today. Funny how a little thing like that makes or breaks a day. Fridays are so confusing. We do flight physical, sick call, medical clinic, surgical clinic, civilian physical, and take care of casualties, all in the same room at the same time. Then some sergeant on a radiotelephone out in the boonies wants to know where a patient is who was admitted six weeks ago. He can be anywhere by now, even home or out of the

Army. We get all the odd calls, like, "What day is it?" and "Can I make reservations on a flight to An Khe tomorrow?"

The phones are a treat in themselves. We call them "The Southeast Asia Phone Company." When I make a call, I yell into the phone, "Working? Working?" Then an operator comes on. Operators in Saigon put calls through to An Khe and operators near the D.M.Z. put calls through to Saigon. Often they are surprised to hear a woman's voice. The guy will say, "Hey, a round-eye." Then I have to stop and talk for a while before he puts the call through. Sometimes, in the middle of a call, there is a third person on the line. Then all three of us have a conversation. When the call finally goes through, we have to do our business first, then visit because disconnects can come at any time. At least the phones provide some humour.

Saturday, June 27, 1970. The indigenous patients who came in the past two days are really sick: falciprium malaria with a temperature of 110, possible cholera, bowel obstruction, bad burns, a Viet Namese woman with a postpartum infection. It is a desperate struggle just to keep them alive. I.V. fluids, antibiotics and oxygen do wonders in forty-eight hours. We can't take care of all of the Viet Namese and Montagnards. The patients we do take care of are either directly injured by American fire or interesting cases or done under the civilian Med-Cap program.

There is a Viet Namese hospital in Pleiku and some missionary hospitals in the area, staffed by Mennonites and missionaries from Australia, Norway and Sweden. The hospitals are very badly equipped: no blood, few medicines, just basic bandages. We take the most serious cases who will not survive in local hospitals. The Viet Namese hospital in Pleiku closes at 3 p.m. on Friday and reopens at 7 a.m. on Monday. During the weekend, patients' families provide the care. We get a lot of admissions over the weekends.

The missionary hospitals are better off. Some of our doctors and nurses work one afternoon a week, holding clinics for civilians and teaching the missionaries. We also give them our extra supplies, our drugs that are about to expire, our equipment that is outdated. If a medic comes in from the field wounded, he has to turn in his morphine. We sign for it and put it in a paper bag for him to claim later. Only he's usually sent to another hospital and never comes back to reclaim it. We end up with a lot of extra morphine we can't account

for. Once a month, the pharmacist comes to inventory our controlled drugs. It is supposed to be a surprise inspection. However, the pharmacist will casually call and say, "I may be seeing you later." Then we call the local missionary hospital and tell the nurse if she wants to come by for tea and happens to see a brown paper bag on the corner of our desk, no one will say anything if she walks off with it. She comes by for a cup of tea, the bag of extra morphine disappears, the pharmacist comes to count drugs and we have exactly the stock we should have. I wonder how the missionaries will survive after we pull out?

Everyone has been on edge lately. Headquarters seems to jump all over us for little things. The I.G. inspection is to be in two weeks and the Colonel is jumping through himself pushing us to the limit to be ready. Most of us don't give a damn if we pass or not. What are they going to do to us, send us to Viet Nam? The wardmaster in I.C.U., the same man who told me not to get too serious about the bodies in the body shed, goes berserk today when a Viet Namese child dies on his ward. They have to sedate him and put him on the Medical Ward in restraints. It does get to us, every little thing, every big thing. We weigh every cutting remark, take every slight, feel frustrated at every death and sometimes at the patients who are saved for no future. We know we are part of a machine, the Big Green Machine, as we call the Army. And sometimes that machine grinds our lives down very fine.

Sunday, June 28, 1970. Having waited two days to write about this day, it's impossible to remember what significant event happened. After forty-eight hours one day is so like any other day that this Sunday is lost forever.

Monday, June 29, 1970. The Air Force major and I have a long talk tonight. He wants inside my pants and I don't want him there. I talk to one of the Special Forces officers about it and he says, "If you want to play with the men, you have to play like a woman." They are such jerks sometimes.

Tuesday, June 30, 1970. Dr. Eli B. arrived yesterday. He was one of our doctors at Ft. Riley and I really like working with him because he's so easygoing and really cares about the patients. Monday was one of those days when everyone was picky about things. The operating room got mad at us about catheter bags, we got mad at post-op for not wanting a Viet Namese patient, they were mad at us for wanting to send him to them instead of to the ward. So it was the one bright spot of the day when the door of the Officer's Club opened and this voice with a New York accent said, "Oh no, not you."

I grinned at him and said, "Hi, Eli. Welcome to Viet Nam."

I am so glad to see a friendly face from back in the world!

…Joan P., my head nurse…

1970 JULY 1970

Wednesday, July 1, 1970. We were paid yesterday so Alice and I walk over to the bank today to deposit our checks. We take the back route, through the A.R.V.N. compound, past some houses that must have been summer houses when the French were here. They are quite lovely buildings of pink stucco with green roofs and green shutters. There are flowering bushes growing in the yard.

I think of when the French were here as if it is a singular time and place, but I know that it isn't. Really, I know very little. The French claimed this country as French Indochina. They were here before World War II; the Japanese invaded during the war; the French came back after the war. We talk about the French having lost the country at Dien Bien Phu. I know there was a siege there in 1954 and then the French pulled out, but I'm not even certain where Dien Bien Phu is other than a vague wave of my hand to indicate north of here.

I know Ho Chi Minh was the leader of the Communists in the north and that we came to this country to prevent his forces from taking over the south. Ho died when our group was at Basic Training last year. I remember lining up in formation on the quadrangle one morning staring at the newspaper in the newspaper box, which had a thick, black headline, "Ho Chi Minh Dead." Those of us in Basic wondered if his death would suddenly mean the end of the war in Viet Nam, if peace would break out before we could be sent here.

The Army doesn't teach junior officers politics. It isn't anything we need to know to do our jobs. I know the old French houses are lovely and that they had gardens. I know that the nuns at the orphanage and the few older, well-educated Viet Namese I have met all speak French. I know that between the French, the Japanese, and us that this country has been occupied for centuries. I don't know what will happen when we leave.

When Alice and I come out of the bank there is this flying crane sling-loading another crane. It looks like two giant praying mantises making love in the air. Alice asks, "Do you see it, too?" I say yes and she says, "Oh, good. For a minute I thought I was drinking too much." Then we both laugh.

There's a Post Exchange on the same compound as the bank. We are issued a ration card every month for cigarettes, booze and soft drinks. Since I don't smoke and drink very little, I let one of the corpsmen borrow my card in exchange for picking up cases of soda for me. That and a fifth of Crown Royal, which costs about $5, will do me nicely for the month.

Thursday, July 2, 1970. Our whole crew scrubs the Emergency Room in preparation for the inspection next Tuesday. We go down on our hands and knees and scrub the floor with a fine brush. We pull every package of supplies and check the expiration date. We move all the cabinets and clean the floors underneath them. We find several pieces of lost equipment and one chart, dated August 1968, behind the cabinets. That Emergency Room hasn't looked so clean since it was built.

While I am down on my hands and knees scrubbing the floor I remind myself Florence Nightingale had to make beds—actually construct them—when she was in the Crimea. I guess if she could do that, I can scrub floors. The room is a shambles while we clean and when casualties come in, there is no place for their stretchers. We tuck stretchers into odd corners, like the admissions clerk's cubbyhole and the bathroom behind the clinic, assign staff to take care of them, and the rest of us go on with our cleaning. Today, of all days, surgery is backed up and we wait four and a half hours to get four men into surgery. Usually the wait is an hour or less.

The zinnias in the flower bed have sprouted and we hoped the Colonel wouldn't take a short cut from the mess hall to his office. Today he and the Chief Nurse are out behind the Emergency Room trying to decide if the body shed needs to be painted before the inspection and he almost trips over the rocks we put around the flower bed. He comes inside and tells the wardmaster, "Get rid of that garbage." One of the corpsmen who was really close to the medic who was killed, tries to explain to him that is our memorial. He gets really angry when the Colonel won't listen and ends up on report for insubordination. He's facing an Article 15, which is one step away from a court-martial. The Chief Nurse is on our side and she finally convinces the Colonel that the flowers should stay. All in all, it is a Number Ten day all around.

There are really only three points on the rating scale. Number one, G.I. is the best, understood by both the Americans and the Viet Namese, especially the kids. That might be the only American they can speak, but they know number one is a good thing to be. Number Ten is bad news. Really bad news is Number Ten Thou. There are no markers between these points and no need for them. Life is either good, bad or very bad. We don't deal in grey areas.

Friday, July 3, 1970. The Emergency Room crew has a Fourth of July barbecue and do a lot of talking about how we are snapping at each other lately. Sometimes we don't trust each other. Some of the corpsmen don't like working for women. Some of the nurses, including me, feel like we went to nursing school and we know more than they do. It's the old-timers, both officers and enlisted, who try to make peace among us. I don't know what good it will do, but at least things are more out in the open.

Saturday, July 4, 1970. Armed Force Viet Nam radio tells us about the Fourth of July celebrations in the States. I suppose all those rallies in support of what we are doing are nice, but there are three hundred and sixty-four other days in the year and by next week all we will hear again is dissent. It's hard to know what the mood in the States really is. Our only contact is the media and we don't trust them.

Sunday, July 5, 1970. The helicopter bring a body into the pad and the crew hauls the big, black plastic body bag into the body shed. The shed is wooden, unpainted, with a tin roof and a strong lock on the door. We take turns having body shed duty and today is my turn. I get the key, go out and unlock the door. At least this is a fresh kill. They get really messy when they have been in the jungle a while. Every time we get one of those, I'm afraid it will be Barry's body and I'd rather not think about that.

This is a Special Forces sergeant, a big man, almost too big for the body bag. His face is a mess and the rest of his body is peppered with shrapnel fragments. Stone cold and hard to move. I wouldn't think bodies could get this cold in hot weather. Anyway, I go though his pockets, pull out any papers, his wallet, his dog tags. I flip the wallet open and realize I had coffee with this man a few days ago at the Special Forces compound. I haven't even recognized him.

Chaplain W. preaches today about making the most of this year by dealing with people. He says love of self is the standard by which we measure love of neighbour. If we do not love ourselves, we can't have enough love to go around to others. He says this relates to confidence, that if we don't have confidence in ourselves we constantly seek reassurance from others. Thus we aren't able to give them something in the relationship, but end up only taking. That part of the sermon moves me because I realize I'm constantly seeking reassurance from others. I think that's what Barry recognized when he said, "I know you think I somehow have all the answers, but I don't. I can't make everything better for you." My confidence in what I can do, the tasks I can perform in the Emergency Room grows every day. I wonder how long it will be before my confidence in myself grows also?

Tuesday, July 7, 1970. The colonel has a barbecue this afternoon, a hail-and-farewell for people coming and going. It's hard to believe I didn't know any of these people six weeks ago. There are a couple of new Dustoff pilots who have just arrived: Ed W. and Don U. Nurses and helicopter pilots tend to get on well together, perhaps better than nurses and other medical people. Perhaps this isn't so strange because we work with the same people all day, every day and don't want to be with them on our time off, too. At least pilots give us a different perspective on the war.

Wednesday, July 8, 1970. The 101st Airborne must have really been creamed. About forty or fifty med-evacs arrived today and we are the third hospital they have filled. They have already been through Emergency Room in other hospitals, so when they come here, they go directly to the wards. We spend a lot of time today directing people and sometimes escorting them to the wards. I've hardly been on a ward since the tour the first day I was here. Sometimes the wards become vague and hazy, an *out there* where we send the patients when we are finished with them in the Emergency Room. I stop today to actually look at the wards: the double rows of iron beds, the metal medicine cart, the orderly daily routine. I feel a little twinge of desire for ward work again, for the order and the routine, but then every time someone with an urgent need comes into the Emergency Room and I know that's the only place I want to work here.

...The 101st Airborne must have really been creamed...

Thursday, July 9, 1970. More rain tonight. It comes as spurts of sudden, blowing rain joined by long, misty drizzles. The lights outside the Emergency Room become foggy and are finally hidden until only the yellow and blue lights on the helipad remain. Dawn sluggishly appears, the whole sky black, then dark blue, purple and finally grey. I go home from night shift under a leaden sky, the mist still falling and the whole world wet. Sometime during the day the clouds break and everything is yellow and blue. There is a beautiful breeze that reminds me of September days in Louisiana when the first cool weather comes.

I'm intrigued by one of the new pilots, Ed W. He is 23, and for the past two days I haven't been able to get him out of my mind. He has curly brown hair, a thick mustache and a body that looks great in a flight suit. For the first time since Barry died, there is someone to talk to, someone who isn't always pawing me or trying to get me into the sack.

283rd Dustoff is our Helicopter Ambulance Unit. Their ambulances, big green helicopters painted with red crosses, are parked in a muddy field between the Emergency Room and the enlisted men's hooches. They fly any time from dawn to dusk, but at night only in emergencies. Sometimes they receive a call just at dusk and we—the pilots, nurses and corpsmen—sit through the night, waiting out a first light mission, knowing there are wounded men on the ground no one can reach. As soon as there is a hint of pale pink dawn one of the ships cranks. They have big turbine engines which start with a low whine and build to a teeth-rattling pitch. Some days the helicopters are a shuttle service, out for a pickup, back with another load. We monitor their radio traffic: "Dust-off six niner. Inbound your location, thirty minutes to the west. Three Victor Novembers and two Uniform Sierras." Thirty minutes to the west usually meant they are coming from Cambodia. Victor Novembers are South Viet Namese soldiers, Uniform Sierras are Americans.

Sometimes when the weather is very hot, we make popsicles in the freezer: a paper cup filled with Kool-aid and a tongue blade for a handle. When the helicopters make run after run, we take popsicles to the crew. One day we forget. The ship stays on the pad after all the casualties have been removed and we

...they look like giant insects...

can't figure out why. Then the radio calls with the message, "I have this really weird message for you. The pilot says to tell you 'Fast Eddy' is on the pad and he's not leaving until he gets one orange and three grapes. Does that make any sense?" We send one of the corpsmen out with the popsicles.

Because they fly red-cross-marked ships, Dust-off crews aren't allowed to carry weapons. Many of them do, sometimes sawed-off shotguns or big Colt .45 Peacemakers, just like old gunfighters. The helicopters are death traps, lightweight aluminum frames filled with magnesium. The fuel, JP-4, is highly explosive. If they are hit they go up in flames. And yet Dustoff flies everywhere, any time, into any situation to retrieve the wounded. To go anywhere is a matter of pride with the pilots. There is a classic tape one of the pilots played for us in Basic Training. The pilot is taking fire and the radio operator on the ground yells for him to pull out, to leave the wounded. The pilot responds, "After I have your wounded." Then there is gunfire and the copilot's voice says the pilot is dead. The man on the ground again tells him to pull out. The copilot's voice replies, "After I have your wounded."

They wear a soft brown flight suit made out of a flame retardant material called nomacks. The suit can't be washed or it loses its flame retardant property. The pilots smell like sweat, oil and JP-4. They also wear maroon baseball caps that say Dustoff on the front and their name on the bottom of the back.

Pilots are Warrant Officers, a rank between enlisted men and officers. The youngest I've met is nineteen and on his second tour of Viet Nam. The old man in the group is "Fast Eddy." He's thirty-two. They decorate their flight helmets and when they pull the visors down they look like giant insects. Most of them have mustaches. Off duty they travel in packs and drink an incredible amount. The pilot who has to fly in an emergency is called the first up.

He doesn't drink that night.

We learned at Ft. Sam that there is a natural affinity between nurses and helicopter pilots. We all congregated in the Pit, our basement snack bar and tavern. The Pit had a ceiling so low the taller pilots had to duck to keep from bumping their heads. We went there for breakfast, rubbing the sleep from our eyes, adjusting our brass and tacking pins in unruly hair. Pilots came in, already in their flight suits, and one of them played "Sky Pilot" or "Ruby, Don't Take Your Love to Town" on the jukebox. The room vibrated with the opening bars and we held on to the tables and to our emotions. In the six weeks we were at Ft. Sam, the group of pilots changed three times. The pilots at Ft. Sam were always just on their way to Viet Nam or just coming back. They had the smell of war on them and it was exciting.

Here they also have the smell of war on them. They go places I can't, are in fire fights and land in hot landing zones. I have been in-country two months. There is no official moment when a person stops being a newbie, but after eight weeks, I feel well past that stage. I'm no longer afraid for myself. I've made it through two months, well on my way to being invincible. But it's not that way for Ed. He's so new here. I hate to see his ship crank, especially for a first-light mission. For the first time I am afraid for someone else.

Friday, July 10, 1970. I am sent, no not sent, exiled, to work on the indigenous ward today. It is very strange to see only Viet Namese patients and I don't like it one bit. I am uncomfortable on this ward, both fascinated and terribly uneasy. I feel as if working here would be a real challenge and perhaps I should try it, but at the same time I have no desire to work here. I wonder what I have done to be asked to leave the Emergency Room? Maybe I'm not a good enough nurse to take care of G.I.s.

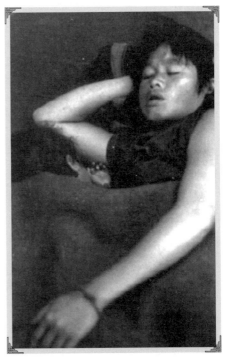

The ward is arranged just like Intensive Care: a shoulder-high wall down the middle of the room with two rows of beds on each side of the wall. The beds are closer together than in the G.I. wards and the lack of space between each bed reminds me of Lafayette Charity Hospital, where I did my clinical practice in nursing school. Every kind of case is on the ward: very seriously ill, orthopaedic, children in croup tents, medical patients. The ward is so noisy, full not only of patients but their families as well. The families are taught to provide much of the care and it seems too informal and disorganized. Children play on the floor, women nurse babies; there's this feeling that they, not us, are in charge here.

The nurses seem to be able to communicate well without speaking Viet Namese or the Montagnard dialects. There is a nurse on this ward who has been trained in Viet Nam; the nurses rely on her a great deal, not only for translation, but to understand what is important to the patients. Captain L., the Head Nurse, comes back from leave today. She enjoys working with the indigents so much she has volunteered to stay an extra six months.

❀ ꕔ ❀

Calgary, Alberta. I thought being in the Army meant to go anywhere, to do anything that was ordered. It never occurred to me to ask my Head Nurse why I was being sent to do ward work. Perhaps she would have said, "I don't like you, I want you out of my sight for a few days." Perhaps she would have said, "You're the kind of person who adapts well to difficult situations." Perhaps she would have said, "No special reason. It's just your turn this time." What actually happened was that I did what I was told and resented it.

Or interpreted it badly. I felt I was being given a subtle hint that they didn't want me in the Emergency Room, that I should ask for a transfer to this ward. My Catholic upbringing had taught me that difficult situations were opportunities in disguise. Perhaps God was suggesting that I give up work I loved for work I hated. I dug in my heels and said no to God.

It took me years to realize what good things were happening on that ward. The nurses there simplified the care as much as possible. For example, heavy plastic bags filled with water were used as the weights in applying traction and families were taught to do dressings with a few materials. They were preparing the people to take care of their families without sophisticated medical care. When Viet Namese casualties came in from the field, having been treated by their own medics, their field dressings were often pieces of cotton batting held on by strips of old-fashioned white adhesive tape. Their civilian facilities weren't any better-stocked; so it was really up to the families to provide care. The families learned complicated care: how to adjust traction, turn a Stryker frame, care for a colostomy, do range of motion exercises, and they were very faithful to see that everything was done on schedule.

I thought Captain L. quite intimidating. She had worked with Viet Namese and Montagnards for a long time, had learned their languages and something about their culture. When the 71st closed, I think she went to M.A.C.-V. as an advisor. Eventually I heard she was decorated for her work with the Viet Namese. I hope that was true. It wasn't until twelve years later, when I began working with Dene Tha in northern Alberta, that I began to understand what she was trying to accomplish: to make the Viet Namese as independent as possible in caring for their families.

I'd often wondered what happened to the Viet Namese nurse, whether she wanted to leave Pleiku before it fell, was able to do that, and what happened to her afterwards.

Saturday, July 11, 1970. The patient who received the long back laceration in the Chinook crash wrote the E.R. a thank you note. It's funny that he thanks us for just doing our job, even for using him as a guinea pig so we could learn to suture. But we appreciate the note and pin it on the bulletin board.

The Air Force Club has a band from the States tonight. It's nice to hear some familiar songs. I go over with some of the Dust-off crew. We do a lot of drinking; Ed teaches me to drink Black Russians, which is his favourite drink.

Sunday, July 12, 1970. The inspection will be Tuesday and the whole Emergency Crew scrubs the place down again today. At least the Colonel can't say we don't try to pass this time.

Monday, July 13, 1970. Some of our guys run into their own ambush last night: one dead and three wounded from friendly fire. It happens too often. It is no one's fault and again everyone's fault. The ambush should have been set up better, there should have been better communication. We just sigh and say, "Shit happens."

Ed is first-up last night, so he gets the call after the ambush happens. The squad leader says he doesn't think a couple of the men will live until morning. So Dust-off flies a night mission. They almost crash while picking up the wounded because the crew has vertigo and can't tell where the ground is.

Ed comes into the Emergency Room after he lands his ship and tells us

about the vertigo in an offhand manner, like it's a big joke. But he's shaking. So we joke him along and hug him and tell him everything is all right. It's early morning now. I'm jotting this down before I try to sleep and I'm still shaking.

Tuesday, July 14, 1970. A ten-year-old girl is brought in today with a small wound in the back of her right shoulder. She is hysterical and I hold her down while one of the other nurses starts her I.V. Then we take her to x-ray. We figure she has a shrapnel fragment in her shoulder, maybe even a collapsed lung. The x-ray tech comes out in a few minutes, almost white.

"This kid has a .38 slug in her heart."

The doctors just look at one another and say, "Oh, God."

We don't have a heart-lung machine, but they try surgery anyway. The membrane around her heart has sealed over the bullet wound and temporarily stopped the bleeding, but the clot gives way while they are trying to anesthetize her and she bleeds to death. The parents take it very hard. The G.I.s think that the Viet Namese are very stoic. It's not true. The men show more emotion than the women. It's her father who breaks down and sobs.

I suppose we passed the inspection. We are too busy with the little girl when the inspection team comes through to notice. After the emotional drain of the past two days, I don't think I have enough energy to care.

Wednesday, July 15, 1970. My best friend from grammar school writes me. Her husband served as a Marine in I Corps a couple of years ago. She is upset because so many people don't understand the people who come home from 'nam. They are labeled killers, and shunned.

We spend a lot of time talking about not going back to the States. Some of the corpsmen want to stay in Viet Nam, some want to go to Germany or South America. Almost every day we talk about the pros and cons of emigrating to Australia or Canada

We talk a lot about what we have left back in the world/back on the block. Mostly we talk about the people, our families, our friends, our lovers, what we want to do when we go home, what we miss most. If we talk at all about ideals, philosophies, patriotism, we make jokes. We take our cue from Frank Burns in *M*A*S*H*. We are what's standing between the free world and the godless hoards of Communism and with us as sentinels, the free world is in a lot of trouble.

It is difficult to believe the enemy is actually out there in human form. I can't equate the person with setting the mine, the human being with throwing a grenade. It's hard to imagine someone actually wants to kill me, not by accident, not by the wrong mortar coordinates, but by intentionally taking my life. Nor do I think very much about the patients we see in sick call or the clinics killing anyone. I know intellectually that they have killed. It just doesn't sink in so that I feel it.

This stage of the war is the "Pacification Program," or as Special Forces puts it, "We're here to win the hearts and minds of the people, even if it means burning their fucking huts down."

I do not disassociate myself from the soldiers in the field. There is no division, them as killers, myself as healer. I am here because I am a soldier and it's a soldier's job, as Patton said, "Not to die for your country, but to make some other poor bastard die for his country." I begin to realize what Barry meant when he said someone taught me to think like a soldier. We often feel ourselves the outcasts, the pariahs. Like garbage collectors, undertakers and policemen, we have taken on those jobs that society needs to survive. I don't spend any time worrying about whether society should need soldiers and war to survive. That's for someone else to worry about. My job is to keep soldiers alive from the Emergency Room to the door of Surgery. My war is fifty feet of blue corridor. There is no going back to who I was before I came here. I don't expect anyone back in the world to understand. The most I hoped for is they will leave me alone. I can't afford to think about going home yet. It's too far away. There are too many days and nights to go through before I climb on the freedom bird. I don't think about how people at home will treat me when I go home. The memory of Kent State, which happened a few days before I left the States, is still fresh and horrible in my mind. If the National Guard can shoot down people who are peacefully protesting, how is my country any different from what is happening here? What are the people who haven't been here going to do to those of us who have been here?

❀ ꇎ ❀

Calgary, Alberta. What is a soldier? How is a soldier related to society? I still didn't know, other than that idea of my war being fifty feet of blue corridor. That is still true. Many of the things I read over the past twenty years, many of the things I heard other soldiers say, confirm that war—that being a soldier— boiled down to whatever fifty feet of territory you were responsible for at the time.

❀ ꇎ ❀

Thursday, July 16, 1970. About nine tonight, Ed knocks on the hooch door. It's raining like crazy and he is soaked. I tell him Ruth and her fiance are probably over at the Officers' Club.

He says, "I came to see you."

He wants to make love. I think, why not? Maybe we are in love. It has happened to Ruth, why not to me? Maybe we'll get married, raise kids and tell them about our wartime romance. And if we're not in love, this is a romp in the sheets with no strings. He isn't married, he doesn't have a woman waiting at home. I've earned it, I've been through the fire. I don't believe in this nonsense of sex making me a woman. If I didn't grow up huddling under the bed during a mortar attack, a man putting his penis into me isn't going to make me grow up. If I haven't become an adult holding men and children while they died, a man holding me isn't going to accomplish it.

So we make love. It is lovely and moving and I am glad I waited until I am twenty-three before doing it for the first time. I feel like I am old enough to enjoy my coming of age. I had no idea I can feel so close to another person. It is terrific, a tremendous release!

Friday, July 17, 1970. It rains all Thursday night, while we sleep holding each other. In the morning we dress and play a little charade for Terri's and Ruth's benefit. My door is next to the back door of the hooch. Ed goes out the back door quietly and comes around to the front door, knocks and asks loudly, "Anyone in here going to breakfast?" Then we go to the mess hall together.

Time to face the consequences. What I did last night is against all the Catholic teaching I have been brought up to believe. According to what the nuns told me, I have sinned. In order to confess I must have the intention of not sinning again and I have every intention of going to bed with Ed again. I am so full of what happened last night that nothing else is on my mind. I float through work today.

Saturday, July 18, 1970.
The plains around Pleiku are blue and gold, washed clean by the rain. A bit of wet haze hangs over the valley, water droplets sparkle on the grass. This morning about eleven, I go into a little side room in the chapel where they keep a statue of the Blessed Virgin. The
window behind her is open and I look out on the lovely, clear morning. My mother tells me that when I was born, she placed me on the altar in front of Mary and dedicated me to her. I've said the rosary all my life. I've been in the Sodality of Mary and still wear the sodality medal under my fatigues. But today I try to pray to her to intercede for me for forgiveness and realize there is an impossible gulf between Mary as Virgin and me. How can a woman who I was taught has been a virgin all her life possibly understand what I experienced Thursday night? I don't think Mary and I have anything left to talk about.

Sunday, July 19, 1970. I am glad to be working today so I don't have to face the decision to go to church. Other than being sick, I've never missed Mass on a Sunday in my life. We have a dispensation here to miss Mass if we are on duty or a priest isn't available, so I won't commit a further sin by not attending. If I do go, I'll have to face the question of Confession again and I don't think I should go to Communion again until I do confess what I did Thursday night. According to the Church's Commandments I must, "Confess my sins at least once a year," and, "Receive Communion during the Easter time." Easter time extends from the beginning of Lent to Pentecost Sunday; I have a whole year before I come up against the deadline.

The Emergency Room is always quieter on Sunday, rather like night shift with the sun shining. We have time to talk to the patients and to relax.

One of the M.A.C.-V. team leaders is in for tests. He's been having bloody diarrhea and no one can figure out why. He tells me about his command. He is one of five Americans living with about 5,000 Montagnards. Even when all the combat troops are withdrawn, advisors like him will still be here. They are the people who are doing the Viet Namization Program, the U.S.'s plan to turn over our equipment and sites to Viet Namese. Most of the people here don't believe the Viet Namese can take care of themselves. Any of the buildings we have already turned over have been stripped of furniture, glass and fixtures. Some people say they sell whatever we give them on the black market. Perhaps they just realize you don't need office furniture and glass windows to fight a war.

The 'Yards are different. They are, in my view, a fiercely independent people. All they want is a little piece of ground to farm, some pigs and chickens and the freedom to roam the mountains. They fight guerrilla war well.

Monday, July 20, 1970. We have two new nurses in the Emergency Room and working with them makes me realize how fast new things become routine. They are having a very difficult time with the same things I did and yet it seems like I've known how to do these things for such a long time. I'll have to be more patient with them. With Sheri working nights and Joan, the Head Nurse, leaving in a few days, it will be all newbies in the Emergency Room. That will be hard for us.

Tuesday, July 21, 1970. Even here, we see the same diseases from the States, such as heart attacks, gallbladder troubles and cancer. A Montagnard man, about thirty years old, is brought in today with bone cancer. The whole head of one femur has been eaten away. What are we to do with him? We aren't able to keep him until he dies. There isn't even any way of explaining to him what is wrong with him. Their idea of sickness is different from ours. He probably thinks he has been inhabited by spirits or something. In the end we give him morphine and send him over to the C.I.D.G. hospital that Special Forces runs. He's their problem now.

Wednesday, July 22, 1970. The Emergency Room staff has another serious discussion tonight. The corpsmen say the newcomers, including me, aren't catching on fast enough. They feel as if they still have to remind us about things we should have known long ago. They feel as if we are stepping on their toes, taking too much for ourselves and not leaving enough for them to do.

It hurts to be told this, hurts even more that they still consider me a newbie. I've been here for two months and I thought I'd proved myself. But they still see me as an outsider. I don't know how to change that.

❖ ☖ ❖

Calgary, Alberta. Twenty years later it still hurt. I am so much better now, in my mid-forties, at being part of a team than I was at twenty-three. Now I would know what to do, how to confront attitudes, how to relax and learn from other people. Then I didn't.

Maybe we were all too young and inexperienced to be doing what we were asked to do. I remember that most days I went to work scared that somehow I wouldn't measure up and that it took me years to get over that feeling.

❁ ♮ ❁

Thursday, July 23, 1970.

Our hooch has a new pet for a few hours today, a tiny white kitten we decide to call Spitfire, because he spit at everyone. We find him wandering around the back of the hooch and think he must have wandered in across the road and through the barbed wire. I take him over to the Emergency Room and the doctors decide he will be a lot happier with them, so they kidnap him for their hooch.

Ed and I are on-again, off-again. Once he doesn't call or see me for three days, but when we are together again he enjoys my company. He doesn't laugh at me because I am inexperienced. Sometimes I think he's not all that experienced himself. We are gentle and slow with each other in bed. We like talking and holding each other.

The guilt hangs on. I tried to make a confession last Sunday and couldn't. I confessed the small, venial sins, but not this one. The lack of confession bars me from communion. It is so hard to sit through Mass each Sunday. I feel dishonest, hypocritical, but if I miss Mass I commit a mortal sin. Every morning I make up my mind to tell Ed what we are doing is a mistake, that we must stop doing what we are doing. And then I look at that wonderful face across the supper table and think what we are doing can't be all that bad.

Suddenly, my religion no longer works. Those years at Catholic school, in the Sodality, training in a nun-administered hospital didn't teach me anything other than there is an absolute right and wrong. That can't be the way the world is. If I have to live in an absolute world, I will go crazy.

Friday, July 24, 1970.

Don U. asks me if I want to go for a ride with them over to Camp Holloway to fuel up. What a trip! The view is fantastic, a photographer's paradise, and I love the sense of moving in more than one plane at once. It feels as if the chopper is part of me. Don flies in the same way other people drive a car or run a boat. The closest I've come to this feeling before is being in a small motor boat skimming at high speed over the Gulf at Cypremort Point. Even the helicopter noise isn't as bad as it sounds on the ground, but the wind that comes through the open doors is so strong that it is impossible to wear a hat or glasses without losing them.

Saturday, July 25, 1970. One of the Dust-off pilots is shot today. One of the other pilots is cleaning his pistol two rooms away and it goes off. The walls between their rooms are only sheets of plywood and the bullet comes through two walls and lodges in his arm. Fortunately, he isn't badly hurt, but he can't fly for several weeks. He is close to going home anyway and they will probably send him home early.

Someone tells me they found Barry's body today, or at least the wreckage is found. I hope they don't bring the remains here. I don't think I could take having them a few feet away in the body shed.

❀ ▷ ❀

Calgary, Alberta. Finding Barry's body was, like many other things there, only a rumour. It was never found.

❀ ▷ ❀

Friday, July 26, 1970. One of the Special Forces majors gives me *The Sensuous Woman*. He has it brought all the way from a book store on Okinawa. It is a funny gift, as if he knows what has happened between Ed and me and wants to celebrate it with me. The major was Barry's friend and took me under his wing after Barry died. It is funny that I look to him for advice. He's not that much older than I am. I ask him why he wants me to have this book. He says, "You're a talented lady, but you have some growing up to do. You might as well start doing it."

Monday, July 27, 1970. Tonight we have the going away party for Joan P. and Louis L. The pool is still closed, but we have the party at pool side and are all dunked in the scummy water.

We have a new Orthopaedic Technician named Prejean. He lived in Lafayette, about two blocks from the university where I went to school. We might have passed each other on the street. It is so nice to hear a Cajun accent again, almost like being back on the block.

It begins to rain again. We have had ten days of dry weather and rumour says Charlie is using the good weather to set up attacks. There are also rumours that our hospital will close in December or January. We are currently operating a hundred beds, only half our strength. Supposedly the surgical "T" will be the last to close and we might become an evacuation point and dispensary. I don't want to think about that. My life is too much here to imagine being anywhere else.

Tuesday, July 28, 1970. Today there are five people working in the Emergency Room and of them I have the most experience here. We measure experience in days, weeks at the most. It takes very little time to become old.

We have two interpreters. Mr. Hai speaks Viet Namese and Sam speaks one of the Montagnard dialects. Mr. Hai has a death in the family and is away today for the funeral. I ask Sam who died and he replies, "I don't know. It's not my family."

Wednesday, July 29, 1970. I still don't know where I stand with Ed. Part of me likes him a lot, part of me spends a good deal of time avoiding him. I want him and I don't want him and I don't understand these feelings.

Thursday, July 30, 1970. Stars and Stripes, our weekly military newspaper, comes out every Thursday. They have a column "Missing in Action/Killed." I look today to see if Barry has been upgraded to killed. He would have been if they have really found his body, but his name isn't on the list. Upgraded to killed—what a funny term, yet we use it all the time, as if being killed is one step up on being missing. I suppose for the families it is better because the uncertainty is over.

We have our first G.I. casualties in a long time. One of them is badly hurt, a broken back with a spinal cord injury. He'll be in a wheelchair the rest of his life. All we have been seeing for days is Viet Namese and 'Yards. The action has been so light here lately that I guess we will be moving in a few months. We don't seem to be needed here any more. If we're leaving, Dust-off will leave also. I hate the thought of Ed going away.

Friday, July 31, 1970. Pay day and I begin to think of all the things I want to buy. I spend hours going over the PACEX catalog. This is the catalogue put out by the Post Exchange system in the Pacific. Those of us who are stationed in Viet Nam, Thailand, Japan, Korea, Okinawa and other Pacific postings can order from it. There are glossy pages full of china, bronze flatware, jewelry, cameras, electronic equipment, carved monkey wood. I fantasize a lot about buying everything in the catalog, but when it comes to actually spending money, I am very conservative. I've set my limit at one piece of camera equipment every one to two months. I already have a Pentax camera and a 50 mm lens. I want a telephoto lens next.

I'm spending time over at C.I.D.G. hospital, not working as I originally intended to do, but just hanging around with the Special Forces medics. I fill my off-duty time with that and with developing pictures at the Air Force Photo Lab.

Tomorrow I begin a week of nights. Time to do penance again.

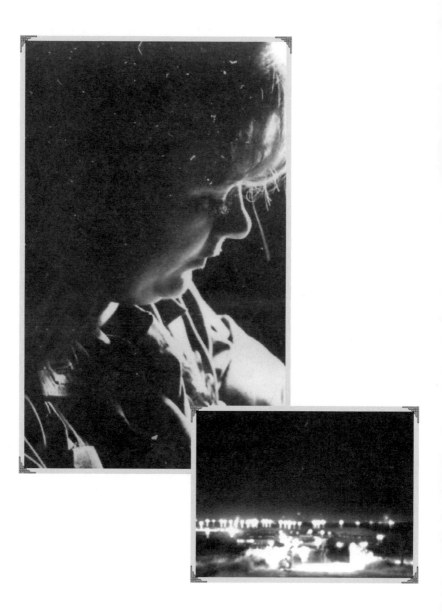

1970 August 1970

Saturday, August 1, 1970. This isn't a hospital, it's a hotel! Six of the pilots from the helicopter unit Ghost Riders who are stationed across town at Camp Holloway come over to the Air Force club and are weathered in. So they spend the night in the back of the surgery clinic. At six a.m. we wake them, give them coffee and aspirins and send them on their way.

Ellis, the radio-telephone operator from Dust-off, has come back from leave. He says Dust-off is definitely being transferred, but he doesn't know when, only that it will be soon. He doesn't want to go. He's been here almost two years and there isn't any other place he wants to be.

Sunday, August 2, 1970. Work this weekend is just like a weekend in the Emergency Room back in the world. Saturday night we had drunks sleep over; tonight we have drunks who have been cut in fights. The doctor on call, the corpsman and I do a lot of suturing.

Dust-off goes out around midnight for an emergency pick-up and when they come back we reward them with popsicles. These pilots are new and I guess no one told them about the popsicles. They have the most surprised look on their faces.

I've become spoiled with night shift being so quiet lately. Actually having patients at intervals all night upsets my cleaning routine. Cleaning is what we do most on night shift. I don't mind it because it makes the night go faster and the Emergency Room looks nice when we finish.

We start night shift at 1900 hours. Often we have patients in and out until about 2300 hours. The typical problems are guys who sprained their ankle during the day and come to see us after they are off duty, or soldiers with medical problems like fever and diarrhea or, like last night, people with cuts to suture. Sometimes E.R. staff who have the day off drop by to pick up their mail and stay to chat.

At midnight we tally the day book, a big green ledger where we make handwritten entries. We call it doing the count. We draw a red line after the name of the last patient seen before midnight and count how many people were seen

during the twenty-four hour period, what was wrong with them, what we'd done with them. Friday's counts are always the highest, rarely below a hundred and often closer to a hundred and fifty. Sunday's counts are the lowest, often less than thirty and once as low as nine. After we count what is in the book, we write in today's date and there is a blank page ready for . . . who knows what?

We take turns going to midnight chow. They usually serve fried eggs, creamed chipped beef on hard biscuits and lots of coffee. We bring back fruit and ice cream, if we can get it, to eat later.

The hospital doesn't observe any blackout conditions and the mess hall windows are lit squares clearly visible in the darkness. It's a good thing Charlie rarely wants to bomb us, because we stand out as a target.

By the time we are back from midnight chow, Armed Forces Viet Nam's Nightline program has begun. We keep the radio on all night unless we have casualties. It's too hard to hear blood pressures or what the doctors want with the radio on, so when the causalities come in, the radio goes off. The program plays mostly music from back home, with breaks for hourly news and sports. We settle down to write letters or read a book borrowed from the Red Cross library. Sometimes I set up my camera and practice with different f-stops or lighting. Sometimes the corpsman and I talk, mostly about home or about people on the compound. Once we are talking about the drug problem and I say I have no idea what marijuana looks like. The corpsman leaves for a few minutes and comes back with this small packet. He shows me the leaves and seeds and tells me how to tell what is high grade stuff. He says, "I'll be glad to share this with you, ma'am, if you want."

I laugh and say, "No thanks, I'd rather stick to booze."

So he wraps his packet and takes it back to wherever it came from. I would report him in an instant if he came to work smelling of hash or his performance were impaired, but otherwise I figure what he's doing is his business.

The nights are long. Sometimes the corpsman sleeps on one of the stretchers in the back room. I wake him up if there are any casualties or about 0400, whatever comes first. The corpsmen offer to cover for me if I want to nap, but somehow I can't do it. I'm supposed to be on duty and it just doesn't seem right for me to sleep.

We start cleaning about four a.m., always the same way, always very methodical. We start with the clinic cubicles because they are out of the way on the left side of the hall. We restock the drawers, wipe the counters with alcohol, empty the trash. I do the restocking and the counters and the corpsman comes behind me with a pail of hot soapy water and mops the floors.

Then we do the room in the back where we put the overflow casualties. I like to put everything in order: full supply drawers, neatly stacked linen, straight rows of sterile packages in the instrument cabinet. The alcohol makes everything smell clean. I take the steel gurneys outside and hose them down while the corpsman mops the floor and turns on the big fans at each end of the room so the floor dries. The room smells wet and cool as it dries.

We take a break when we are about halfway through, usually just after we finish the back room. We aren't supposed to cook, but we do. We have a bent, dented electric skillet. No one seems to know how long it has been here or where it originally came from. In our packages from home we get pizza mix or popcorn or Kraft dinner. We make a pizza or some Kraft dinner and make a batch of popsicles for the next day. We like the pre-sweetened Kool-aid, but lately all we have had is the non-sweetened kind. It makes lousy popsicles. The corpsman is going to see if he can't liberate some sugar from the mess hall tomorrow night.

After our break we do the front room just as we did the back room. By the time the last gurney is washed it's almost 0600 and it's just dawn outside. We listen for the sounds of a Dust-off ship cranking for a first-light mission and if there is no ship going out, we know we'll have time to finish everything. The second to last thing I do is line up all of the gurneys in formation, with a stethoscope and a fresh intravenous bottle hanging at the foot of each one. The last thing I do before the day crew arrives is make

fresh coffee and wipe down with alcohol the sink where we wash our hands, so when the wardmaster arrives the Emergency Room smells like hot coffee and every-thing shines.

The wardmaster usually arrives first and the nurses and corpsmen drift in between 0645 and 0700. At seven we give report, which is usually mercifully short. Most mornings I go to breakfast because it's my favourite meal. Then back to the hooch for a quick shower and into a warm, dry bed. I keep the electric blanket on low all night while I'm away so the sheets don't feel clammy in the morning.

Before I go to bed I drop my dirty fatigues, socks, underclothes and boots in a pile outside the door. My mama-san collects them during the day, so that when I get up there are polished boots and a pile of clean, dry, ironed clothes outside my door. If I'm lucky I sleep until five or six in the evening. Most of the time I work nights I have time for a quick supper and then back to work. I am usually on night rotation for five to seven shifts in a row, so that by the time I finish a whole week has gone by in which I've done nothing but work, eat and sleep.

Monday, August 3, 1970. I am in the middle of a long string of nights and am too tired to write anything coherent.

Tuesday, August 4, 1970. Barbara K. and I were sworn into the Army at the same ceremony. She was also a nursing student at the University of Southwestern Louisiana; she was the only one in our class who fainted in surgery. I haven't seen her since basic a year ago. Today a note is delivered by one of the chopper pilots. Barbara has just arrived in An Khe, just a little ways down the road from us. If things stay quiet and our Dust-off ships keep making runs down there I'll go and see her. Or perhaps she can come here for a day. As she says in the note, now that we are so close it would be a shame not to keep in touch.

Wednesday, August 5, 1970. Jeanne, my best friend from high school, writes me a letter in which she says I'm becoming very brief and noncommittal in my letters to her. I'd planned to write long, detailed letters to her, describing the war and the people here. But it's so hard to give any kind of a picture of what it's like here. She will have to be satisfied with brief sketches. I'll send her some pictures. Perhaps that will help.

Thursday, August 6, 1970. I make another M.A.R.S. call home today. Only John is home. He seems to be feeling well after his open-heart surgery. It is a funny conversation. We have seventeen thousand miles between us and we are yelling back and forth about the dog and the cat. As with Jeanne, he doesn't know what to ask me and I don't know what to tell him.

Friday, August 7, 1970. Star Trek is on Armed Forces Viet Nam Television tonight. Watching it is just like being back in the world. It is hard to remember at times that we are in the middle of a war.

Around 0100 it becomes a lot easier to remember. An Khe is hit by sappers. We hear that one medic, possibly two, are killed. I can't help thinking this is some reception for Barbara. She has been in-country only a couple of weeks and this happens to her.

Saturday, August 8, 1970.
A few days ago I went to one of the other hooches to find one of the nurses. I was startled to see the condition of their hooch. They have painted it, hung curtains on the windows and turned their empty room into a small kitchen. I wonder why we haven't done anything about our hooch. Our rooms are comfortable enough, but the bathroom is still green with mould and we've never done anything about creating a common room.

One of the reasons I like spending so much time at the Civilian Irregular Defense Group (C.I.D.G.) compound is that the team hooch there is more comfortable than my own hooch. I can walk in at any time and make myself at home. I like the Special Forces medics and never feel at all self-conscious around them. They are a rough lot, but what I like best about them is that they accept me and they accept being here. They seem to think that as long as we have to put in time here, we might as well make the best of it.

I can't walk to their compound from the hospital because there is some civilian territory between us and them. But when I call them someone always comes over to give me a ride. Sometimes, if I stay over there late and I have a day off the next day, I curl up on their couch in the day room instead of going back to the hospital. We are supposed to sign out and be back by curfew, but no one ever checks the books. Or if they do, they never say anything to me.

Sunday, August 9, 1970. There is a practice alert tonight, while I am over at C.I.D.G. Everybody plays soldier for a while: puts on their helmets, takes their weapons and set up a perimeter defense. I stay out of their way, which I think is exactly what they want me to do.

There is a film on television about the Army Nurse Corps. Ruth and Anita are in it. It is a lot of propaganda, all about how we are saving lives in Viet Nam. I think they are going to use it as a recruiting tool. They are using the line in their ads, "The most beautiful girl in the world is an Army nurse." Anyway we had a good laugh out of it.

...everybody plays soldier for a while...

Monday, August 10, 1970. I am so sick today, I have to leave work and go on quarters. I feel bad about that, as if I am shirking my duty. But I just can't keep throwing up and stay at work.

I'd forgotten the hustle of days. After the solitude of cleaning and no patients on nights, there are too many people, too much noise and confusion on the day shift. Some of the medics have been away on leave and are back now. There are so many people on the day shift that we trip over each other.

I've received two letters from people I knew at Ft. Riley. One is down in Na Trang and the other might be moving to Da Nang. Both seem to be doing well over here. I've been away from Ft. Riley five months, but it seems as if I left there a lifetime ago.

Tuesday, August 11, 1970. Dr. B. has a birthday party tonight. I like working with him even better here than I did at Ft. Riley. He's such a good doctor and he's terrific with the patients. All of the doctors here are assigned some specialty and Eli is Snake Bite Officer. He turns on his Jewish, New York accent and says, "I'm a kid from the Bronx. The only snakes I've seen are in the Bronx Zoo. So what do I know about snake bite?" But he sent to the States for some books and read up on it and now knows a lot about treating snake bites.

During the party I am dunked in the swimming pool again. I feel as if I'm spending more time in the water than on dry land.

Wednesday, August 12, 1970. Special Forces are trained for guerrilla warfare and they train the locals to carry out that kind of war. They fight in small teams, called A-teams, usually composed of two officers and ten enlisted men. Mike Force and the Civilian Irregular Defense Group (C.I.D.G.) are the two indigenous groups they are training and supporting in Viet Nam. There are A-teams in the hills around Pleiku, places like Dac Sien, Dak Toe, Plei Gerang, Plei Mie. Pleiku is their regional headquarters and the people stationed here are part of the next level, the B-teams. B-teams are supposed to provide support services; most of the people who have a B-team assignment were on A-teams on their last tour of Viet Nam, so the men here in Pleiku all have stories to tell.

I spend a lot of time in their team hooch, eating Rue's barbecue, drinking at the bar they constructed themselves, sometimes even tending bar. On the wall of their hooch is a framed sign:

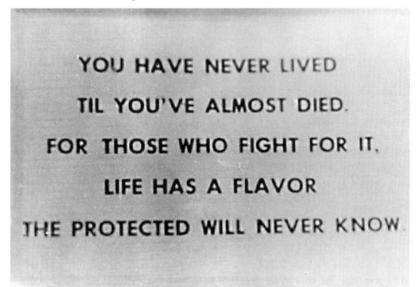

One way to interpret the first sentence is that you've never experienced a real rush until you've almost died. The second way is you don't know how special life is until you've faced death. I choose to believe the second interpretation. For those who fight for it. It's not just fighting this war or even fighting in a military war. That has to do with fighting for life, for making life what you believe it should be. I think about Douglas Bader when I read that. I guess it was his biography, which I read when I was in junior high, that made be a believer in fighting for life. I like what this sign says. I have a picture of it hung in my room and the second sentence engraved on my lighter. I don't smoke, but everyone gets a lighter here, so I did, too.

One of the Special Forces medics gave me one of their war medals. It says

War rather than Peace. I wear it under my fatigues, next to my dog tags. It makes me feel as if I'm accepted by them. I eat with them, drink with them, fend for myself when they fight and, most of all, I sit and listen to them.

Many of them are from the south. They come from the Appalachian hills, from cotton land in Georgia, from poverty and the inner cities. Some of them are in the Army because a judge said, "Jail or the Army." Some of them are here because they really believe in what we are doing here. Some of them are here for the adventure or the money or the opportunity not to be hassled. Some of them haven't been home, other than on leave, in ten or twelve years. They keep requesting overseas assignments in Viet Nam, Thailand or South America.

There is a legend that if you stay long enough in Special Forces you acquire four things: a gold Rolex watch, a star-sapphire ring, a case of the clap and a divorce. Some are already alcoholics. Some are burned out on adrenalin. Some have a wife from a second or third or fourth marriage back in the States. It seems that the smart ones, the lucky ones, get out of the business of killing and go back to other careers, families, homes. The others stay, circulating from Viet Nam to Germany, Thailand, or Panama and, when they can't stay away any longer, go back to Ft. Bragg. About three times around the circuit and a guy can retire.

They tell me stories about Ft. Bragg, about their club on Smoke Bomb Hill, about the pawn shops on Bragg Boulevard, about the drinking, the fights, the divorces. They tell me about the statue of the Green Beret in front of Special Forces headquarters. He stands almost twelve feet tall and his booted foot pins the head of a snake. In his right hand he holds an automatic rifle, but his finger is on the safety, not on the trigger and his left hand is extended in friendship. They say a block down the street, at the Smoke Bomb Hill Chapel, there is a stained glass window, a memorial to the men who have died. They laugh and say the prayer on the window can best be translated as, "God protect us while we are kicking the shit out of the rest of the world."

They tell marvelous stories. Some came to Viet Nam for the first time when the tour of duty was six months long and A-teams came together, fought together and went home together.

When I go in tonight, the Master Sergeant says, "Go congratulate Jim." So I trot down to Jim's room and say, "I"m supposed to congratulate you, but I don't know why. So congratulations. Now tell me what for?" He smiles shyly and opens his dresser drawer to show me the Silver Star he has just been awarded. All I can think of to say is, "Oh, my God."

I wait until he has gone to bed to ask the others what he did. The last time he was here he was in an A-camp about to be overrun. The officers had been killed and most of the team members, including him, were wounded. He organized the 'Yards and defended the camp for two days until they could be relieved. Even this group, who have a fair number of decorations among them, tell this story in a hushed, reverent manner.

There is one of Merle Haggard's tapes that starts with "Montego Bay" on one side and "Mama's Hungry Eyes" on the other. This evening, after they finish telling Jim's story, we drink a lot of beer, play the tape and sing harmony. Then we talk about home, about the South, about how we wish we were there tonight and about why we never want to go back.

Saturday, August 15, 1970. Jeanne sends me a tape of her playing her guitar and singing some of our favourite folk songs. There's "Ash Grove" and "500 Miles", "Michael Row the Boat Ashore", "Canadian Wilderness" and "Cruel War." There are so many memories attached to these songs. Jeanne and I sang them late at night at her house when I slept over. We sang them on the train going to Girl Scout Senior Round-up in Idaho in 1965, around campfires and early in the morning driving to Texas one weekend. We sang them together the week before I left to come to Viet Nam. I miss Jeanne. I miss Girl Scout camp and sleep-overs and sitting on her bed at two o'clock in the morning, eating Fritos and talking about our futures. I've forgotten what it's like to not drink every night. I've forgotten what it's like not to be responsible for other people's lives.

Sunday, August 16, 1970. Dustoff brings in five 'Yard patients late this afternoon. Sam, our 'Yard interpreter, doesn't work on the weekends and they don't have any casualty tags or medical records. We aren't even sure what their names are. My 'Yard is limited to, "What village are you from?" We finally get a consistent answer and put that on their charts. With a lot of pidgin English and hand waving we learn that a Special Forces medic sent them to us, but not why. There is only so much hand waving and yelling can accomplish. We begin to treat it as a puzzle, relying on what we can find on physical examination. Three of the five have a fever. All of them are sleepy and thirsty. The doctor orders malaria smears, blood counts and chest x-rays. Everything is normal.

The doctor keeps saying, "I wish Sam was here. If we could only talk to them, maybe we could figure this out."

I have an idea. I know where there are people who speak 'Yard. I call C.I.D.G. hospital and explain the situation to Bill. He goes down and brings one of their ward orderlies to the phone. I motion to this old papa-san to come over to the phone. I'm not sure he's ever seen a phone before, but he trots over and I hold it up to his ear. He listens and his eyes dart sideways, towards the phone receiver, and he backs away from it. I encourage him to come to it again and show him how to hold it. Pretty soon he's jabbering away in 'Yard.

Finally we get the story. The Special Forces medic is giving immunizations in his village today. After they have their shots, these five men develop fevers and complain of chills and pains, so the medic must be afraid they are going to have an allergic reaction. He gives them some medicine—probably Benedryl—calls in the helicopter and sends them to us. There isn't anything we can do except let them sleep off the effects of the immunizations and the Benedryl. I ask the orderly on the phone to tell them to go to the tent for the night and that we will get them back to their village tomorrow. Papa-san listens and nods, then goes back to the group and says something to them. All five gather up their bundles and quietly follow the corpsman out the back door.

They must think we are crazy. So far today someone has stuck a needle in their arm, given them a pill that makes them thirsty and sleepy, and loaded them on a helicopter, which takes them farther away from their village than they have been before. Then people yell and wave their hands at them, take blood out of their arm and have them take their clothes off and stand in a dark room while a camera is pointed at their chests. Finally a disembodied voice from a piece of black plastic speaks their language and tells them go to a tent for the night and that they will be fed and taken care of and go home tomorrow. And they just go off in a docile manner, following a stranger.

Monday, August 17, 1970. The compounds around us take incoming for about half an hour tonight. I am sitting on my bed talking to one of the Special Forces sergeants when the siren goes off. He laughs at how it takes me all of one second to dive under my bed when the siren sounds. But after the second one hits, he is under the bed with me. We lie there and wait, counting the seconds, trying to decide if the action is over. I don't get called in to work in the Emergency Room, so maybe nothing has been hit.

Tuesday, August 18, 1970. The incoming last night was a mistake, one of those involved situations that can only happen in the Army. We have a brand new Second Lieutenant from the Medical Service Corps. M.S.C. is that part of the Army where they put people with a university degree in biology or chemistry or anything that seems remotely connected with health sciences; the officers do administrative and support duties in a hospital. So this guy arrives a couple of days ago with his B.S. in biology, a set of shiny gold Lieutenant's bars and six weeks experience in the Army. The Colonel assigns him, among other duties, to be Hospital Safety Officer. Not knowing what a Safety Officer does he reads the manual which lists the duties for that position. One of the duties is to make sure every person who pulls perimeter guard fires his weapon once a month to check its accuracy.

Most of the guys who are on perimeter guard are either pot heads or trouble-makers. They are on guard duty to keep them out of everyone's hair: they work during the night and sleep during the day. We don't care if they have accurate rifles. Sometimes it worries us that they have rifles at all. Anyway, this officer discovers that they haven't fired their rifles according to schedule, so he organizes a firing party for after dark. Only he doesn't know he should inform people that there is to be firing. After dark he collects six or eight soldiers and their rifles and takes them to the far end of the hospital compound.

"Where do you want us to fire, Lieutenant," they ask.

He waves his hand in the general direction of the darkness, towards an area where there are no buildings or lights. "Oh, just fire in that direction."

What he doesn't know is that there is a perimeter trench in that direction and a patrol of South Viet Namese soldiers in that trench. They are fired upon so they set up their mortar to counter the attack. This means the mortar is pointed towards the Engineer's Compound and the hospital. That's when we took "incoming".

We're just lucky that both sides are bad shots and that no one is hurt. The Second Lieutenant is shipped off to somewhere in the D.M.Z. this morning. It's a real shame. It isn't his fault. Of course, he should have had better sense, but someone should have shown him the ropes, too. We all think it will be a shame if he gets killed up north just because of a stupid mistake.

Saturday, August 22, 1970.

Three of the Special Forces sergeants have their goodbye party tonight. Out in the small hut beside the team hooch, they have a big jug of 'Yard rice wine with a reed in it for a straw. There is a small split piece of bamboo across the mouth of the jug, with a second smaller piece set in the split at a peg. They adjust the peg and, to earn a 'Yard bracelet, I have to drink down below the peg. I do it, but it tastes awful, rather like soapy dish water. I've heard I can catch hepatitis from rice wine, so as soon as I drink it I go to the bathroom and make myself throw up. With the warm, soapy taste still in my mouth, that isn't that hard to do. Anyway, I come back to the team area and everyone pats me on the back and puts a brass bracelet on my arm. A lot of people who have worked with the 'Yards wear one and I'm quite proud of mine.

Sunday, August 23, 1970. The party is still going on this afternoon when I go back to C.I.D.G. I've had time to go home, sleep, work a shift and come back and they are still in the same place I left them, only a lot drunker. Even in university, I didn't think it was possible to party this hard. I guess we play so hard because we work so hard.

I have to come home early tonight. We have a 2000 hour curfew and I think tonight they mean it. Charlie is reported to be active in the area and with the false incoming a few nights ago, we are all jumpy. I guess going to bed early is a small price to pay for the long lull since May.

Tuesday, August 25, 1970. I spend most of the evening developing pictures at the Air Force Base lab. Some of the going-away party last weekend come out very well. I plan to give them to the guys that are leaving as souvenirs. A goodbye gift.

At least we don't have a 2000 hours curfew tonight. I enjoy every chance I have to be off the hospital compound. Except for that one brief helicopter ride with Dustoff when they went over to Holloway to fuel up, I haven't been more than a mile away from the hospital for three months. As soon as the weather turns nice, I want to go up to An Khe and see Barbara. That's a whole thirty miles away!

Wednesday, August 26, 1970. My cousin, Roland, sends me a beautiful letter, which arrives today. He is really my second or third cousin, an old man I've never met. He lives in Cannes, France, and we have exchanged a few letters ever since I studied French at university. I write to him in French and he answers in English. His English is much better than my French. He fought in World War I and

was a member of the French underground in World War II. He writes how impor-
tant he thinks my job is and how I should be very proud that what I do helps soldiers.
It is such an charming, European letter, almost something from another century. It
means a lot to me because no one has said those things to me before.

Thursday, August 27, 1970. One of the sergeants that just left C.I.D.G.
was an outstanding cook and now that he's gone home, the guys at C.I.D.G. are
complaining about having to take turns doing their own cooking. So I say I'll
make them some chicken gumbo. I unfreeze two packages of chicken—the Army
bulk packages that I can hardly lift. I substitute bamboo shoots and pieces of new
bamboo for the okra and the rest of the ingredients come dehydrated, courtesy of
the Army mess hall system. As it is simmering, one of the medics sticks his head
in the kitchen and asks if I need anything.

"A bag of rice."

He brings back a twenty-five pound bag of rice.

Friday, August 28, 1970. It seems if I'm not sleeping, working, or at C.I.D.G.,
I am in the darkroom at the Air Force Base. It's about a ten-minute walk, through
the back gate behind the Emergency Room, across an open green field, down by the
Air Force chapel. The processing lab is in a tiny tin building, with most of the inte-
rior dark behind a double black curtain. It's almost like a Halloween fun house
trying to bat my way through the curtains and into the unlit room.

I like what I do here because it's my own ritual. I try to go when the place
is empty, often about three in the afternoon. It must be the effect of all of those
night shifts, but I never find the lab clean enough to suit me. I usually spend
the first half hour cleaning all the developing trays and capping bottles and
lining up the equipment in exactly the order I want to use it. Three months ago
I didn't know a thing about developing pictures. One of the corpsmen told me
I could develop negatives by stapling them to an unused piece of x-ray film and
running the film through the x-ray machine. It works, but the metal runners in
the machine make streaks on the negatives, which I don't like. So I sent away
for some books on developing from Kodak and have learned to process nega-
tives, make contact prints, print pictures, and develop my own slides. I like
doing black-and-white pictures better than slides. It's a lot more fun to have the
anticipation of whether or not the negatives will turn out well and then to play
with the enlarger and try different effects. Slides always come out pale and
bleached looking. The lab tech says it's because water temperature must   be
accurate and consistent for colour and we don't have that luxury.

I've been going through my still-life phase: taking pictures of barbed wire
and banana trees and the bunker outside my hooch at sunset. I'm learning to see
all kinds of patterns like the different clouds over the Mien Yang pass at differ-

ent times of the day or how the Air Force gate looks when the early morning fog is rolling in or the perspective of the beams in the covered walkway that connects the wards. I'm beginning to be brave enough to take pictures of people at work. Sometimes I wish I were a really good war photographer, like those people who photographed World War II for Life Magazine. There is so much drama in the Emergency Room, so much I would like to record on film, but I can't bring myself to photograph the patients. It seems an invasion of privacy.

Of course, having the camera at all is illegal. We're not supposed to photograph anything, but everyone over here has a camera. The Post Exchange even develops film for us and I've never heard of any pictures not being developed, even those of naked women. I imagine they might not develop pictures of something that was of strategic importance or that was secret, but I can't imagine anything here that hasn't been photographed.

1970 SEPTEMBER 1970

Tuesday, September 1, 1970. Half the phones in Pleiku are out today due to the rain. It is so difficult to carry on normal business without phones. When an outpatient comes from one of the other compounds their buddy usually drops him off, leaves and returns to pick him up when we call to say he's finished. But with no phones the only way to get in touch with people on other compounds is to get in a jeep and go look for them. At one point we are so backed up with patients who can't get back to their own unit that we load them on one of the ambulances and run our own taxi service. Thank goodness the phones on the hospital compound are still working. We have enough trouble finding the doctors when we need them, even with the phone working. We constantly make calls: to the lab, the mess hall, the wards, post-op and surgery. The wardmasters are organizing runners, just in case the compound phones do die.

I am supposed to go over to C.I.D.G. this evening, but with the extra work because of non-working phones I am too tired. One of the medics comes over to pick me up. He's had a hard day, too, plus having to drive over here in a pouring rain, so he's not in a good mood. I tell him I won't be going back with him and he says, "Then why the hell didn't you call and tell me not to come?" We stand staring at each other and burst out laughing.

Wednesday, September 2, 1970. There are new rumours every day that the hospital will close before the end of the year. We know by now that Dustoff is leaving, but not when or for where. Ed and I are on-again, off-again. We make love; we don't speak to each other for days. Our schedules frequently don't match and when we are together either he is tired or I am and we fight. Sometimes he dates other women and I am quite jealous. He doesn't like me spending so much time at C.I.D.G. I am trying very hard to deal with the idea that if I make love with a man, we don't own each other. I want to be mature and sensible about the whole thing; I want his body in my bed.

Thursday, September 3, 1970. After supper tonight, we are sitting in the common area at C.I.D.G. when this 'Yard man knocks on the door. His wife is outsid, ready to deliver. Bill delivers her. He barely has time to glove before the baby's head crowns. Starkey and I take pictures of the delivery. I love watching the birth; love how exciting it is. I haven't seen one in almost two years, not since I had Maternal and Child Health in nursing school. There are a lot of things here that seem exciting: the absolute panic when a mortar round goes off close-by; the fear of seeing blood all over the floor of a chopper and wondering what pieces someone is in; the pure adrenalin of the Emergency Room full of casualties and working well. But there is no sheer joy like seeing this baby born. This is a pure, clean moment for her, a moment before malaria, tuberculosis,

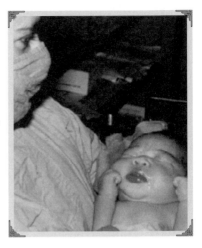

malnutrition and the war. And in that pure, clean moment, they let me hold her.

Friday, September 4, 1970. A little while after the mother and baby are settled in a bed, with her husband and son sleeping beside the bed, we have another red alert. Nothing hits near C.I.D.G. and, after the sirens and the shelling have stopped, none of us can sleep. I stay up until three in the morning talking with some of the medics. Perhaps because of the birth, or perhaps it's the birth and the red alert coming so close together, we are all vulnerable tonight. They tell me very intimate stories about what they have been through during other tours they have done in Viet Nam.

Saturday, September 5, 1970. I'm back on nights and the Hospital Commander has had a bright idea. The night nurse in the Emergency Room is now the Night Supervisor for the whole hospital, and tonight is my first taste of supervision. I make rounds on all the wards and am supposed to be available to help the staff make decisions in emergencies or unusual incidents. I graduated from nursing school sixteen months ago. I haven't done anything that would help me help the staff make decisions. Me being Night Supervisor is as ridiculous as putting the potheads on perimeter guard and probably results from the same psychology: we're going to be up all night anyway, so why not give us something to do? I wish they would leave me to just my few patients and the cleaning.

It is not a quiet first night:

A Viet Namese women dies in post-op in spite of a tremendous effort to save her.

One of the wardmasters is admitted to the hospital with a heart attack.

One of the wards asks me to start a difficult I.V. and the patient has seizures as I insert the needle in his vein.

It rains all night.

One of the corpsmen bites a patient. I try to keep a straight face while I explain to the nurse that she has to write an incident report.

At 0730, after I've given the change of shift for the Emergency Room, I have to give the Night Supervisor's report to the Hospital Commander. I'm so tired I'm not sure I remember my own name. So I walk into the Colonel's office, salute and mumble out the report. He seems to think the report is satisfactory. Then I go home and sleep for twelve hours.

…shift change report…

Sunday, September 6, 1970. Becky C., one of my classmates from nursing school, writes me a letter. She is involved in missionary work for her church and is leaving soon for West Africa. Her letter is full of news about our classmates.

My mother has a theory that about every four years a class comes along that is brighter, more cohesive, more aggressive. That was our class of '69. It was as if we hit the floor running. Someone in our class was always doing something, getting into some mischief. It came together in our junior year when our class, en masse, threatened to resign unless problems with some instructors were resolved.

A year and a half ago we were a tight group. Now we are spread out over south Louisiana, over the South, even over the globe. I'm really proud of what Becky is going to do. If I had more religious faith I might give missionary work a try, but I think it's better that she do that and I do this.

I think about nursing school at lot. Sometimes I even remember particular classes or conversations. I try to imagine how Mrs. A., our Nursing Arts instructor, would have solved a problem or if Mrs. N., who pushed us so hard to be clinically competent, would pass me for the work I do in the Emergency Room. Mostly I think about my Public Health Nursing instructor, Mrs. S. She is a tall, thin, gracious lady who is close to retirement. One time, to illustrate her point that often nurses make a difference by encouraging small gains, she told us about one of the soldiers she nursed during World War II. Her patient was badly burned and depressed. She worked for a long time to convince him he should let her write a letter for him to a girl he had been fond of in high school and talked of constantly. When he finally agreed and the girl's first reply arrived, full of love and hope for their coming life together, he began to heal. A couple of years later he sent Mrs. S. a Christmas card: he and the girl had married and he said that if she hadn't encouraged him to write that first letter, he probably would have died.

That was the only time she talked about being an Army nurse. She kept her memories to herself, but I had a sense she was proud of what she had done and at peace with herself. I like that idea.

Nursing school seems so normal, so civilized, such a long time in the past.

Monday, September 7, 1970.

One of the Special Forces medics has decided we aren't in good physical shape, so the C.I.D.G. doctor puts him in charge of organizing a physical fitness program. We play volleyball with the 'Yards today and then do exercises. I don't think this newfound energy will last. We like to drink more than we like to sweat.

I have a wedding announcement from Jerry H., who lived in the apartment next to mine at Ft. Riley. She and Howard were married August 29. There must not be any of us left at Ft. Riley. Jerry is out of the Army and married. Lee is probably out on a medical discharge; he and Debbie will be married soon. Tom has finished pilot training in Texas and is probably back in Viet Nam. Al is here. And Darcy. And Sharon J. And Larry. And Eli and I are here in Pleiku. I wondered where we will all be a year from now?

Thursday, September 10, 1970. Two years ago today Capt. Carolyn C. swore Barbara and me into the Army. I try to call Barbara in An Khe so we can celebrate, but it is her day off.

Civilian and A.R.V.N. casualties seem to be picking up. There are a lot of rocket casualties, so apparently Charlie uses the rainy season to set up more rocket sites. So far there hasn't been any great push on U.S. troops, though M.A.C.-V. and Special Forces have reported some scattered action. Everyone wondered if Charlie is building for another push or waiting to see how many troops will pull out.

Friday, September 11, 1970. I am so depressed. I go to work. It rains. I go over to C.I.D.G. It rains. I go to the photo lab. It rains. Four months of the same places, the same faces. A month of the same rain.

I'm getting careless: my room is a mess, my letters home unwritten. I'm not interested in doing anything after work except sleep. Even my work is beginning to suffer. I can't concentrate. I miss things. I feel almost as disorganized as I did when I arrived and I lack confidence in what I'm doing.

Saturday, September 12, 1970. Today is even worse than yesterday. Thank heavens there are only two more days until my day off. Talking to Barbara is the one bright spot. If the weather is nice next week, I am going to An Khe to see her. Perhaps a change of scenery will do me good.

Terri has a hard day also. She comes by the room and wants to talk and I think, just go away and leave me alone. So I ignore her for about fifteen minutes and she goes away. I must apologize to her tomorrow.

Sunday, September 13, 1970. I finally have a good night's sleep and feel better. Maybe I haven't been depressed the past few days, just tired?

Monday, September 14, 1970. A Marine helicopter crashes today and we have an Emergency Room full of patients again. Almost all the people in the Emergency Room are new and this is our first test as a team. Things go pretty smoothly; in fact, while the mass casualty is happening I feel better than I have in weeks. What was it Barry said? War is ninety-eight percent boredom and two percent sheer terror and the boredom is the hardest part. Boredom is what has been wrong lately. I came here to work. I want to work, to be challenged, to learn and improve. There haven't been many challenges lately and I feel myself growing stale.

I only hope we never have to prove ourselves like they did last April. Everyone who was here then talks about that as a real hell. They worked eighteen hours a day, seven days a week. In one week, in the Pleiku area alone, they had a Killed-In-Action count of fifty-three G.I.s in one week. They must have had them stacked like cordwood in the body shed.

Tuesday, September 15, 1970. Today makes four months in-country. I celebrate by sleeping in late because it is my day off and then go to the Air Force base to develop pictures. I have supper with Marie and Alice tonight. I don't do that often enough, just go out and socialize with the people I work with.

Wednesday, September 16, 1970. Oh, God, are we busy today! An A.R.V.N. truck hit a mine and we are full of casualties. As usual, the corpsmen are terrific, but we have a new Commanding Officer and a new Chief Nurse and that doesn't make it any easier. They aren't familiar with the way we work and seem to be at odds with us and with each other. There are orders and counter-orders all day. We are building up a lot of resentment, among ourselves and with the wards. Sometimes I wonder who the enemy is?

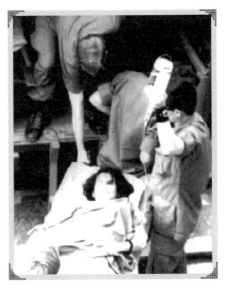

My aunt's care package arrives today, full of food from back on the block. We share the homemade cookies and bags of candy and today she is one of the Emergency Room's favourite people.

Thursday, September 17, 1970. Dustoff will leave at the beginning of next month. This is the first sign that we really are leaving. I hope to be able to stay until the beginning of December. A lot of the Special Forces are leaving then; C.I.D.G. hospital is closing and the place will be deserted. I don't know where I want to go. Nowhere really. I just want to stay here and have life go on as I have become accustomed to it going on.

Friday, September 18, 1970. Some of the Special Forces medics who were here when I first arrived have gone home. Bill and Ed have gone to Kontum. The exercise program at C.I.D.G. has petered out and the place is very quiet. I stayed over there so late last night there was no point in coming home. And it isn't safe on the road. So I spent the night on the couch in the day room. They have formation every Saturday morning at 0600. Someone goes through the hooch waking everyone up. Someone shakes me and says, "Want to stand formation?"

"NO!" I say as I turn over and bury my head in my pillow.

So they allow me to sleep.

Saturday, September 19, 1970. A pilot is brought in from a chopper crash today. His name is Glenn H.; he is from Jeanerette; he was at U.S.L. at the same time I was there. I write his name down because this is the first time I have been able to take care of someone I went to school with and I want to remember his name.

There are so many of us here, from so many different places. A dozen or so state flags hang from the Emergency Room ceiling. The Louisiana flag is here, but everyone except Prejean and me are from somewhere else. We even have a doctor from Montreal: he was studying in the States and got caught up in the draft.

Earlier this week Lou S. finished building the new bar at C.I.D.G. It is a lovely thing. The medics found some leather to line the front of the bar and two refrigerators, one for the beer and the other for food and soft drinks. They have been getting ready for the bar party all week. Yesterday we pooled our September's ration cards for beer, liquor, soft drinks and cigarettes and bought everything we could at the Post Exchange. Then they went downtown and bought a young pig, which they butchered last night. The 'Yards dug a huge pit in the back of the team hooch and roasted the pig all last night and today.

It is a wonderful party. The Special Forces chaplain, a huge man with a shaved head and a scar running down his right cheek, blesses the opening of the bar.

Most of the hospital staff are invited over for the pig roast. The word has gone out that this is an open house and at one point we must have a hundred people in the team hooch all eating, drinking and dancing. I spend most of the evening tending bar and dancing. If someone didn't contribute their ration card to laying in the stock, he or she is supposed to make a donation for their drink. So I spend a lot of the evening wheedling money out of people for their drinks.

It is a little after 2200 when I look up from the bar and sitting across from me is Jimmy W.

"Hi, young warrior."

He looks at me hard for a minute as if trying to recognize me, then smiles and says, "Hi, pretty lady."

It was our third day of basic training. Our class of four hundred nurses was assembled in the auditorium and had already sat through classes on the Army Staff, Organization of the Medical Field Service School, Military Leadership and the Code of Military Justice. A young officer with blond hair walked on stage past the podium and did a sharp right face, coming to parade rest in the middle of the stage. He wore spit-shined jump boots, a uniform so starched we saw the creases from the back of the auditorium, a green beret and a chest full of medals.

"Good morning, ladies and gentlemen. My name is Jimmy W. and I'm your instructor for compass and map reading. I'm a Green Beret. In case you don't know what that means, it means I go places where I can get hurt. And when I'm out in the field, hurt, bleeding, and call you on the radio and say hey, pretty lady, I need help; when you reply, 'Just tell us where you are, young warrior, and we'll send help' it's to my benefit that you can read a compass and a map. So believe me, you're going to learn it before I let you out of here."

There were two rumours about Jimmy W. One said he had messed up in Viet

Nam, gotten some of his men killed and been sent to Ft. Sam to teach him humility. The other was that he had been wounded and had asked to come to the Medical Field Service School to repay the nurses for saving his life. Probably both stories were apocryphal, but what was real was that he made jokes, spun stories, called us pretty ladies and was there, smiling and cheering us on when we came off the map course at Camp Bullis.

I would sit in the San Antonio August heat, listening to other instructors drone on about the Introduction to Military Preventive Medicine or the Values of Drill and Ceremony, and have day dreams about Jimmy. Once he was behind me in the cafeteria line at the Pit. He leaned across me to get some cream for his coffee and said, "Excuse me, pretty lady." I was so flustered, all I did was turn red.

Now he sits across the bar from me. We talk and he helps me tend bar for a while. We are all pretty drunk by now. Most of the guests have gone home, someone puts a country music tape on the tape player and the evening is winding down.

I pour myself a shot glass of whiskey and take out my lighter. Jimmy takes it from me, reads the inscriptions and smiles. He lays money on the bar and says, "I'll bet you can't drink it and leave fire in the glass."

I light the whiskey, toss it back in one swallow and set the empty glass on the bar. A faint blue flame cups itself inside the glass. Jimmy pushes the bill towards me.

"Where did you learn to drink a Flaming Hooker?"

"Barry H. taught me."

He describes Barry.

"That's him."

"We served together. I didn't know he was back here."

"He isn't any more."

"You going with him?"

"No. We were just friends."

"How come it's not more?"

"Because he bought the farm."

Jimmy picks up my lighter, turning it over and over between his fingers.

"I'm sorry. I'm so used to everyone around here knowing it. It was in June. He was out flying reconnaissance with the Air Force and their plane was shot down." The story rolls by then and, seeing Jimmy's pale face, I want to give him some kind of comfort. "When search and rescue found the plane, they said Barry and the pilot had died instantly in the crash. I mean he didn't suffer, at least that's something."

Jimmy presses the lighter into my hand. It is warm and he holds his hand over mine for a few seconds. "Yeah, at least that's something."

I want out of there and make some excuse about finding someone to take me back to the hospital. A couple of the medics are out on the porch, leaning into each other, almost asleep. I tell them I want to go back. One of them moves his arm back and forth, trying to focus on his watch dial.

"Can't. It's after curfew. Besides, none of us are sober enough to drive."

I find an empty room and a sleeping bag and crawl into a drunken sleep. A hand shakes me awake. I squint at the green shutters and see it is dawn. Jimmy stands beside my bed, dressed in combat fatigues. He puts his bag on the floor and sits on the bed.

"You awake?"

"Yes."

"I talked to some of the guys. They said Barry's body hasn't ever been found. Why did you lie?"

"I guess I thought it would make you feel better."

"Don't do that again." He puts his arms around my neck and hugs me. "Goodbye, pretty lady."

"Goodbye, Jimmy."

Sunday, September 20, 1970. The Emergency Room is so quiet today: only thirty-seven patients, but some of them are really sick. The wife of one of the civilian engineers is admitted with postpartum hypocalcemia. Her baby is admitted also and is being spoiled by the I.C.U. staff. We also have a guy with abdominal pain and a temperature of 104°. He probably has appendicitis, so they take him off to surgery.

I haven't had any mail in a long time. I know everyone is busy with school starting and I do owe people letters, but it would be nice to get something at mail call.

Monday, September 21, 1970. I think I am coming down with the flu. All day I am lost in a fog and not much help. I am constantly forgetting to do things and have all of the ambition of a slow turtle.

Mama's care package arrives and now my fridge is stuffed with cheese and jam and cans of Vienna sausage.

Today is the ninth anniversary of Fifth Special Forces Group being in Viet Nam. Terri and I were going to a party over there, but I just feel too lousy to go.

Tuesday, September 22, 1970. One of the C.I.D.G. medics brings in a very sick Montagnard baby today. The child has pneumonia and dies later that day. Arthur has kids of his own at home. He says he can take anything here except what this war does to the children. We spend a lot of time talking about his family and how much he misses them. Sometimes I feel like a social worker. It seems everyone comes to the nurses with their problems. It reminds me of a Peanuts cartoon that I cut out of a Sunday paper when I was in nursing school.

Snoopy sits on his dog house, dressed in his World War I flying outfit. He says, "This war is madness. It's never going to end. Maybe one of the nurses at the dispensary will talk to me." So he goes off to see Lucy in her psychiatric booth. Maybe if we charge five cents like Lucy does we'd go home rich.

Wednesday, September 23, 1970. I spend most of my day off reading old copies of the American Journal of Nursing that my mother forwards to me. I'm never certain how long I will be at one assignment, so I have never changed my address so that the journals are mailed directly to me. I'm beginning to look forward to a fixed address after I leave here. Anyway, she sent me three or four back issues as padding in the last care package. There is a whole different world in them, a world where nurses go to school and write papers and live for more than just getting though the day. There is an article about some hospitals allowing their nurses to wear pants suits at work. It's about time. I've become so accustomed to working in pants that I don't know how I'll ever go back to those starched white cotton uniforms the Army supplies stateside.

Ed comes over today. He'll stay away for weeks, then suddenly want to spend time with me. He will be leaving soon anyway, so I guess it doesn't matter any more.

Thursday, September 24, 1970. Sometimes we sit behind the Emergency Room and watch the Pink Teams—two Loches and a Cobra gunship—work out in the Ming Ying Pass to the east. The little Loches, we call them flying sperm, fly very close to the treetops. They try to attract ground fire. The Cobra waits above them. The corpsmen tell me that when the Cobra sees the flashes of fire from the ground, it screams in with its machine guns firing. That hasn't happened while I've watched. The Loches tree-hop, with the Cobra waiting above them, and after a while they turn and go off somewhere else.

Casualties are picking up in the area, so far all civilians. Rumour has it that Charlie is on the move. But that is only rumour and we have lots of those. The Special Forces A-camps are not under siege. That is my barometer for the Central Highlands. If the camps are quiet, the Highlands are safe. M.A.C.-V. reports some scattered action. The Ming Ying pass is quiet.

I am never sure whether this sounds like a fledgling military expert or just our version of talking about the weather. After four months in-country, the military jargon rolls easily through my mind. I have learned to believe only what I see. It saves a lot of wear and tear on the emotions. In the space of one day I usually hear at least a dozen rumours, sure guesses and inside information. Sometimes I wonder how much of it might be true, how much information we accidentally give Charlie.

Jerry H. and I talk about that. Jerry is the M.A.C.-V. captain who comes to us every few weeks for more tests. We have never found out what causes his bloody diarrhea and we've never cured him. But one of the doctors has taken an interest in his problem and tries this medicine or that and Jerry recovers enough to go back to the field for a few more weeks. We'll probably never find out what his problem is because he goes Stateside in fifty-three days; we both hope that just being home will make him better.

We talk a lot about war, about the concept of being an officer. It's different talking to him than it is to the Special Forces medics. They know what war is like in the field on a day-to-day basis. Jerry talks about the long-term implications of this war. He says that no one at home understands it because they don't have any idea what the history of Indochina is. They try to understand the war through western values and that just won't work. I'll miss him. His visits provide some intelligent conversation.

Friday, September 25, 1970. Most of the time I work seven nights in a row, but this is a two-night stretch. Nights are becoming my favourite duty because there are so few people around and they are usually the same people. There is also time on nights to take more time with the patients and to get caught up on paperwork. Thank goodness for A.F.V.N. radio. Without it, staying awake between 0300 and 0500 would be impossible.

Ellis, the Radio-Telephone Operator for Dustoff, usually works night shift also. I try to bring him some midnight chow whenever I am working. It means a long, dark walk down to the bottom of the hill where the radio room is located, but nothing has happened so far, so I keep doing it. I really got a talking to from the Head Nurse today. She says that has to stop and gave me a direct order not to do it again. I have the feeling I am on very thin ice with her.

❀ ꕤ ❀

Calgary, Alberta. It took me years to realize why she was mad at me. I only thought of the physical dangers, of Charlie attacking or the dangers of walking through a dark area. I was too naïve to realize that a woman going down to see a man alone at midnight gave all sorts of wrong impressions. For all our sophistication about war, we were awfully childlike at times.

❀ ꕤ ❀

Saturday, September 26, 1970. One of the pilots, Bob F., comes by and tries to start a water fight. He is in a playful mood, but after having the law laid down to me yesterday, I'm not and I tell him to go away, that I don't want to play. That makes him mad and he leaves in a huff.

Sunday, September 27, 1970. I stay awake all night talking to Lou, Ed and Carl. Today is Carl's last day in-country and we pour him on the plane this morning. Somewhere early in the morning, when we are pretty muzzy from alcohol and lack of sleep, Ed says, "There's this great bakery. I can't remember what country it's in, but they make the best bread." And Carl said, "I know the place, you turn left at such-and-such, et cetera." Ed agrees that's the place and they discuss possible countries for a while without actually deciding where the bakery is. I think how wonderful it must be to have traveled so much that you can't remember what country your favourite bakery is in. Someday I want to have traveled that much.

Monday, September 28, 1970. I plan to go to An Khe to see Barbara today, but the weather closes in and I spend most of the day sleeping instead.

Ruth is on R & R and Anita and Terri are working nights so the hooch is very quiet this evening. Guess I can go over to the club, but I stay in my room. It is really hard to take crowds some times. One or two people at a time aren't bad, but it seems all I have done for the past few weeks is drink in a noisy crowd. What I would really like is a nice, quiet library. There is a bookshelf over in the Red Cross room, mostly western and adventure paperbacks, but that's not the same thing as a real library with quiet corners where I could sit and just think.

Tuesday, September 29, 1970. I put in for my next assignment: Ft. Bragg, North Carolina. I hope I get it. Not only does it have a great reputation as an orthopaedic hospital, but there will probably be a lot of familiar Special Forces faces there.

Wednesday, September 30, 1970. Ellis gives me my own Dustoff cap today. It's maroon with Dustoff on the front and Short-Round on the back. That is his nickname for me, I guess because I am short and round. A short round is a shell that goes off unexpectedly, before it is set to go off. I guess that's me also.

1970 OCTOBER 1970

Thursday, October 1, 1970. Today is actually cold. I never imagined that Viet Nam would be cold, but it is.

A year ago today I was a brand new Second Lieutenant, just finished with Basic Training and reporting to Ft. Riley, Kansas. It was so exciting to drive up to the front gate of the post and announce that I was assigned there. The private at the gate didn't seem as impressed as I thought he should be.

I loved the old cavalry post. Its old sandstone buildings were on tree-lined streets. There was a street called General's Row that had big Victorian houses and green lawns. Civil War generals had lived there. So had Pershing and Bradley and Patton. Around the corner from General's Row was a little house that Captain George Custer had lived in and captains still lived in it. They didn't house senior officers there because, in spite of the sign in front saying it was a private residence, tourists trooped though at all hours, taking pictures and asking for a tour. I loved to drive around those older parts of the post and look at the old-fashioned buildings, especially in the fall when they were surrounded by red and gold trees.

Last fall was the first time since I left Shreveport that I'd seen fall colours. Last winter was the first time I'd ever seen snow, at least snow that came and stayed. I made the other nurses in the Bachelor Officers' Quarters build snowmen and make snow angels with me. They were all from Minnesota or Vermont, so snow wasn't as much of a novelty for them as it was for me.

A couple of weeks before Christmas my roommate and I drove to Kansas City to do Christmas shopping. I had worked night shift the night before and by the time we started back to the fort from Kansas City, I was dead tired. I went to sleep and woke up as the ten p.m. news was starting on the radio. I expected to see the lights of Ft. Riley, but there wasn't anything but black prairie. We had missed the one turn between Kansas City and Ft. Riley and we were lost and almost out of gas in the middle of the prairie. We finally found a lone gas station and were told that we were on the Kansas Turnpike, headed toward Wichita. Because we didn't have leave, we were only allowed to be away from the post until midnight and, if we had to turn around and go back to the junction at Topeka, there was no way we would make it back on time. The man at the gas station told us about a Turnpike exit, which was barred and locked, but he assured us that if we stopped at the barricade and blew our horn, someone would come to open the gate. That road led to a back road which came in at the back of the post.

By the time we reached the Turnpike exit, a thick fog had formed. We stopped on this absolutely deserted blacktop road and honked the horn. In a few minutes a bright yellow Volkswagen with a big sunflower and the words Kansas Turnpike Authority painted on it appeared out of the fog. A man got out and without a word tipped his hat to us, opened the gate, locked it behind us, got back in his yellow Volkswagen and disappeared into the fog from which he had come.

The road wove up and down, past black fields and widely-spaced farm houses, most of which were dark by now. On a particularly black stretch of road my roommate said, conversationally, "Have you ever read *In Cold Blood*?" We arrived at the hospital at 2358 and signed in with two minutes to spare. While we were signing in the sergeant in charge of the book asked our blood types. We were both A-positive and the lab was desperate for A-positive blood because there had been a multi-car accident earlier that day and they had used up all of the blood available. So we donated blood before falling, exhausted, into our beds.

In the spring I took long rides on the prairie, stopping in small town cafes for chicken stew or coffee and pie. I went to the Eisenhower museum and remembered how my father had taken me out to the airport when I was five. Eisenhower was campaigning for president then, and I had shaken his hand. It was only years later that I realized my father had wanted me to see him not because he was a presidential candidate, but because he had brought the U.S. through World War II.

We had a good time at Ft. Riley. The people in our Bachelors' Officers Quarters were in each other's apartments as often as in our own. Every Friday night we went to happy hour in the Officer's Mess; then upstairs for a steak and lobster supper. Every Saturday night we took turns cooking; we drank gallons of wine or sangria; talked and played board games until the early hours. Looking back on it, we seemed to have had such normal lives there. I miss that normal feeling here.

Friday, October 2, 1970. The best time every day is mail call: it has evolved into a daily ritual. The people who are off duty drift in about 1445, bringing Cokes and candy bars. If we aren't busy we put our feet up, gossip, discuss the patient load. One of the doctors is building his white man's dap and he grabs whomever he can for a practice session.

The dap is a complicated set of hand movements, performed in synchronous motion by two people. It's part recognition and greeting and part secret ritual. The blacks use it as a way to exclude whites. For example, two black soldiers will stand in the mess hall doorway and dap. A really complicated dap may take five minutes. As they finish a third black soldier comes along and they begin again.

Because they're standing in the doorway to do this, no one can enter the mess hall until they're finished. If they are interrupted they'll claim black culture is being discriminated against.

So our doc, who is white, has decided to build his own dap. It only lasts a couple of minutes at this point, so he has quite a bit of building yet to do.

The wardmaster goes up to headquarters at 1500 hours. He carries the canvas mail sack back with him. We watch him come down the hill, hoping he has it over his shoulder like Santa Claus because that means it is heavy. He dumps everything on the counter and we scramble to find a package or envelope with our name on it. The people who don't have anything hang around the edge of the group while those of us with letters read silently. Then the packages are opened. We share the pictures, Peanuts and Doonsbury cartoons. If we are really lucky, someone gets a care package full of home-made cookies, pre-sweetened Kool-aid, chocolate bars and pizza mix. We eat the cookies and chocolate bars and put the Kool-aid away for making popsicles and the pizza away for night duty.

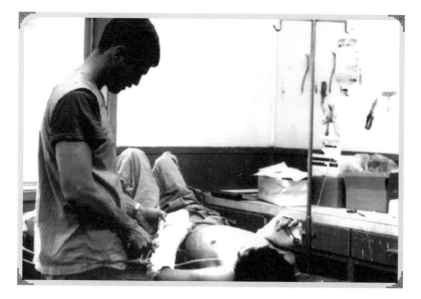

Saturday, October 3, 1970. Arthur loses another child today. I sit with him for a long time and just let him ramble. He tells me not to be involved with people over here, not to worry about them. We both know that's impossible.

Sunday, October 4, 1970. I break down and cry at C.I.D.G. tonight. Arthur holds me and lets me cry myself out. I tell him I can't stand it here any longer. He asks what I can't stand.

What I can't stand is that people are constantly on the move. The hospital is a hub, a place people like Barry, Jerry H. and Jimmy W. always come back to. We are their security, the place they know is always open, where the coffee pot is always on. Sometimes we have an hour or a day to visit, then they go away again. There is no secure place for us to go.

Monday, October 5, 1970. We are at other compounds to give flu shots today. All day is a steady stream of bare arms, of jokes about passing out. My fingers are all wrinkled from having them in alcohol all day.

Tuesday, October 6, 1970. Marie, the Head Nurse, is still getting complaints about my work. I don't know how to change, how to be any better than I am already.

Wednesday, October 7, 1970. Today is Military Payment Certificate (M.C.P.) conversion day. It takes almost three hours to get the exchange certificate. The new currency won't be issued until tomorrow so there is literally no money on the compound. The Post Exchange and the clubs are closed. We are confined to the compound and no Viet Namese are allowed through the gate. The whole hospital is strangely quiet and deserted.

There are three kinds of money in 'Nam. Our U.S. greenbacks are collected when we come in-country and we are issued Military Payment Certificates, which look like Monopoly money. Some people keep greenbacks because they have such a high value on the black market. There are rumours—there are always rumours—that money spent on the black market ends up in North Viet Nam and is used to finance the war. Piasters are the third currency: the money we pay to the Viet Namese.

Everything we buy from American sources—goods at the Post Exchange, drinks and food at the clubs—is paid for in M.P.C.s. Our mama-sans and the other Viet Namese workers are paid in piasters. We aren't supposed to give any of the M.P.C.s or greenbacks to them. A lot of money changes hands for legitimate services; for prostitution and drugs; for the black market. Money is sometimes stolen by the Viet Namese workers. Consequently, a lot of M.P.C.s end up in Viet Namese hands. The M.P.C. Conversion Day is an attempt to make all the money in Viet Namese hands worthless.

Without warning, all the compounds in the Pleiku area are closed to the Viet Namese. Armed guards patrol the perimeters to make sure there isn't any contact through the wire. We are ordered to report to the old movie theatre with all the money we have. The theatre is a damp, dark building with a dirt floor and rats running through the grass amid the seats. The seats are really movie house ones. No one knows where they come from. Probably someone got a good deal in the States and managed to have them shipped here. Like the pool, the movie house is never open. Movies are shown in the Red Cross rec room.

In the theatre we form two lines and at the head of each line, down where the movie screen once was, are two tables. Pay officers sit at each table, flanked on either side by Military Police. The pay officer has lists of how much money everyone is paid and how long they have been in-country. If a person comes to the table with an unusually large amount of money, one of the policemen takes him away for questioning. The pay officer takes all of our money from us and records the amount in a pay book.

The gates will remain closed until the paymasters bring in the new Military Payment Certificates, which will be a different colour. We don't believe this slows the flow of illegal money one bit. It's a game to be played, like standing in the registration lines at university. The Army says we must do it, so we do it.

❀ ꧁❀

Calgary, Alberta. It was almost as hard to write about the past few weeks as it was to live through them.

I had a sense, erroneous as it was, that I knew what war was all about. It was about losing friends. It was, as we often commented in the Emergency Room, ninety-eight percent boredom, punctuated by two percent sheer terror. It was about having meals cooked for me, clothes washed for me, all of my responsibilities except work taken care of by someone else. It was about being hassled by the brass about an inspection that didn't really matter because we were closing anyway. It was about alcohol and drugs and ducking fist fights. It was about constantly being on display with the ratio of men to women about 600:1.

In spite of constantly being in hot water with my Head Nurse, my nursing skills were improving. The problem was that I was such a perfectionist that nothing less than a perfect performance was good enough for me. It took me a long time to get over that.

My relationship with people was the part I wished I could do over. I missed something in those days in the photo lab, in those nights drinking with Special Forces. I missed ever becoming a real part of the team I worked with.

The people skills were the hardest to learn. It took me a while to realize that the world didn't revolve around me and that people often had their own agendas. I wanted everyone to be open and honest and up-front with me. And, sometimes, they weren't.

❀ ꧁❀

Thursday, October 8, 1970. Dust-off is leaving tomorrow for Tua Hoa; they are having a going away party tonight and the whole hospital is invited. I refuse to go because I can't bear to admit to myself that they are leaving. I shut myself off from them so I won't miss them so much. I won't see Ed any more, won't say goodbye.

Saturday, October 10, 1970. Yesterday, as a farewell, Dust-off did a low fly-bye low over the hospital. In close formation all of the helicopters flew a few feet above the hospital buildings. On their final pass they dropped smoke grenades in the pool. The water is now pink.

My aunt sends me a Christmas box and the Sears Christmas catalogue has arrived. It is hard to believe Christmas is only about ten weeks away. So many people back in the States feel compelled to do something for us. The boxes have already started arriving, some sent through the Red Cross, some simply addressed to Any Army Hospital, Viet Nam. There are cookies and fruit cake, ditty bags made by different Red Cross chapters, and lots of other gifts. The women who work for the Red Cross are already distributing the food that will spoil before Christmas and then packing the rest of the gifts away to give out at Christmas.

Sunday, October 11, 1970. A few weeks before they left Dust-off moved its radio room from the little building at the bottom of the hill up into the Emergency Room. I like that. I can talk to Ellis again on night duty without getting into trouble.

He gives me two small pieces of ivory jewelry. There is something incredibly romantic about being brought ivory from Bangkok. It makes me think of weather-beaten houses on the Maine coast and an old sea captain presenting his wife the ivory from half-way around the world. Or the shops on Royal Street in New Orleans where I only dared look and not touch because the prices were so high.

Monday, October 12, 1970. Someone comes up behind me in the Emergency Room this afternoon, puts his hands over my eyes and says, "Surprise." It is Bill L., one of the Special Forces medics who is stationed in Kontum. He and Ed P. are in Pleiku for a few hours. They look dirty, tense and completely exhausted. I grab and hug both of them. I wish we could spend the evening getting pleasantly high tonight, but they have to be back to Kontum.

With Dust-off gone, we have begun the process of shutting down the hospital. I am on the list to be transferred, but don't know where I will go or when my transfer will happen. How can I leave here? This is the only home I've had for months. I want everything to go on as it has been, but even if I stay, it won't be the same. Dust-off has gone, the other units will soon leave. Bill and Ed are talking about Special Forces pulling out of their A-camps. Security is our main topic of conversation at meals. Which units have gone, which ones are still here? What is Charlie's strength? Is he going to let us leave or wait until we are down to too few soldiers to defend the compounds, then attack? Will Charlie attack a hospital? Will they evacuate the nurses? Will we refuse to leave if the doctors, corpsmen and patients must stay behind? Will they take nurses as prisoners? We are watching the units leave one by one and expect any morning to wake up to a blood bath.

1970 NOVEMBER 1970

Sunday, November 1, 1970. I am up at dawn this morning, lying in bed under my warm electric blanket, reading a novel set in the South. The tin flaps over my screens are tightly closed against the cold and the room is very quiet. Reading in the silent early morning before anyone else is awake is almost like being back home.

When I think of back home, back on the block, I don't think of my parent's house. They moved to Mandeville after I was in university and, aside from spending two summers there, I never lived in that house. Back on the block to me is my grandmother's house in New Iberia.

November weather in Louisiana is the same as we have had the past few days in Pleiku. Since the weather has turned cold, I am homesick for Graume's house. I always stayed in the front bedroom on the left side of the house. It was a huge room with nine-foot ceilings. The only heating was an open-front gas heater which was placed in front of the sealed-up fireplace. I turned the heater off at night because my grandmother would not permit anyone to sleep with gas burning. She was afraid there would be an explosion or the flame would go out and we would all be asphyxiated by the gas. In the morning the bedroom would be very cold and I would dance across the freezing floor in my bare feet and light the heater with big wooden kitchen matches. The gas would catch with a whoosh of blue-tinged flame. Then I'd race back to bed, snuggle under the blankets and wait until the room warmed, just like I am doing this morning. Only here there is no heater, only an electric blanket on the bed. Our hooch, which was quite comfortable in summer, is downright cold and it will be several hours before the sun on the tin roof warms the room.

Electricity had been added to my grandmother's house long after the house had been built, so a braided, insulated strand of electrical cord hung from the middle of the ceiling and a single bulb in a parchment shade dangled at the end of the cord. There were six bevelled-glass mirrors in the front bedroom: three in an old dressing table, one in each of the two free-standing clothes closets and one over the dresser. The front bedroom faced the railroad tracks which ran through the centre of the street in front of my grandmother's house.

When I was younger there were still steam engines on freight trains and one would pass the house about every two hours. When I lay awake early in the morning, reading and waiting for the room to warm, as I am doing here this morning, I could hear the train from a long way off. The engineer would begin to blow his horn at each railroad crossing as he entered the town. As he got closer and closer the suspended light began to vibrate. All six mirrors picked up the light from that single bulb, split it and threw pieces of it across the room. Then the bed would begin to vibrate: just a little at first, then more and more, and I would begin to hear the gates going down, softly at first, then the second one down the street and finally the one two houses away.

I could not continue reading while the train passed; the light vibrated too much to see the page. I would close my book and feel the train; listen to the wheels singing on the track; smell the slightly musty smell of hats stored in mothballs in the armoires; look at the pictures on the dresser: my own, taken at age three in my pink coat and hat, and the pictures of my two uncles in their Army uniforms during World War II. My Uncle Ward was a lawyer with the Judge Advocate's Office; he served only in the States. My Uncle John was in the Infantry. He fought in France. I wish I could write to them; I wish we could talk about our wars, theirs and mine, but I have never talked to them about their lives. I don't know what I want to ask them; I don't know what I want them to tell me unless perhaps that they understand what I am doing here, that they are proud of me.

I received my new orders on Friday: the 67th Evac Hospital in Qui Nhon. That's almost due east of here. I'll leave on November 24th, a little over three weeks from today. Terri and Ruth are going there also. At least that's some consolation.

Monday, November 2, 1970. The past few days were windy, like March weather at home. They just cut the grass again, so it seems more like spring than November. The nights are cold and clear, very different from the thick, foggy nights of monsoon season. There are bands of clouds on the horizon at sunrise and sunset. Some of the sunsets are quite dramatic with the clouds catching and reflecting shades of yellow, blue, violet and orange.

It must have been lovely here before the war, when people came from the cities to vacation in little whitewashed cottages in the mountains. I like to think that the hills were always green then and the air always clean. I wonder if anyone will ever come here for a vacation again?

I feel safer with the clear nights. There is less chance for Charlie to sneak in under the cover of the fog. One night during monsoon season, just after they moved the Dust-off radio into the Emergency Room, we were monitoring radio traffic from the Air Force Base. There was a plane having trouble finding the runway lights in the fog. We heard him making a couple of passes over the Emergency Room, then he said, "All right, tower, I have your blue lights in sight."

"Roger. Cleared for landing."

The noise of the plane grew louder and louder and the radio operator and I realized at the same instant what had happened. The radio operator grabbed the microphone and yelled, "Pull up, pull up. Our helipad lights are blue. You should be seeing yellow lights, repeat yellow lights."

Then there was this tremendous noise and the plane just cleared the top of the Emergency Room.

Tuesday, November 3, 1970. Today is election day at home. I didn't vote. Being here is too far removed from home to be able to know what the issues are. My friend, Sharon Anne, has been working very hard for the Republican Party. We have known each other almost fifteen years, ever since second grade at St. Joseph's. She always said she was going to get involved in politics; I always said I was going to war. Funny how we guessed what we would do.

Wednesday, November 4, 1970. I seem to get the weirdest night shifts. Our first patient is a postpartum dog in convulsions because of hypocalcemia. The owners can't find the vet, so they bring her and her puppies to us. In our log book, we list the rank of all patients, so we list her under K-9. The corpsman gets one of the warmed blanket out of the shock cabinet and makes a nest for the puppies and while I call around and try to locate the vet. Finally I call the doctor on medical call. He comes over, starts an I.V. on the dog, gives her some intravenous calcium and owners, dog and puppies go home happy.

Then there is this drunk brought in by a buddy who is concerned because his friend is breathing funny. If I'd had as much to drink as this guy, I'd be breathing funny, too. He sleeps it off on a stretcher in the back of the Emergency Room.

About midnight, just as the Air Force Officers' Club closes, the corpsmen and I are sitting on the bench behind the Emergency Room. We watch a chopper take off from the club, turn and land on our helipad. A major comes over and asks, "Do you have the key to the Air Force gate?"

"Yes, but I'm not supposed to open the gate at night."

"Well, ma'am, I have to get back there. I lost something as the chopper was taking off."

"Look, Major, it's dark out there. Unless what you lost was really important or classified, can't it wait until morning?"

"No, it can't wait, because what I lost was my drinking buddy. He fell out of the chopper as we were taking off."

So I find a flashlight and the key and we all go to look. There, sprawled in the field, unhurt, is his drinking buddy.

The night isn't all funny. We have a new Dust-off unit, the 498th; they are here temporarily until the hospital closes. Tonight while they fly a night mission their main rotor almost comes off. After they land, the two pilots come into the Emergency room. They are white and shaking. We go out to look at the damaged ship and, even at night, we can see the rotor just hanging there, held intact by a very thin strip of metal. One of the pilots and I hug each other for a long time, not saying anything, just holding one another.

The Commanding Officer enjoys my Night Supervisor's report. He says I provide comic relief in an otherwise dull week.

Friday, November 6, 1970. Tomorrow I start packing for the move to Qui Nhon. Or at least shipping home the things I don't need any more. I am resigned to the move now and am caught up in the mechanics of doing it. This will make my sixth move in eighteen months: home from University for two months; to Ft. Sam, Texas; to Ft. Riley, Kansas, back home for a month's leave and then to Pleiku. I feel like everything I own is scattered over two continents and that I am constantly living out of a duffel bag.

Saturday, November 7, 1970. I spend almost all of my off-duty time at the C.I.D.G. hospital. Jim S., the medic who was awarded the Silver Star, takes me up on the water tower to try out my new telephoto lens and extenders. We take some pictures of MIKE Force across the road and some other compounds farther down the valley, including the P.O.W. camp for North Viet Namese prisoners. All the pictures we take are, of course, illegal. We aren't allowed to photograph military installations. I'm not sure we're even allowed to photograph anything here. But everyone does it and no one ever checks our film.

Sunday, November 8, 1970. I am banished to work on the indigenous ward again. It is incredibly hard to work with a ward full of patients again. In the Emergency Room the patients are with us from a few minutes to an hour. Even when they are there for the hour, we aren't constantly working with them. We do the initial care, go to someone else, come back to check on them. Here there are all of these people for the full twelve-hour shift. I feel lost, drowning in a sea

of people with constant needs. I know the Emergency Room routine, not the ward routine, and am constantly stumbling over tasks not done on time. If I do the medications on time, the treatments lag. If I do the treatments, the meals aren't out on time. There are so many forms to fill out, so much charting to do and I don't have the luxury of a ward clerk. There are days I feel tired and overwhelmed. On those days, I hide behind the paperwork and the routine and minimize my contact with the patients. Maybe Mary is right, maybe my work just isn't good enough, maybe that's why she banished me to this ward.

❀ ⌂ ❀

Calgary, Alberta. There were so many changes in my life—Ed leaving, my own upcoming transfer—that being sent to another area was one too many changes to cope with. I felt that I somehow hadn't measured up in the Emergency Room, that they couldn't bear to have me around for the two weeks I had left and had sent me off so I wouldn't be in their way. It took me a long time to realize that the hospital wasn't functioning around my needs. They needed someone on that ward, I was available and I went. If I had it to do now, I would be proud that I could switch from an Emergency Room to a ward on such short notice.

❀ ⌂ ❀

Monday, November 9, 1970. Barbara K. comes to visit for a couple of hours today. She has been working in the Operating Room of all places and she really likes it. She is being transferred to the 95th in Da Nang, so we both realize this is probably the only time we will see each other in-country. She's very proud of what she's doing here. Her father died in the Korean War. I think she's trying to make sure other daughters won't have to grow up without a father as she did. I'm very proud of what we are both doing here. We've done our nursing school proud; we're part of a tradition. There is Barbara and myself from the class of '69, Charlene from the class of '68, Anna and Pat from the class of '67: all of us have served here, all of us have made a contribution.

I have been instructed to begin out-processing and the Sergeant in the Chief Nurses' office has given me my out-processing sheet. I have a whole page of blank lines, places to go and people who must sign that I have no outstanding business with them. When the Finance Clerk is checking my records so that my pay can be forwarded to Qui Nhon I see the form I signed six months ago that says I want my pay to go into a fund if missing. It's funny now to think that idea scared me then. I know now that I'm not going missing.

I've decided not to send any baggage home; there are too many stories about packages being lost forever in the mail. I'll leave the small fridge, the fan and the electric blanket in my room, just as someone left them for me. But this time there won't be anyone moving into my room because the hospital will close in a month and everyone is being transferred out, not in. I'm the end of the line, the last person who will hide under the mattress during a red alert, the last nurse to be awakened for a mass casualty by the phone and choppers, the last woman to dream and live here. Pack up and move, leave things behind, that is what the Army is teaching me.

Wednesday, November 11, 1970. My orders for captain come through. They will take effect December 16, long after I am in Qui Nhon. I wish I was going to be in Pleiku when I am promoted. I'll miss getting a beer bath from the medics at Special Forces. As it is, they are all kidding me, addressing me as Captain Grant, and throwing me salutes.

It's Veterans' Day. Are women, are nurses real veterans? Sometimes it doesn't seem as if we should be. We live in hooches, eat in a mess, work under conditions that are at least comfortable. We don't have to wade in rice paddies full of leeches or spend the night in a tree waiting to kill someone. There is so much that the guys do in the field that I can't imagine myself doing. Seeing the results is bad enough.

For every one man in the field here there are five of us non-combatants backing him. We drive trucks, do the payrolls, work in the Post Exchange, run the radio stations, order supplies, cook food. The guys in the field call us R.E.M.F.s: Rear Echelon Mother Fuckers. I don't like being called that. It is demeaning, as if we aren't doing anything important here.

What we do here is important.

Thursday, November 12, 1970. When we had a party over at C.I.D.G. last weekend, Chuck P. had a new monkey. There is a rule that any animal kept as a pet must be examined and vaccinated by the vets, but Chuck bought the monkey late Friday night after the vet's office was closed; he was going to take him to the vet on Monday.

Friday night we were drinking and teasing the monkey and he nipped about ten or eleven of us. The monkey died Saturday morning and, as a joke, Chuck sent the head off to be tested for rabies. The tests came back positive!

At first the Emergency Room crew doesn't believe me. They think I am playing a practical joke when I request rabies vaccination. Dr. S. at C.I.D.G. calls them and tells them I really do need rabies shots. The shots themselves aren't as bad as people said they are. They are given in the stomach, one every day for twenty-one days. The only problem so far is the spot where they give the last shot itches like crazy about twelve hours later.

We have created such an uproar. Chuck has to write a long report about why he didn't taken the monkey to the vet. The hospital flies in extra rabies vaccine for the eleven of us. The worst part is listening to all the jokes. The word spread rapidly and everyone feels he has to contribute some levity to the situation. We usually retaliate by threatening to bite them.

The Emergency Room submits a daily report to the Commanding Officer after every shift. Any hospital personal in the hospital or receiving any treatment must be listed on that sheet. The embarrassing part is I will be on that report for twenty-one days.

Friday, November 13, 1970. One of the Special Forces medics drives over to Camp Holloway today and asks me if I want to come for the ride. This is the only time besides going to Colonel N.'s house in June that I have been more than a mile away from the hospital compound, have seen anything other than American installations. Six months in an area one mile by one mile. It is also the first time I see the city of Pleiku and, since I am leaving in ten days, I imagine it will be my only time to see it.

There are no real buildings, which I find surprising. Occasionally there is a pink stucco shell of a building that once belonged to the French. What do the Viet Namese do with window glass? The first thing they do when they take over a building from us is to take out all the windows. No one seems to know whether it's an obvious protection against shattering glass in an attack or if they are selling the glass somewhere.

From a distance, I see the infamous Pleiku hospital, a low white building surrounded by a stone wall. We think of it as infamous because they close every Friday afternoon at three and open again Monday morning. All of the staff goes home and the families must care for the patients, or at least that's what we've heard. We don't drive close enough that I have a close look, which is disappointing. I also see a church and a market square. Pleiku is the market

town for surrounding farms. I never really think about how people live here.

There is stark poverty. Most of the houses along the road are shacks made of cardboard and odd scraps of lumber. It is obvious there is no water supply and no sewer. I see people urinating into an open ditch beside the road and a little further down, a woman draws water from the same ditch. Most of these people are refugees, brought into town by the A.R.V.N. troops from their farms outside the city. When we pull out, when the Viet Cong take over, there is no place for these people to go. The nearest city is An Khe, sixty miles away through the mountains and the Ming Ying pass. I wondered what will happen to them, where they will go.

I have thought day shift on the ward merely irritating. This is my first night shift here and I am actually scared. What if I forget something? What if I miss something? It isn't just cleaning and a few patients with minor complaints like it is in the Emergency Room. This is a ward full of real people, some of whom are quite sick. And I start nights on Friday the 13th!

Saturday, November 14, 1970. Last night wasn't at all bad. The corpsmen help a lot. When I was back in the world I used to dream of being in charge of a sleeping ward full of patients in Viet Nam. That was the romantic streak in me. Now that I have experienced it, that kind of responsibility is romantic, but it's sobering and funny at the same time. With most of the lights out I trip over almost everything.

I used up a lot of energy last night, more than I have used on night shift since the first night I was Night Supervisor. So instead of going to bed in my own room this morning, I hitch an early morning ride over to C.I.D.G. and curl up to sleep in an empty room. I have just gotten up and am fixing myself some breakfast when we hear about Ed P, one of the Special Forces medics.

Ed P. was flying with Bernie today and they were shot down. By some miracle, both of them walked away from the landing. I feel stunned and relieved; they came so close to meeting the same fate that Barry did. If that had happened twice, I didn't know what I would have done.

Only this time I don't go through the waiting alone. We are all together at C.I.D.G. from the moment we hear they are down, through people hurrying in and out with the latest news, trying to keep their voices calm, putting the news in the most positive light, to the time when we hear they are safe. When Ed walks in the door, pale, with a shocked look on his face, Bill L. grabs him and hugs him, and then turns everything silly by putting his tongue in his ear. When it is my turn to hug Ed, we are both shaking and trying not to let the other person know. But we do know. When I look up into his blue eyes, I think they are the most beautiful eyes I have ever seen.

Everyone, except me, gets silly, roaring, happy drunk. I have to stay sober because I'm working tonight. We pierce each other's ears. Bill does mine. Only when I am on my way to the ward this evening I meet the Chief Nurse. She sees my new earrings, tells me they are against regulations and makes me take them out. I guess the holes will close up and I'll have to have them pierced again.

Monday, November 16, 1970. I have been the search girl at the main gate several times. I really hate doing it. I never find very much-the girls pass the word when they realize that there is a woman in the gate house and those down the line get rid of whatever they have. I am sure it must be a game to them, to see how much they can fool the Americans. Most of the G.I.s don't want to find anything, until they had something stolen themselves. Then they become really hyper and want us to do strip search.

The Viet Namese girls line up by the gate. Almost all of them are young, slender, dressed in close-fitting ao-dias and black silk pants. They carry pointed straw hats and bundles wrapped in newspaper. Occasionally there is an old woman, her face stretched to brown skin over bone, her teeth black from chewing betel nut. For the equivalent of ten American dollars a month the women clean hooches, wash clothes by hand, iron fatigues, polish boots and scrub the green slime from the bathroom. Some of the women work in the hospital laundry or the mess hall. The women come in one by one to have their packages searched.

Most of the bundles are the remains of lunch, cold rice, cakes wrapped in newspaper, bottles of nuoc mam sauce—a smelly concoction made from dried fish. The women who work in the mess hall have silver lard cans of leftovers. Sometimes there are clothes the women bring to wash along with the fatigues. Once in a while I find a new American dress or a package from Sears or Montgomery Ward.

If the enlisted man at the gate is in a bad mood, he picks a girl out of line and points toward the back of the shed. "In there."

I take the woman behind the curtain and strip her. The woman takes down her hair, pins clattering on the hard dirt floor. We do not look at one another while I run my hands through the woman's hair, probe her vagina and rectum with my rubber-glove-covered fingers. The woman looks at the floor, I stare out the window to the green fields around the Air Force Base. I hand her the clothes, saying, "Di di mow." It meant, "Get the hell out of here."

When the whole line of women have passed the gate and are shuttled to waiting Lambrettas, I go back to my hooch, shower for a long time, wash my hair, and put on the clean clothes mama-san had ironed that day.

❀ ▷ ❀

Calgary, Alberta. A fictional character, Pepper—Elizabeth Anne Pepperhawk—was eventually my way into writing about Viet Nam. She first developed as a character some time in the mid to late 1970s, when I was living in Asheville, North Carolina. I began to listen to Pepper tell me stories: first, stories of her own that were fiction, stories that had never actually happened to me, but might have. Gradually she began to tell me my own stories reflected back as her stories. The first time I wrote the story about searching girls at the gate, it was Pepper's story, told in the third person, as if it didn't belong to me at all. That fiction took me to the place where I could admit the new American dresses were real. The women were real. The strip searches were real. I did them. I would not do them again.

❀ ▷ ❀

Tuesday, November 17, 1970. I didn't think my day off would ever come; working two weeks on night duty is too long a stretch. One interesting thing happened this week. Bill V., one of the Operating Room techs, wanted to go out with me, but I got sick. So Terri went out with him. They came by after they had been on their first date to tell me they are engaged to be married. Right. It is all this moving, everyone being transferred, the hospital closing down. It makes everyone unsettled. I'm sure they will get over this idea when they have a little more perspective.

My going-away party is tomorrow night at C.I.D.G. I'm glad I'm getting a party. It makes me feel like they will miss me as much as I'll miss them.

Wednesday, November 18, 1970. A heavy mist covers the ground. The night is dark and there are no stars. In the brick barbecue at the Special Forces hooch the fire burns down to red coals. Grease drips from the thick iron grill and a fire flares occasionally. The smell of coals and steak smoke mixes with a lingering odour of corn-on-the-cob, reminders of my going-away supper.

Surrounded by cigar smoke, four of us sit on the porch: myself, Ed, Carl and a friend of Carl's whose name I can't remember. It is very late, past midnight, and I am going to stay the night curled up in a sleeping bag in an empty room. I have spent a lot of nights here and long ago stopped worrying about being back by curfew.

It is very cold on the porch, but no one moves. To our left, men walk back and forth in the hall of the team hooch. The same bar I have spent many evenings tending stands between us and the hall. There is a small red light over the bar and occasionally a figure slips into the dim red light to mix a drink or get a beer.

Ed is in his thirties with salt-and-pepper hair. He has magnificent, penetrating eyes. Carl has a very sharp face and close-cut hair; he wears a striped t-shirt. The fourth person is only a blur on the edge of the group. We are drinking/drunk, wanting the night to go on forever, suspended, knowing time has run out, counting the minutes. Ed and Carl talk about their experiences in Special Forces. They disagree on some minor point, getting stuck on it as drunks do. Ed gets mad, insists he is right. Carl tells him to drop it.

Then they are at each other. Broken glass and liquor is over everything, including me. A chair breaks and the door screen is torn as the men fall against it. They hit each other over and over, repeated sounds of fists on flesh. I scramble out of the way. They rolled toward the barbecue and its hot grill. Behind us come running feet. Arthur yells, "Fight!" and the porch is suddenly full of people pulling the men apart. Carl yells, "The motherfucker started it."

Arthur tells every one to shut up. They lead Carl away, still yelling. Everyone looks disgusted, surveying the damage. The rule is you drink only as much as you can handle. Ed and Carl have broken the code. No one asks me if I am all right. The unspoken rule is if you hang out with Special Forces you take care of yourself. I have just as much right to duck blows as anyone else.

Ed and I are alone on the porch, sitting on the bench of the picnic table. Blood covers his face and hands and, in the light from the coals, the blood turns black. His hands shake as he lit a cigarette. I feel him draw inside his anger, shut me out, shut out the world. Hate physically pushes us apart.

Inside I am screaming, "I have so much I want to say to you and now I don't have the chance. Can't you leave the fighting alone for one night? I'm going away, I'll never see you again. Why did this happen tonight?"

We say nothing. The fire, the night, most of all a feeling inside of me grows cold. I tell Ed I have changed my mind, that I want to go back to the hospital. He asks Arthur to drive me back, which I both understand and hate.

I know that when I go back tomorrow afternoon I will find people shaking their heads, cleaning up broken wood, mending the screen. Arthur will shake his head, "My God, what a night." It is always that way after they fight among themselves.

Thursday, November 19, 1970. Tomorrow we close Ward 5, the ward I have been on for the past two weeks. Then the hospital will be down to twenty-five bed capacity. We have only thirteen patients on the ward today, which would seem like a dream to some nurses working in an overcrowded hospital in the States. There isn't very much to do and we have a lot of free time during the shift. I spend a lot of the day talking to the corpsmen. We talk about where we are going, how much time we have left in Viet Nam, what we are planning to do when we get to the States. The same old topics.

Friday, November 20, 1970. I keep saying good-bye to the people at C.I.D.G. I try to spend a little time with each of the men there, telling each one how much I have enjoyed knowing him, what I will remember about him. I thank Arthur for all the times he has been willing to listen to me when I needed to talk. I tell Ed how glad I am he is still with us. We don't talk about what happened Wednesday night. I just hug Jim and thank him for all he has taught me about photography. We have never talked about his Silver Star. Bill is out in Kontum; I won't be able to tell him how much his steady confidence, his ability to just smile and carry on has meant to me. I can't believe I'll never see them again. Maybe I really will be assigned to Ft. Bragg and maybe some of them will be there. Not all of them because some of them are getting out of the Army when they go back to the States. All of us will never be together again the way that we have been here. There is so much about them that is etched into my memory. I love them.

Sunday, November 22, 1970. We went on alert last night. The incoming was quite close. I just rolled under the bed, pulled the covers and pillow with me and went back to sleep. I stopped struggling with my flak jacket and helmet months ago. They are also under my bed, covered with dust. My only thought between waking up in bed and falling back asleep under the bed was, "What the hell does Charlie mean by breaking up my sleep?"

Plei Mei is under siege. I hoped Stevens is all right. He is one of the few Special Forces I know who are still at an A-Camp. His camp has been turned over to the A.R.V.N. Rangers and he stayed on for a while as an advisor. Last month we joked about his camp coming under siege and him having to be a hero to save it. That idea isn't so funny tonight. What's going to happen to people like him, to people like Bill who are in the field when this hospital leaves? I go over and over the situation in my mind and know there is nothing I can do, not for

Stevens, not for Bill, not for the men who are left here. Someone else is going to have to take care of them for me.

Monday, November 23, 1970. Today goes really slowly. I have finished work here, finished out-processing, finished packing. Just like the Army: hurry up and wait. I spend most of the time today writing Jeanne a letter telling her about Arthur, Jim, Ed and the rest of the people at C.I.D.G., telling her what they are like, what I feel about them. I hoped she will keep the letter. I write it as much for my benefit as for hers. I said goodbye to them last night for the last time and I can't bear the idea of not seeing them again.

Stevens is out of Plei Mei, dirty, exhausted, with dark circles under his eyes and a pinched, drawn face. But he is out in one piece! He came to the hospital late today; he said he wanted to hug me one last time. That hug is my going-away present. I want to get drunk with him tonight, listen to his story, give him a chance to talk. We will never have a chance to do that again.

Pleiku is over. I walk around looking at the compound and the mountains for the last time. Dragon Mountain and the Ming Ying pass are etched in my head. I feel as if I have seen them all my life. They are the first to catch the sun at dawn, the first sign that the long night shift is over.

I have grown up here. It hasn't all been good times. I have been so tied up in leaving, I've forgotten what other emotions feel like. I don't want to go to Qui Nhon. I want one of the hot spots like Hue or Phu Bi. I have done the best job in Pleiku that I can, and that seems far from enough. I know I should feel better about what I have done here, but there is a constant anger inside of me. I have been fighting to be the best for so long, I no longer remember what peace feels like.

The goodbyes are said, the packing done. I walk around my room one last time, hoist my duffel bag and climb in a jeep to the helipad.

❀ ⌂ ❀

Calgary, Alberta. There were two postscripts to this day. About a year after I left Pleiku, I was working on an orthopaedic ward at Ft. Bragg. There were big windows around the ward and through them I could see the other wing of the hospital and the neatly manicured lawns surrounding the hospital.

About 1400 hours one afternoon I was distributing medications. I looked out of the windows and saw, not the green lawns of Ft. Bragg, but the Ming Ying pass and the mountains outside the Emergency Room. They were absolutely there, not my imagination, but there.

Then one of the patients, who had also been to Nam, tugged on my arm. "You okay, Captain?"

I shook my head: the mountains disappeared and the lawns reappeared. "What?"

"You got this funny look on your face. You okay?"

"Yea, I was just having a flashback."

The patient looked really concerned. "Should I get someone for you?"

"No, I'm really okay. It was quite pleasant." And it was. It was a moment that made me realize that all flashbacks aren't bad ones. I was lucky. That

view of the cool, green mountains was the only true flashback I ever had. I've spent a lot of time thinking about Viet Nam, dreaming about it, writing about it, but never another experience where I was actually was completely, totally back there.

The second postscript to Pleiku took place in May of 1982, just a couple of weeks before I left for Canada. I was again working night duty in an Emergency Room. One of the nurses came down from C.C.U. and said, "Want to hear something funny? My boyfriend said he knew someone with your same name in Viet Nam."

"Oh, who's your boyfriend?"

"Bill L."

"Bill L.! As in the terrible trio: Bill L., Harry M. and Arthur T.?"

She had also met Harry and said, "My gosh, it was you."

Bill had become a Physician's Assistant, left the Army and was working for one of the orthopaedic doctors in town. She was supposed to wake him up early to assist in surgery. She gave me his phone number and I called him at 6 a.m.

"Sgt. L.?"

I could tell I had woke him out of a sound sleep because he mumbled, "Yea, right, what is it?"

"This is Lt. Grant over at the Emergency Room. I've got three 'Yards for you to pick up."

There was this long pause, followed by "Holy shit."

They invited me to dinner and we talked about old times. Jeanne had kept the letter I'd written that day and I showed it to him.

The rain is the same. Some days it rained in Pleiku and we sat in the team house and listened to it beat on the tin roof of the hooch where the men took the girls at night. That night we sat and listened to the rain on Bill's plexiglas patio roof.

Twelve years ago in Pleiku I wrote a friend a letter, asking her to keep it because one day I might want it back. She did and I did. Tonight I let Bill read it, qualifying the gift. "Remember I was twenty-three, naïve, and you guys were my hero."

What I didn't say was the framed beret on his hall wall still made my heart beat faster. Bill was 20 pounds lighter than he was 12 years ago, dressed in a faded jeans, a greasy white t-shirt saying Seacoast, blue Nikes.

So I gave him the letter and watched his face as he read it, hoping in spite of my disclaimer that what I wrote was okay with him. *The Great American Hero* was on the TV in the background, setting up a resonance that was almost too silly and bittersweet to bear. Bill's son wanted to tell me knock-knock jokes. So I sat there, hardly breathing, watching Bill's face and pretended to laugh at the jokes. He read to the last page, where there was the part about him.

SFC William L. is Ed's best buddy. Bill is now team sergeant with the 4th Battalion MIKE force in Kontum. A short G.I. who tends to be stocky, he is one of the ones I really worry about because he is out in the field so much. Whenever he comes in, he looks exhausted. He never complains, just takes a deep breath, smiles and goes on.

After he had finished reading the letter, I said, "When you had to go back to Kontum, I physically hurt every time you left. All I could imagine was pulling you off a chopper. I couldn't tell you this then."

He shrugged his shoulders. "I had to go."

"I know. I knew it then, too."

We hugged each and twelve years disappeared. He felt the same, he smelled the same. In that moment, Pleiku was there and not there, a double vision that told me I had finally moved beyond it. "I'm glad you were there." He whispered low into my ear, so his son wouldn't hear. "I knew that if anything happened to me, you'd be there. I knew I could trust you."

After twelve years the circle that was Pleiku finally closed.

❀ ꕳ ❀

Tuesday, November 24, 1970. The helicopter ride to the 67th is noisy and bumpy, but not long. I have time to eat a leisurely breakfast in Pleiku and say one final round of goodbyes to the people in the Emergency Room before I climb on the chopper. The chopper is very noisy; I don't know how the pilots stand the noise. I spend most of the ride with my camera outside of the window: this is my chance to see more of the countryside than I've ever seen. I've been in Viet Nam for six months and today I see my first rice paddy. They are lovely from the air, sometimes perfectly square, sometimes contoured to fit the hillside, and they glimmer and glisten in the sun. I think about water a lot once we are over the Ming Ying pass and out of the dry highlands. The country seems so wet and, at the end of the journey, there is Qui Nhon and the ocean.

I've been inland all of my time in the Army: San Antonio, Kansas, Pleiku. We say that when we Cajuns are away from home for a long time the webbing between our feet begins to disappear and mine feels almost gone. When I see the ocean I remember Wes B., my friend from New Iberia. We went fishing off Cypremort point the week before he left for Viet Nam and the week after he came back, and the week before I left for Viet Nam. I'm looking forward to going fishing with him again the week I get home.

We land on a concrete helipad at the end of the air base and, as soon as the cool wash from the rotors stops, the heat and the humidity roll over me like a wave. I've forgotten how muggy the air is near the ocean.

The hospital is bigger, more formal than I'd expected: the 67th Evacuation Hospital, Qui Nhon. Their-our-motto is painted on a big rock outside hospital headquarters: *Mihi Portate Vulneratos—Bring us your wounded.* I think the Latin is pretentious. There is nothing pretentious about the 71st's good English motto in Pleiku: *To Conserve the Fighting Strength.*

The first thing I have to do, of course, is report to the outpatient clinic to get my daily rabies shot! Now I will be on their daily report for six more days until I finish my series of shots. This hospital does things differently than we do in Pleiku. They have a separate walk-in clinic for the non-emergencies, open only during the day. We run the walk-in clinic as part of the Emergency Room. I think I like our way better, though I admit their clinic is cleaner and brighter than ours. It is almost like being in an outpatient clinic back in the world.

I walk over to the nurses' quarters after my shot. Mass is being said in the chapel when I pass by there. I peek into the chapel and think that ours in Pleiku is prettier. This one is a wooden building, not much ornamentation and the altar looks plainer.

The 67th is apparently taking staff who are transferring from all over the Central Highlands as hospitals close and there isn't enough room for the nurses. Terri, Ruth and I are in what was, until yesterday, the nurses' recreation room; we have three newbies with us in the room. It feels strange to be one of the old-

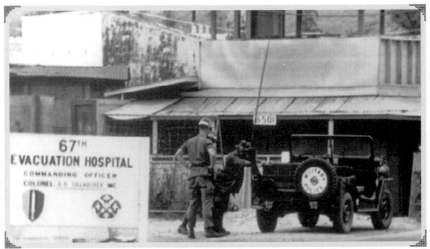

timers. The newbies ask us questions like what a mortar attack sounds like and will they be able to recognize one. We tell them that they will.

I am more tired tonight than I have been in a long time. I feel a sense of being so dislocated.

Wednesday, November 25, 1970. I spent hours today in-processing and meeting people. The different places I have to go to in-process are spread out over several distant compounds. It isn't like Pleiku where we could walk from one compound to another; I have to arrange for a jeep and driver in order to get to all the places.

The 67th Evacuation Hospital is at one end of the air field in what had been barracks for the airmen. A double row of barbed wire surrounds the air field. On the other side of the wire is a road and the city itself. After the long green vistas of Pleiku, the city presses in on me from all sides. The threat of sappers—Viet Cong who come through the wire with explosives strapped to their bodies—is real here. The snipers can also sit in the windows of buildings just outside the wire and hit people or equipment on the air field. One of the nurses says they rarely do that, but the idea they can is always with me today. Last night I heard the crack of a Russian AK-47 quite close. Living this close to the city feels like living on a razor's edge.

The hospital is much larger than in Pleiku, but I don't consider it as pretty. There are eight wards, each holding thirty-six patients, spread out over four two-storey buildings. I am to work in Wards 2 and 4, the first wards at the top of the ramp on the second floor. Surgery and Recovery Room are directly under my wards. A long, steep ramp has been constructed to the second floor. It takes two and sometimes three corpsmen to push a patient on a stretcher up the ramp from surgery on the ground floor to the wards on the second floor. I watch them push several stretchers up that long walk today and am afraid each time that the stretcher will slip and crash down the ramp and into the wall of Recovery Room.

There are special departments: a psychiatric ward, a physical therapy department, a neurosurgeon and an eye surgeon. We are told that the hospital does elective surgery on the Viet Namese, part of the Med-Cap program to build public relations. The hospital is so big, so structured that after being in Pleiku I feel lost. At least at the 71st I knew everyone's name. Here even the mess hall is divided, with enlisted personnel on one side of a small wooden half-wall, officers on the other side. We never segregated ourselves in Pleiku.

Mail call isn't nearly as much fun. They have a mail office, a small window in a trailer next to the Chief Nurse's Office. We have to pick up our own mail, line up, present ourselves one-by-one to the clerk at the window. No one shares their packages from home.

Our quarters are crowded. With hospitals closing down in the area a lot of nurses have been transferred to Qui Nhon. Our quarters are a square of wooden buildings around a central grassy area, just beside one end of the runway. At least in Pleiku we felt like our hooch was our house. Here it is more like having a room in a motel. There are no windows in any of the rooms because the building is air-conditioned. We can't see daylight or weather and I miss the open windows and smell of grass that I had in Pleiku.

Thursday, November 26, 1970. Thanksgiving Day. We are served a huge Thanksgiving dinner in the mess hall. The Red Cross and the U.S.O. women decorate the room with cut-outs of turkeys and cornucopias and brown-and-yellow crepe paper. The Commanding Officer and the Chief Nurse stand at the door to shake our hands and the Chaplain says grace before the meal. We have turkey, dressings and all the trimmings. I think a lot about sacrifice today, about what people have given up so we could have this day and I have a lot of mixed emotions about sacrifice, country, honour that I'm only beginning to sort out.

Friday, November 27, 1970. I began working on Wards 2 and 4 today. When I went to Ft. Riley, I worked only two weeks on the Orthopaedic Unit before I was transferred to the Emergency Room. When I went to Pleiku I worked only two weeks in I.C.U. before I was transferred to the Emergency Room. In

Kansas and in Pleiku the trauma of the new posting as well as the rapid assign-
ment changes at work made me feel as if I was treading water. Here in Qui
Nhon is the first time I've been really comfortable in a new assignment since
I joined the Army. When I was in nursing school, we did our clinical practice
in large, open wards at Charity Hospital in Lafayette. They were just like the
wards here and I feel at home in this open room with rows of beds. Now if I
can just work here longer than two weeks before they transfer me to the
Emergency Room.

At least the familiarity of the wards offset some of the strangeness of our
living conditions. Most of the nurses live two to a room and we have been told
that we will be provided with our own rooms as soon as they are available. In the
mean time, the six of us christen our room *The Swamp*, after the doctor's quar-
ters in *M*A*S*H*. Our swamp has been a recreation room for the nurses and they
are upset because now they have no place to talk together and socialize. Not only
are we six living in one room without privacy, but the washer and dryer for all
the nurses is accessible only by going through our room. A constant stream of

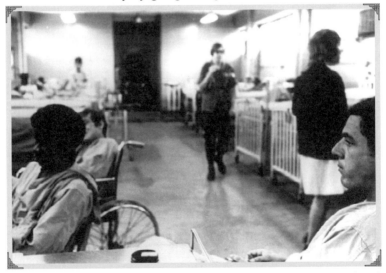

people parade through, people who don't know the recreation room has been
converted to quarters, mama-sans who lug baskets of dirty laundry through to the
washer and who sit in the laundry room and laugh and talk as they iron clothes.
I wonder: how will I shut out the constant voices when I work night duty?

There is a tremendous gulf between the newbies and we veterans of five-and-a-
half months. They talk about movies and records we have never heard of. The usual
jargon—M.A.C.-V., evac'ed, frag wounds—which Ruth, Terri and I use easily is a
foreign language to them. They have brought bottles of their favourite shampoo or

nail polish from the States. We use whatever we get at the Post Exchange. I have a brief thought today of sending a list of my favourite brands to Leslie or Jeanne and asking them to mail them to me, then discard the thought because it's just too much trouble. The newbies have trouble rolling their fatigues while our sleeves fall into automatic creases. Their underwear is white, ours various shades of green, yellow and grey. They are squeamish about small bugs in the bread, we eat anything that doesn't move. They are excited about going on Med-Cap trips to the orphanages and the leprosarium. We don't owe anyone any of our off-duty time.

Most important, we think we have a sense of what the war is really about, about which wounded are going to survive and when it is better if they don't. They think us callous. They say they won't get like us, won't call the Viet Namese "fucking gooks," won't swear or make racial jokes. They are shocked we pay the mama-sans the equivalent of fifteen dollars a month. For that, the mama-sans clean our room, wash our clothes, iron our fatigues, polish our boots. I think how easy the mama-sans have it here because they have a washer and dryer and I think of the women in Pleiku who did our laundry by hand, often without hot water. The new nurses try to talk to the mama-sans, pick up a few Viet Namese words, ask about their families. I am long past being polite to the mama-sans, learning their names, asking about their children. I think them thieves at the worst and con artists at the best. In Pleiku I could laugh off them working for us during the day and the Viet Cong at night. Here the city is too close, the sound of the AK too near, the possibility of sappers too real. I feel like if I find any of the women pacing off our compound, I will probably beat her.

And yet there is a small, gnawing feeling deep inside, that we are all women together, suffering from the war in ways men cannot understand. The newbies, we old-timers, the Viet Namese women, we are all victims and powerless to relieve each other's suffering. Sometimes I yell at my mama-san over something like getting back the wrong socks. She yells back and we wave our arms and swear in different languages. Then we dissolve into laughter at how absurd this all is. I think if the two of us could just get away from all of this, go somewhere by ourselves, we could be friends.

Saturday, November 28, 1970. It has been cloudy, hot and muggy ever since I arrived in Qui Nhon. I wish the weather would break. I come home every day exhausted. The ward work is hard and we don't get many breaks. Pleiku had me spoiled. I have become accustomed to taking a couple of hours off in the afternoon if things are slow. Here I begin work at about 0645 and leave the ward only for a twenty minute break in the morning and a half hour for lunch until I leave about 1915 in the evening. Like Pleiku we have one day off a week, unless we are working nights. Then we have a sleep day and a day off.

Sunday, November 29, 1970. One of the chopper pilots, Stan, came over to the room last night and kept us in stitches. He managed to keep six women entertained at one time by telling us funny stories that have happened to him and his crew. That is no mean feat.

We have so little privacy. The newcomers are still taking it well, but we old-timers are a lot crabbier.

Sunday, November 30, 1970. The rumour is Pleiku is getting a lot of action. I call Starkey tonight. He says they are all right. I've had my last rabies shot today! Yeah! No more being listed on the daily reports. I can sink back into the woodwork again. I'll be so glad when my stomach stops itching.

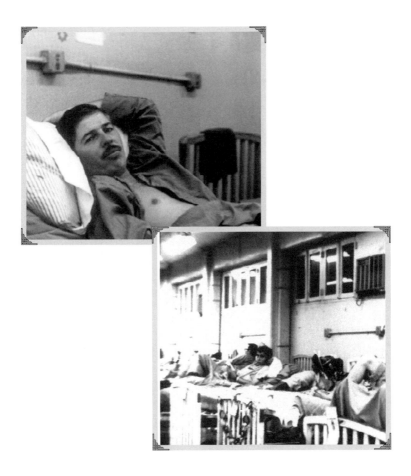

1970 DECEMBER 1970

Tuesday, December 1, 1970. Qui Nhon is a port on the South China Sea, a city on a small strip of land between the ocean and the grey rock hills beyond. There are long, white beaches and piers where dozens of ocean-going ships dock. Some Naval officers invite half a dozen nurses, including me, to lunch on their ship today. We wear our fatigues and ride to the docks in an Army truck.

In the city there are paved streets, shops, restaurants, and apartment buildings. The noise and confusion overwhelms me after living six months so far up in the hills. The weather is always much hotter here than in Pleiku and I haven't become accustomed to it yet. I think it's a great joke that someone who took Louisiana summers without a complaint feels so uncomfortable in Viet Nam.

On the way to the Navy ship my new head nurse, Mary S., points out small fishing boats riding at anchor outside the harbour. She says the Viet Cong hide on the boats during the day and come ashore at night to attack the compounds. It is one more reason to make me think this place is more unsafe than Pleiku.

The ship is wonderful, a miniature city with everything on a small scale. The officers have tiny staterooms with bunks covered with tightly-tucked blankets, small lockers and a little row of books, secure behind a railing over their desk. Everything is clean and fresh, and our Swamp with six nurses, laundry and mama-sans seems almost uncivilized by comparison.

The doctor who has invited us to lunch has a full, black beard. I realize I haven't seen anyone with a beard for months.

We have a lovely, quiet lunch. There are white tablecloths and shiny cutlery. The food is excellent. Our talk centres around picnics on the beach and the movie being shown at one of the compounds. In Pleiku our idea of a night out was to go to a neighbouring compound, barbecue and sit around in our dirty fatigues getting drunk. All of a sudden I am back in civilization and I'm not sure I know how to behave.

Wednesday, December 2, 1970. This hospital is here to move the G.I. patients through to other places. Because we are located at one end of the airfield, we can load the casualties on the evac planes practically at our front door. Men who are expected to recover within a month go to Medical Holding Companies in Cam Ranh Bay. Those who will take longer to recover or who have less than a month left in-country are sent home. The really sick ones go to Japan, Guam or Okinawa, sometimes to die there. Or they will spend months in Intensive Care there before going home. Mary says there is a special ward in Japan for critically ill men who won't survive the trip back to the States. The Army flies their families to Japan so they can be with them when they die. I wonder if that doesn't help some of them survive.

Wards 2 and 4 are on the second floor at the head of a long ramp. Ward 2 is a post-surgical floor for American casualties; Ward 4 has sixteen beds for urinary patients, including the venereal disease cases, and sixteen beds for post-surgical Viet Namese patients. The arrangement of our Nightingale wards hasn't changed since Scutari. The nurses' station is a small island located in the centre along one long wall. Supply shelves form small barriers surrounding the island and isolate the desk and medicine cabinet from the beds on either side. There are eight beds on either side of the desk and sixteen beds along the opposite wall. There are no screens, no drapes, so the nurses and corpsmen are seen by all of the patients. Every one of the thirty-two patients is part of our lives just as we are part of theirs.

The wards are arranged like the letter "H" with the wards in the longer parts of the H and the shorter crossbar housing the bathrooms and supply room. Small square windows are placed too high in the walls to see anything but sky and one light pole. The ward walls are green and there are banks of fluorescent lights. Everything in the wards is blue or green: sheets, pajamas, linoleum floor. The metal beds are white and the paint chips easily each time someone hits them with a stretcher. The beds have heavy cranks at the foot on which I crack my shin at least once a
shift. The drawers in the bedside stands stick and then come open with a loud, metallic bang. There isn't shiny chrome here or the latest equipment. The supplies are bulk-packaged, wrapped in green cloth wrappers and stored on open

wooden shelves. There are glass intravenous bottles and large bottles of sterile water with black rubber caps. It's not fancy, but what we have does work.

The supply room is also our change of shift report room. There are no chairs in the supply room. We sit on the concrete floor, cardex spread on our knees, and give report. Behind us, across the hall, there is always a background of slapping wet feet on the bathroom floor. Sound carries from the concrete and metal room, so we keep our voices low if we are passing on some confidential information about a patient.

The television at one end of the ward is always tuned to the Armed Forces Viet Nam TV Network. They run tapes of every football game, baseball game, golf match and other sporting event televised in the States. We are still watching baseball in December. The patients' two favourite programs are reruns of *Star Trek* and *Combat*. They guys like to do critiques of how Sgt. Saunders leads his patrols. In addition to the television, there are usually a radio and a couple of boom boxes playing; there is a constant card game in progress.

At least in the Emergency Room, the patients came and went. Our relationships with them, often intense, were over in an hour. On the wards here if a patient is difficult or grates on my nerves, he is going to be there the next day. My only hope is that he is posted on a med-evac soon.

Noise, constant coming and going of patients, phones ringing all the time, the banter of voices and the roar of televisions, radios and tape players are common to the twelve-hour day shifts. Sometimes it is an hour or so after I leave the ward before the noise stops in my head.

Thursday, December 3, 1970. There is a regular bus service in Qui Nhon! I guess they have to have it since the compounds are so spread out over the city. The bus goes to the hospital, to the Post Exchange, to the bank, to the U.S.O., to several other compounds, including the Engineer's Compound where the photo developing lab is located. I've even become adept at remembering bus schedules and being at the stop in time to catch the bus.

One of the things I've noticed riding the bus to the photo lab or the Post Exchange is the number of students. Many of the little children wear blue shorts or skirts and white blouses. The older boys wear all-blue uniforms and the girls at the University have white ao-dias over white or black pants. From the window of the bus I see groups of young children leaving school. Sisters walk with little brothers. Many carry book sacks under their arms. One boy carries a sweet potato vine in a glass jar. The children cluster around dirty, umbrella-covered stands to buy pieces of sugar cane or bottles of sticky orange soda. They are so like the children back in the States except here the schoolyards have no grass, only brown dust and barbed wire built into the fences around the schools. The school buildings are marked with black smoke from grenades. At fifteen, most boys have to leave school to join the Army. Some of the girls go to University, some go out on the streets as hookers. There isn't much of a future for them, there isn't much of a future for this country.

Friday, December 4, 1970. We go to a party on the beach tonight. Amid the waves crashing into the sand, lights twinkle on a ship in the harbour and when the moon darts behind clouds, the sand changes from silver grey to a deep black. The beach is surrounded by barbed wire and Viet Namese boats patrol the harbour. We can see the fishing boats anchored just outside the breakwater. The Viet Cong on the boats can see us, too. I have stopped worrying about being so close to the city. Nothing seems to happen, so I suppose I'm as safe here as I was in Pleiku.

I don't have a very good time at the party. In Qui Nhon the nurses stay mostly with other hospital people or with a few pilots from the Cav. There isn't as much visiting back and forth between compounds as there was in Pleiku and there are more compounds and more men here. American women are a prize and the men in the other units go to great lengths to have a little of our time. That's the reason for the party tonight: some Navy types come into the Officers' Club, and kidnap all the nurses there with a promise of a party. It is just like being back at a fraternity party in college. The officers are drunk, they have a belching contest, their hands are constantly pawing at us. I won't let myself be kidnapped again.

Saturday, December 5, 1970. We have a twenty-two year old captain on the ward who is blind in one eye. Both eyes are bandaged. I spent a lot of time with him, explaining what I'm doing, just talking with him. I remember Jim, the first patient I took care of in Pleiku. Perhaps there is always one patient at the beginning of each new assignment that I will remember, someone who marks my way into the new assignment. I like the intimacy with Captain W., the sense that he is my patient.

Sunday, December 6, 1970. Six months here has made me think a lot about living in the States. Many of the people I've met here don't want to return to the States. We don't like what is happening there: the demonstrations, the marches, the firing on Kent State students. It sounds crazy, but what we often talk about in the middle of this war is how much we have come to hate violence. I think about not going back, finding a job somewhere, anywhere to just not have to face the problems in the States. I don't want to live with racial tensions, high prices, crime. I am trying to balance that idea against running away because the going is getting rough. I think about my parents having through the Depression and the Second World War and all the wars my grandmother has lived through. But I don't like their solutions. I don't like the profanity my father uses to describe black people. I don't like that poverty and war and torture exist and that we know they exist and don't do anything about them. I see what I have compared to the people in this country; those differences don't seem fair and I don't have a clue what to do about the unfairness. Now that I've stopped worrying about the city being too close and the Viet Cong attacking, what I'm afraid of is that somehow I'll go home and lose what I'm beginning to learn here about people.

❀ ᛒ ❀

Calgary, Alberta. I was beginning to get restless, even then, with the idea of being an American. Somehow it just didn't fit for me, thought at the time I was only beginning to see where the mismatches were. This whole idea of other cultures, other ways of doing things was just beginning to open up my life. And, though I didn't know it at the time, it would eventually lead me to Canada and a far different life than I was imagining for myself that December.

❀ ᛒ ❀

Tuesday, December 8, 1970. A school child was killed by a G.I. yesterday and there are riots in the city. The mayor orders a curfew and we are on Yellow Option III. That means we pull our dust-covered flak jackets from under our beds, try to find our helmets and take the jackets and helmet to work with us. Tear gas is tossed into the compound this evening, so we go to the supply room and draw our gas masks. They don't let us keep them all the time because they are afraid we will lose them. I haven't had one on since basic and wondered: do I still remember how to use it? Here the newbies have the advantage on us; they were at Ft. Sam only a little while ago so they remember how to handle these blasted things.

On paper we are authorized a .45 pistol, and I jokingly ask the supply sergeant if he is issuing pistols to the nurses. He says, "With all due respect, ma'am, I'd rather shoot you than issue you a pistol." We have been told if there is trouble, we are to go to the ward and wait to be evacuated. Everyone is jumpy. We don't think the Viet Cong will attack the hospital, but the byplay of a general riot would be just as serious for us. The wind doesn't discriminate where it blows tear gas. I wonder if they will evacuate the patients along with the nurses if things get hotter?

Wednesday, December 9, 1970. None of our Viet Namese workers are allowed into the compound today. It makes me aware of how much they do for us. Our small Post Exchange and snack bar are closed; the mess hall is serving sandwiches and soup instead of full meals; our laundry isn't being done and the are no repair services available for the equipment. If this goes on much longer, we will have to detail some of our corpsmen for laundry and mess hall duty. They are already pulling extra guard duty and come to work exhausted because they are up most of the night.

The hardest thing is working without the two women who usually care for the Viet Namese patients and do the translations. We are making do with a few phrases and lots of sign language. It is especially hard on the babies who have had cleft lip repair. We can't explain to them why the women, whom they hang on to like mothers, are not here. They cry all day.

I wonder what the news services are saying about the riots? My guess is that what is really happening here isn't what is being reported in the States. I only hope my family isn't worried, because I'm not really in any danger.

Thursday, December 10, 1970. I extended in the Army for an extra year today. I like what I'm doing and keep hoping I can be assigned to Womak Army Hospital at Ft. Bragg. I've always wanted to work in orthopaedics and Ft. Bragg has one of the best orthopaedic experiences in the Army. I guess it has something to do with all those people from the 82nd Airborne jumping out of planes there. If I don't get Bragg I have thought about asking for another overseas assignment, perhaps Okinawa, Japan or Belgium. But I think I really want to go back to the States, to be stationed somewhere I've never been before and see more of the country. The Army offers a lot of courses: surgical nursing, public health, midwifery. Maybe I can take one of those. I think I'd like public health and it might be nice, after I've done orthopaedics for a time, to work outside of a hospital for a while. I don't know if I want to become a career officer or not. Some days I can't wait to get out and other times I think this is a pretty good life, so why not stay?

Friday, December 11, 1970. There is an official announcement today that the traditional Christmas, New Year's and Tet truces are to be observed. With minor violations, I imagine. The violations aren't actually mentioned, but everyone knows they will be there. Rumour has it that Tet will be bad next year. I only hope the rumours aren't true. I remember the pictures of Tet in '67 and '68, with the Marines being evacuated out of Hue on tanks. We feel so vulnerable here sometimes, especially with the pull-out and so many units down-sizing or stand-ing down. A lot of us feel that if a big push happens, as we are told happened in '68, there just won't be enough troops in the field to win this time.

The Viet Namese workers come back today. I don't know what their feelings are about the local troubles. I am sure many of them must be resentful and afraid. They also put themselves in danger by working for us. At least if there is a big push at Tet we American women are to be evacuated. The Viet Namese women must stay here and the Viet Cong will rape, torture or kill them for having worked for us. We are putting them in that kind of danger so we can have our food cooked, our laundry cleaned, our work made easier.

Saturday, December 12, 1970. The slides from the last few weeks in Pleiku come back today. I feel funny looking at them. I have a curious sense of detachment, as if I have known those people but don't any longer. Three weeks ago, I thought it would break my heart to leave that place. Now I still marvel over what the mountains look like at dawn, but it isn't the same feel-ing as having the wind sting my face and knowing the bone-weary fatigue of my sixth night on nights. I look at the pictures from the last party at C.I.D.G., but it isn't the same as hearing Starkey's voice or Arthur's laugh. I am surprised at how quickly I've lost the feel of it.

Sunday, December 13, 1970. Captain W., the man who is blind in one eye, went out on air evac today. I don't know if I helped him and will never know. I hope he remembers me. Most of the time I don't think about being remembered. The patients come and go and a few days after they have gone I don't remember who they were. But there was Jim, who was my first patient in Pleiku, and Glen H., who came from Jeanerette and went to U.S.L., and now Captain W. When things are quiet I'll think about one of them and wonder where he is and how he is.

❀ ᛈ❀

Calgary, Alberta. When I reported to Ft. Bragg, we had a Captain W. on our ward. I thought it couldn't be the same person, but when I looked at his chart, he had been evac'ed from Qui Nhon in December 1970. He had one of the semi-private rooms down the hall. I went into his room and wasn't sure I recognized him because he looked so fit and healthy. He had a black patch over one eye. I introduced myself to him and said, "I think I knew you in Qui Nhon?"

He smiled and said, "I think you did, too. I recognized your voice."

He was all right. He was about ready to be fitted with an artificial eye, though he wasn't sure the patch wouldn't be less trouble. Then he was leaving the Army and going back to school.

That was almost the only time the circle was completed like that. The only other patient that I met both in 'Nam and in the States was a young man who came up to me one day in the canteen at Womak Army Hospital at Ft. Bragg. He introduced himself and told me he had come through the Emergency Room at Pleiku and that I had started the I.V. on him. I didn't tell him that I didn't remember the incident, but I did tell him how grateful I was that he remembered and had stopped to talk to me.

There were times that I wished I had met more of my ex-patients, that I knew they were all right and had come back and gone on with life. I thought about this the most when I traveled down to the States, when I see a man my age with scars, or a prosthesis, or sitting in a wheelchair. I wondered, "Were you one of them? Did I know you a long time ago in another place?" It felt like stories without endings.

...I don't remember his name...

❀ ☊ ❀

Monday, December 14, 1970. Some of the hospital staff have decided to go caroling for Christmas. Going Christmas caroling is bred into nursing students. I haven't found any nurse, including myself, who wasn't expected to dress in her student uniform with an especially starched apron over it and go singing among the wards at Christmas. So some of the nurses drag doctors and corpsmen to our first practice tonight so that we will have some deeper voices. The Red Cross is trying to get candles for us so we can do a candlelight procession. We practice in the chapel. There are the usual jokes about not being able to sing. Then the organ begins and we try some familiar lyrics and suddenly Viet Nam seems very far from everything that is familiar.

This is the first time I have been in the chapel. I am not hypocritical enough to confess sins I'm not sorry for. I figure I have already done enough to send me straight to hell. I just don't worry about it any more. The carols are nice and singing with other people is nice and that is all there is to it.

I have begun my Christmas shopping from the PACEX catalogue. I think I'll send my parents a set of Noritake china and my brothers some binoculars. All I have to do is send PACEX a check and they mail everything to the States for me. It's the easiest Christmas shopping I've ever done.

It's going to be a lot harder for my family to shop for me. I've got so much money in the bank right now that I can get myself almost anything I want. Part of being able to do that is not wanting big things. I couldn't afford furniture or a new car or really expensive clothes, but I can afford things right now I've never been able to afford before. What would I really like? A good tape player? My little reel-to-reel is just about worn out. They have these huge tape players in the catalogue, some reel-to-reel that look like they require an engineering degree to run and some cassette players with double cassette heads and mini-speakers. A lot of the black soldiers buy those. I want one that is small, light, portable. There's this cute little one, hardly bigger than a paperback book. It comes with a set of earphones and costs $100.00. I'm still trying to decide if that's too much to spend on a tape player. I've put it on the list after the camera equipment and after the trip to Bangkok in March. But besides that I don't know anything else I want for Christmas.

Tuesday, December 15, 1970. Today I have been in the Army a little over two years; on active duty seventeen months and seven months in-country. I'm over half way through my tour here and time is passing so fast that it will be time to go home before I am ready.

It's hard to find things to do on a day off. There are shops and restaurants in Qui Nhon, but the town is off-limits. The places I am allowed to go are confined to the area bordered by the barbed wire fence surrounding the air field: the air field cafeteria, the U.S.O. and the Cavalry compounds. The air field cafeteria serves a terribly greasy breakfast: fried eggs, hash brown potatoes, toast swimming in butter. Sometimes I go there for a treat. The U.S.O. shows movies, runs bingos and has a small library, though most of the books are adventure or war novels. On Thursdays, the women from the U.S.O. bring tubs of ice cream to the wards and we have either strawberry or hot fudge sundaes. That is often the high point of the week.

I spend most of my off-duty time in the photo lab over at the Engineer's Compound. Developing pictures requires more planning than it did in Pleiku. There I walked from the hospital compound to the photo lab. I'd stay as long as I wanted and walk back. Here I have to make sure I'm finished by the time the last bus runs in the afternoon.

There is an old man who picks up trash on the Engineer's Compound. Someone dressed him in a Boy Scout uniform, complete with badge sash. He beams with pride and salutes all the officers he passes. I hate seeing him go around the compound, dressed in his uniform, with the garbage sack over his shoulder, smiling his toothless grin as he salutes. He is something of a tourist attraction. People come over to the compound just to take his picture beside the garbage dump. I want to take his picture, also, but there is some kind of tact that prevents me from doing this. It is the same feeling I had in Pleiku that prevented me from taking pictures of casualties, as if there are some times when privacy should be preserved.

It's quite strange to ride the bus through the different compounds, to visit a large P.X., to look at the ocean from the bus windows. The afternoons are hot and lazy and there is a strong smell of hot tar streets and of white buildings reflected in the strong sunlight. Sometimes I close my eyes and the heat feels like Louisiana on a summer day.

Flashback

Sky-blue Tuesday.
Behind white buildings,
the South China Sea breaks.
Rows of silver pentagons flash on water.
Lazy breakers take grey waves.

If this is a war,
why am I swaying in a hammock,
painting my nails coral, planning a tan?

Wednesday, December 16, 1970. A convoy is ambushed today and we are just finishing working through a mass casualty. It's so strange to hear the choppers, to find out secondhand how many casualties have been brought in, not to be down in the Emergency Room myself. I don't like it because I feel confined on the ward, out of the way, out of the action. But I console myself that some of the casualties are on our ward and I have an opportunity to take care of them.

We don't take care of critically-ill patients in our wards; they go to Intensive Care. Or maybe after being nineteen months out of nursing school, my definition of critically-ill has taken on a new meaning. The ward is full of patients with I.V.s, chest tubes, stomach tubes, and all of the hardware that is just routine to me now. I have burn cases and consider them minor because only a quarter of their body is burned. Critically-ill now means to me that the patient isn't going to die that day.

What a guy wants is a million-dollar injury: to be hurt badly enough that he can go home, but not badly enough that he will be crippled or maimed. Even the ones who are slightly wounded don't want to go to Cam Ranh Bay. After they have recovered, they probably won't be assigned to the same unit they came from. The don't want to go to the field with strangers, to learn to fight with new units.

Sometimes a man asks me or the doctor to exaggerate a little on the chart, to say he needs to go home instead of Cam Ranh Bay. When we say no, some of them shrug and say, "Oh well, no harm trying." Some of them become quite angry and say they are going to die if they go back to the field. Sometimes they are right. Twice we have had patients on our ward with minor wounds, sent them to the Medical Holding Company only to have them come back a few weeks later with both legs blown off.

I feel like I'm a part of this 'conspiracy' for lack of a better word: this conspiracy to get men crippled or killed. Sometimes I think I should say "no", make some kind of protest like refusing to send someone back to the field. I know I'd last about thirty seconds if I tried that. Whatever I do has to be sneaky and subversive, like coaching the patients on how to answer the doctor's questions or learning which doctors are more likely to send some-one home. I feel like it's us, the patients and the hospital staff, against them, the Army. It's not going to hurt the Army in the long run to send a few guys home early. It might kill them not to go home. We do what we can to help.

I've read about people who take draft dodgers or deserters across the border to Canada. I can't go along with that. If they believe the war is wrong, they should stand for what they believe, even if it means going to jail. I guess I think our guys here are different because they haven't run away. They came to Viet Nam even if they didn't want to or didn't believe in the war. But I think I know how those people feel who help them across the border. They are doing what they can to help, too.

On Ward 4 we have the resistant venereal disease cases. Some of the guys think getting clap over and over is a joke. One patient wants to set the record for the getting it the most number of times. He's been admitted six times so far. There is a rumour going around about black clap. It's supposed to be incurable and there is rumoured to be a mythical naval ship off the coast where they ship guys who have black clap because the military won't let them go back to the States for fear of spreading it. Between the patients who don't take the illness seriously enough and those who are terrified by the rumours, it's hard to teach any real health information.

We have to act tough when the humour gets vulgar because if the patients think a remark embarrasses a nurse, she becomes fair game for harassment. One of the favourite games is for a patient to ask in the middle of the open ward, where all the other patients can hear, "Lieutenant, can I get clap again if I . . . ?" and proceed to recite in graphic detail what he plans to do. I've learned the best response is to smile enigmatically and walk away. The patients' behaviour gets old very fast, but even with that kind of behaviour, I like taking care of the G.I.s better than the Viet Namese.

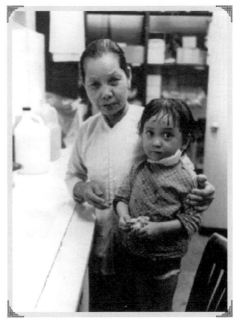

We have two Viet Namese women who are translators, housekeepers and ward aides. They provide most of the care for the Viet Namese patients. We have a lot of children on Ward 4 because we do cleft lip repairs as part of the Med-Cap program. Some of the children are casualties, usually victims of our own fire.

We have a little two-year old girl who is burned. Her parents stole aviation fuel from the airfield and tried to use it for cooking. It exploded. When she came in, the

doctors thought her whole face was going to be scarred. But now, after six weeks, she requires only a skin graft the size of a dime on her neck and will heal without scars. She is almost ready to go home, but her parents have disappeared. They stopped coming to see her about a month ago. One of our translators says her parents have lost face because of stealing fuel and they are also afraid the Americans will punish them for the thefts. If they don't come back, she will be sent to the nuns at the orphanage.

The corpsmen become attached to the children and it's common to see one of them going about his rounds with a baby tucked under his arm. We have no lack of help in comforting the children. The patients play with the babies and rock them to sleep at bedtime. They buy clothes and toys for the children and agonize over what will happen to the children when they return to their families.

Sometimes there are Montagnards, too, usually evac'ed from the Central Highlands because there is no more American medical care there. The Viet Namese aides have little to do with them. When food trays are served, we watch the aides to make sure they don't give all the food to the Viet Namese patients and none to the Montagnards. Some of the nurses and corpsmen are fascinated by the 'Yards. They have only seen them in the hospital, and Qui Nhon being so far from the Highlands the families can't be with them as they were in Pleiku. The people here have no idea of how the 'Yards live. One of the corpsmen asked me if it was true that they are cannibals.

We had a young woman on the ward recently who had been wounded and evac'ed from Kontum. The corpsmen were all laughing at her the morning after she came in and they wouldn't tell me why. When I examined her I saw that one of her breasts was swollen, while the other one was normal size. I palpated her breast to see if I could find what was causing the swelling and milk came out of the nipple. I remember how the women would carry their babies in a wrap, like a sling, so the baby could nurse while the mother was working. I tried the few words I knew and realized she had a baby a few days old in Kontum. We called Pat Smith's hospital and they had the baby, but no mother. I explained to the supervisor what I'd discovered and she made arrangements for the mother to be evac'ed back to Kontum about an hour later.

I miss Ba, the 'Yard interpreter we had in the Emergency Room. There is no one here who can talk to the Montagnards. Some days I come to work and find all the Montagnard patients huddled squatting in a corner terrified of all that is going on around them.

Thursday, December 17, 1790. Each evening when I arrive for night duty about 1830, the shock of the ward's noise hits me. I scan the rows of beds, calculating how many have gone on med-evacs, what kind of action there has been during the day, who are the sickest patients. My corpsman and I sit on the floor of the supply room taking report. Usually the combined census of both wards is about fifty patients, both G.I. and indigenous. After we've finished report, the day shift goes home and we make rounds, and check I.V.s. Then I have to set up the medicines. In nursing school we were taught to set up medicines in a quiet place so there would be less chance of errors. In Qui Nhon we don't have that luxury. I line up rows of small cards for each patient and pour the medicines from the big glass bottles into small paper cups. If we have a high census, completing all the setup of all the medicines takes me almost an hour. The medicine cart has one stiff wheel and if, after pouring all the medicines, I turn a corner too sharply, pills jump from one cup to another and I start over.

The patients' supper comes from the mess hall in deep stainless steel buckets and the nurses and corpsmen prepare the trays and distribute them. Ambulatory patients help. For a while the smell of hot food replaces the usual ward smells of iodine solution, wet skin and cigarettes.

After supper the wards become quieter. The television, radios and tape players are constantly on. The Red Cross workers sometimes come over after supper, to play cards or put together puzzles or write letters.

There are a lot of wounds to dress: some just small frag wounds, hardly bigger than a pimple, some gaping wounds that expose muscle or organs. A wound any size can become infected so we do a lot of wound care. The soaks, dressings and other procedures take most of the evening. Our work is close and intimate. The beds almost touch each other. The patients can see what we do, hear what we say. What I do involves touching: changing dressings, turning helpless patients, back rubs, sometimes just a hand on an arm or holding a man's hand. There aren't any pictures of me doing this. Sometimes I am embarrassed to have others ever see me do it. I want to be private about caring. This is the hard part of nursing. I've gotten good at the routines: the medications, the treatments, the I.V.s. I'm getting better at organizing my work and at supervising the corpsmen. Those are  nursing skills, management skills, and they can be pretty impersonal. There's something terribly personal about the intimacy of some of the care I give. That kind of care is just as important as the medications and the treatments and the I.V.s. I don't understand it yet, but I know it's one of the reasons so many of the wounded survive.

Ward work is exhausting. It isn't just the new medicines and the treatment routines, but what is more tiring is the intensity of those contacts. We are visible, available twelve hours every shift. On night shift the two of us, one corpsman and one nurse, move from one ward to the other and there is never any private place.

The corpsman and I spend the hour before lights out at 2200 giving back rubs and settling people for the night. About 2130 I walk out on the porches outside the end of the ward and tell everyone to come inside. Sometimes I think about what good targets we make in the lit porches, on the second floor, and I think we're just lucky that no one gets shot there. I have to take a deep breath before I go outside and not breathe too deeply while I'm out there because some nights the smell of pot is very strong. I think the stash may be on the ward, but I don't want to know.

After lights out there are rounds to make every hour. I've learned to tell from the way the blankets move or don't move who is sleeping. If the man is awake two hours in a row, I stop and talk to him. Sometimes he needs morphine and doesn't want to ask for it. Sometimes another back rub helps. Sometimes he's accustomed to being up all night waiting in ambush. Sometimes he just wants to talk. Those late nights talks are intimate. I know how to keep my voice low when we talk. We talk about home, about his chances of being sent Stateside, about how he was hit, about life in the field, about buddies who haven't survived. We talk about where we're from and what we miss and what we look forward to when we go home.

It's always a long night. We chart, straighten the supply shelves, go to midnight chow and still have six hours until change-of-shift report. I write letters or read. Sometimes the corpsman takes a nap. At 0630 the corpsman stands at the far end of the ward with his hand on the light switch and I stand by the radio. There is a tape of an announcer on the A.F.V.N. Radio who starts every day with a most enthusiastic "Good Morning, Viet Nam!" We have the timing down to a fine art. At exactly the same moment he says "Good Morning . . .," I turn on the radio and the corpsman hits the lights. We wake the whole ward in less than a minute.

Like faint background music I am learning the rhythms of the ward, the changing shifts, the coming and going of the patients, the rattle of the medicine

cart's stubborn wheel, the endless card games, the sounds of football and Captain Kirk, the Viet Namese children, the lewd remarks, the rounds, the "Good Morning, Viet Nam" that start each day. It's like a waltz, slow and flowing in three-quarter time. I've been dancing to this music a long time now. I wanted to keep dancing as long as the men do. This routine of night shift, as long and hard as it is, suits me just fine.

❀ ♫ ❀

Calgary, Alberta. It took me a long time to not be embarrassed by the closeness of caring. My own sexuality was too inexperienced to be able to understand and separate out what I felt when I participated in the lewd conversations, what I felt making love with Ed and what I felt with the patients: to know what was pornography, what was love-making, and what was caring. Years after Viet Nam, I found a quote in *Testament of Youth* by Vera Brittain, who had worked as a V.A.D. in World War I. She wrote

> Short of actually going to bed with them, there was hardly an intimate service that I did not perform for one or another in the course of four years, and I still have reason to be thankful for the knowledge of masculine functioning which the care of them gave me. . . . From the constant handling of their lean, muscular bodies, I came to understand the essential cleanliness, the innate nobility, of sexual love on its physical side. Although there was much to shock in Army hospital service, much to terrify, much, even, to disgust, this day-by-day contact with male anatomy was never part of the shame.

That hadn't changed. It was as much a reality in the Viet Nam war as it was in World War I. It was one of the things we learned about ourselves as women and what we learned about the men we cared for and about.

❀ ⌘ ❀

Monday, December 21, 1970. I am down at midnight chow and one of the cooks comes running to my table and says there's an emergency on my ward. The long way from the mess hall to the ward is around recovery room and up the long ramp, but there is also a short cut: the fire ladder at the back of the ward. I take the short cut.

It's the patient with a dog bite on his leg. He's in the hospital because the wound is infected and also because there's some question if he can take the rabies shots. When I arrive he is in convulsions and I think, "He's having an allergic reaction to the rabies vaccine and he's going to die." Then I don't know what happens but something clicks. I remember taking the rabies shots myself and the side effects the doctor told me to watch for and somehow I just know this wasn't an allergic reaction. So I send the corpsman for the doctor on call and talk to the patient. I know if I stay calm, everything will be all right. The doctor comes right away and decides the patient has worked himself into an anxiety state because he thinks he might have a reaction. After the patient calms down, he looks sheepishly at me and says, "Sorry. I didn't mean to frighten you." I think of my quick trip up the fire ladder—and my fear of heights—and burst out laughing. I guess this is what they mean by gaining experience.

Tuesday, December 22, 1970. Last night was my last night shift for a while and I try to sleep all day today. Having six nurses in the same room, all on different shifts, means someone is always trying to sleep. We try to be as quiet as we can, but this is getting very old and I hope they will do something soon about more rooms for us.

I have heard that C.I.D.G. hospital is closed and all the medics are transferred to different places. It feels like having a piece of me break up.

Wednesday, December 23, 1970. Our ward has a Christmas party with Wards 6 and 8. The corpsman I've been on duty with this last stretch of nights draws my name. He doesn't know what to make of me. I don't know what to make of him. He comes from a big city, Detroit, I think. Sometimes it doesn't seem like we speak the same language and we certainly haven't had many common experiences. But he does work hard and he's good and kind with the patients. He thinks I'm funny because I thank him for his work at the end of each shift. He tells me he really doesn't understand me. Anyway, he drew my name and he gave me a lovely 'Yard pottery bowl.

We take some food to the people who have to work during the party. There are a lot of casualties recently and one is admitted to the ward while we are up there. Everyone immediately rushes to get him settled. It must be pretty strange for him to wake up surrounded by people dressed in party clothes.

So many church groups, Red Cross chapters, Scout troops have sent us gifts and cookies. The Red Cross lounge and the U.S.O. are full of packages and good things to eat. There is a magnificent Christmas tree at the U.S.O. and we have our own smaller version on the ward. Someone has a blow-up plastic Santa Claus and we put him in one of the beds, with an I.V. of Jack Daniels for him.

Stan, the helicopter pilot Diane is dating, cut us a tree for The Swamp. It's a strange, tropical-looking thing, hardly in keeping with the evergreens we are accustomed to having at Christmas, but we have some lights from the Red Cross and it looks pretty good.

...and he gave me a 'Yard pottery bowl...

Thursday, December 24, 1970. Christmas Eve. Some Viet Namese student-teachers and city officials come to bring us gifts and cards today. The teachers are learning English and some of them speak it quite well, much better than my Viet Namese. The student-teachers are all women because men their age are in the Army. We take them on a tour of the wards and have a reception in the mess hall afterwards.

I'm caught off guard by their visit and am angry the whole time they are here. I remember how I strip-searched women in Pleiku and realize how little I have learned about the women here. When we pull out, when we lose this war as we are sure to do, these women are going to be killed. By being teachers, by learning English, by being friendly towards Americans they have almost insured their own deaths. We are going to climb on planes and ships and go away. They don't have that protection. So we play this damned charade: exchange gifts and pass out hard candy and have eggnog and cookies in the mess hall afterwards.

This evening we go Christmas caroling on the wards. We sing "Peace on Earth, good will to men" to a twenty-year-old man with both arms blown off. Diane was with him when he woke up from the anesthetic. He said to her, "What do I do with my life now, stand in a corner?" She said, "You do whatever you want to do, whatever you have the guts to do." Then she came back to the hooch and cried and we held her.

I hate this war, hate everything about being here. It isn't just being away from home, but also not understanding the war or what we accomplish by being here.

At midnight we have a Christmas service with music and poems on the theme "Let's Get Together." I sit next to a Negro. We share sheet music for the carols and when the church bells ring, we hug, kiss and wish each other "Merry Christmas." My parents would die if they knew I'd done that.

Friday, December 25, 1970. Christmas Day. I work Christmas Day and am happy to have something to do. I have no desire to spend the day moping in my room. We have turkey and all the trimmings at lunch today. There are decorations on the tables and the Commanding Officer and the Chief Nurse have a receiving line as we come into the mess hall. Later in the afternoon the generals from the units we support come to see their men. They thank us for what we are doing and bring us boxes of candy.

Bob Hope is in-country. He isn't very popular around Qui Nhon. We support the 173rd Airborne Infantry, commonly known as "The Herd." Bob Hope supposedly gave them that name. He was asked to perform for them one Christmas. At the time there were rumours about atrocities the 173rd had committed against civilians. He is supposed to have said he would never perform for a herd of animals like that. Like a lot of stories here, it may never have happened, but the name stuck. The 173rd takes it as their nickname as a mark of defiance. He isn't popular, but we still listen to his show on the radio. When they sing "Silent Night" at the end, I am hanging a bottle of I.V. fluid on a patient who had just come back from surgery. We look at each other and both cry.

Monday, December 28, 1970. I never have to spend a lot of money in the bar. It's always possible to tell, from the vehicles parked outside the Officer's Club, who's inside. I've learned who's a likely prospect for buying drinks.

If I play Liar's Dice with any of the pilots from the Air Cav I don't usually buy my drinks. Liar's Dice is played with five or six dice in a cup. I roll them out, being careful not to let anyone see what they are. Then I'll announce what I've rolled. The person I'm playing with can either call me a liar or not. If I have lied and he calls it correctly, I have to buy a round of drinks. If I've told the truth and he thinks I haven't, he has to buy the drinks. Most of the time I come out ahead, I buy one round and get four or five bought for me.

Tuesday, December 29, 1970. I had a flaming hooker last night. One last one for Barry. He's been gone almost seven months now. I guess he's made some kind of an impression on me that I'm not likely to forget. Perhaps it was the circumstances, being new in-country and impressionable. His death brought the war home to me in a very real way.

Wednesday, December 30, 1970. I had a chance to go to Pleiku with one of the Cav pilots today. I made all the arrangements, then just didn't show up at the air field. I guess that means I am finally breaking the emotional ties with the place. My only regret is not having been able to show some of the guys at C.I.D.G. the last set of slides. I think my photography is getting pretty good.

Thursday, December 31, 1970. New Year's Eve. I am drinking a great deal more in Qui Nhon than I did even in Pleiku. I was really drunk last night and, in the Officers' Club, I poured a drink on a Captain's head. The bartender threw me out. I'm barred from the Officers' Club for a week. I don't know why I did it, just for some excitement, I suppose.

I am so tired of riots and demonstrations, so tired of newscasts that start with Viet Nam, so tired of people not giving us the support we need to win. We have already lost this country. Our guys patrol, keep getting shot over the same piece of territory. We never hold anything.

I am angry because of the people who will die without their deaths meaning anything. Every time I look at the patients on the ward I want to yell, "Enough! Stop!" It isn't just the G.I.s. There are enough booby traps and mines to kill farmers and their water buffaloes and their children for a hundred years. They are all going to die: our mama-sans, the teachers, the old man in the Boy Scout uniform, prostitutes, officials, children—especially the children. I am tired of seeing children missing arms and legs. Hundreds of half-American children live on the streets unless they are among the fortunate few taken in by nuns or missionaries. They survive a little longer, until they are old enough to go into the Army or onto the streets.

There is a boy on our compound who shines shoes. Three years ago one of the corpsmen tried to adopt him. The paperwork is so complicated that it has dragged on for three years without resolution. Now he is almost fifteen. When he is fifteen he will be needed for the Army. Any day I expect him to disappear. Why can't they just let go of one small boy?

I am angry at the waste, the death from drugs. When I first came in-country we averaged one death a month from drug overdoses. Now we average one death a week, usually from heroin cut with strychnine. I've learned to ignore the drugs, to not care that there must be pot hidden on the ward, to check a casualty for needle marks so he can be sent to the psychiatric ward before he goes into withdrawal. One of my corpsmen was busted the other day about 1500 hours. I stood on the porch outside the ward, looking at the two Military Police make him stand against the jeep while they frisked him. Then I went inside and called my Supervisor and told her she'd have to send me a corpsman for the rest of the shift because mine had just been carted off by the police. I was more worried about who was going to help me take temperatures than that one of my corpsmen had been busted.

Some C.I.D. men came to see me once in Pleiku. They thought one of the nurses was stealing narcotics and selling them on the black market. They wanted me to work for them undercover to try to trap her. I told them to go to hell. Then I went and told my head nurse, who had her transferred to work in the Central Supply, where there weren't any drugs.

I am tired of the white phosphorus burns and the smell of pseudomonas infections. I am tired of tubes and transfusions and doing malaria tests. There are times I think I hate the Army, but when I'm really honest with myself, I am most angry because deep inside I like what I'm doing. I like the order, the structure, like having my rank on my collar and name on my shirt, First Lieutenant Grant. It tells me exactly who I am. I like the power of planting my size five, combat-booted feet at the door of the ward and saying to two captains and a sergeant-major, "You're not coming in here to visit until you go downstairs and check those weapons." I think a lot about making the military my career. I feel like I'm trapped in some middle ground, not really a soldier, not really a civilian any more. If it weren't for war I could like this military life very much.

End of the year. End of the year I left the States and I don't know if I ever want to go back again. End of the year when Barry died and I still miss him. End of the first full year that I have been out of nursing school. I'm getting pretty good at what I do. I like it. I almost like the Army. Almost. Not quite. Never quite enough.

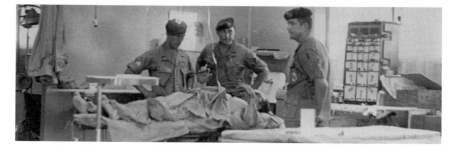

1971 JANUARY 1971

Wednesday, January 6, 1971. Terri has a party tonight to celebrate her promotion to Captain. At the party is a New Zealand Red Cross worker named John G. He's a small man, with a full black beard, who is at ease around us military types. He's not exactly what I think of as a Red Cross worker. He says he was a Major with the New Zealand Army in Malaysia and I wonder what made him go to work for the Red Cross. I also wonder why New Zealand sends Red Cross workers to Viet Nam. In any case, I like John. He has an easy manner and I find him very charming.

We go back to the Red Cross' house in Qui Nhon after the party and are discussing the pros and cons of going to bed together. He's pro and I'm con. All I want is a little cuddling, being held. Then the sappers hit. The first blast is close. It rattles the walls and shakes plaster from the ceiling. The lights blink and come back on again. John takes a .45 out of the closet, checks to make sure it's loaded and hands it to me. He doesn't ask me if I know how to use it, just makes the assumption that I do know. I take it from him and check it a second time because my father taught me never to trust someone else's word about whether or not a gun is loaded. John smiles when I do this.

The second explosion hits what I find out later is the A.R.V.N. ammunition dump and a whole series of explosions go off, each one rocking the small house and lighting up the sky. John dresses in khaki shorts, knee socks and a bulky tan sweater. He straps on a second pistol and says, "I have to see if our workers are all right. Get under the sink in the bathroom and if anyone comes through that door who doesn't have a New Zealand accent, shoot first and ask questions later."

Thank goodness for being only 4'11". I am able to climb under the sink without any difficulty. Outside the sky is bright orange and the night sounds as if the world is exploding. John handled the pistol like a professional. I wonder more about who he might be, about what he might really be doing in Viet Nam. I wonder if it really matters. I'm crouched under a sink with a loaded pistol in my hand and orders to use it. After seven months in-country, I didn't think I could be this scared. I'm scared all right. I have only two thoughts. First, if a Viet Namese comes through the door, will I shoot? I have visions of one coming through the door, of me killing him, only to have the ones behind him kill me. My second thought is that my mother will never forgive me if I am killed like this in a man's bedroom at three in the morning.

In about twenty minutes John comes back, all cheerfulness and smiles. He's whistling happily under his breath as he takes me to the kitchen and makes coffee. A girl who is barefoot and wearing only a light green towel pokes her head in the kitchen and says, "The blast knocked a live wire loose in the ceiling. It's just hanging there, making sparks. Will somebody fix it in the morning?" There is also Peter, another Red Cross worker, a friend of John's. The last I see of Peter that morning he is climbing on the roof to take pictures of the explosions.

By now the ammo dump has been exploding for half an hour. John and I drink our coffee, then lie down on his bed. Almost getting killed has made me horny. It is some kind of a reaction, an affirmation of life to want to bed a man. Now I want John to make love to me. Instead he's now sleepy as if the excitement has been a substitute for sex. He turns over and goes to sleep.

❀ ▷❀

Calgary, Alberta. I think a lot in my life broke loose in that night in the Red Cross house. In the months following that night I often thought about the woman in the green towel. She was my age and yet she had a self-confidence I knew I didn't have. I thought about how sheltered I was living on a barbed-wire-enclosed compound, eating my meals in a mess hall, not daring to venture out into the city, while she lived in the city, bought her food in the same markets as the Viet Namese, went anywhere she was needed. I wondered: how had she been able to do that and what would it take for me to have the same self-confidence?

John would say to me, "You Americans think you're the only bloody people who go to war. You don't even know about Malaysia." Then he told me about the war the Commonwealth had carried on there for years and I realized I had to look at the idea of Europeans and Americans fighting in Asia from another perspective. Sometimes I'd ask other people at the table in the mess hall, "Do you know anything about the Brits fighting in Malaysia?" They didn't; some of them didn't even know where Malaysia was. I began to feel that I'd had a good American education which made me woefully uneducated about the world. I thought back to the Special Forces in Pleiku. The world they had seen, being stationed in Panama, Thailand, Germany, and Viet Nam, was still essentially an American, military world. I began to wonder what else was out there.

Once John was digging at me, in a friendly way, "You don't know anything about Suez, about Dunkirk, about the Battle of Britain." "Oh, yes I do," I said and told him everything I knew about Dunkirk and the Battle of Britain. He didn't know that Douglas Bader was one of my heroes. When I finished he smiled at me just like he'd done when I checked the pistol a second time and said, "You keep up with me better than most Americans." I learned a lot about New Zealand arrogance, too.

❁ ᛁᚩ❁

Thursday, January 7, 1971. I've recovered from the effects of last night and fortunately no one checked to see if I was on the compound. I think I will stick closer to home for a while. It is pressing my luck to be out after curfew again because our Chief Nurse gets more upset about that than the one in Pleiku did.

The explosions blew out many of the ward windows and took the back off the

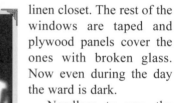 linen closet. The rest of the windows are taped and plywood panels cover the ones with broken glass. Now even during the day the ward is dark.

Needless to say, the explosion scared everyone on the ward. All the patients got under their beds and the nurse and

corpsman crawled under the nurses' desk. We have been ordered to bring our flak jackets and helmets to work. I don't know where mine is, but I finally find it in the corner of a locker in our room.

Friday, January 8, 1971. I'm writing letters telling everyone at home not to worry if they hear about the dump going up, that it was really terribly dull. I write the truth to Jeanne, a seven-and-a-half-page letter, but when I read it, the letter sounds like a war story. I'm not sure why I feel such a need to explain the events in detail. I feel a terrible need to go over the whole night almost minute by minute and only after that letter can I clear the events from my mind.

❁ ᛁᚩ❁

Calgary, Alberta. I loved the line above: "I've recovered from the effects of last night. . . ." I was actually innocent enough to believe all there was to recovery was to sleep well, dust my hands of what had happened and get on with life. War is only for the young. Those of us with a few years behind us simply don't have that kind of resiliency.

I don't know what I did with the letter to Jeanne, whether I mailed it or tore it up because it sounded too fantastic, too much like a war story. I also wonder how I managed to compress the whole evening into only seven and a half pages.

❀ ♫ ❀

Saturday, January 9, 1971. This is the first day I have felt really at home on this compound. It is so nice to be able to walk from the mess hall to the quarters and know people's names, to have them know mine, to stop and chat with people. I'm beginning to make decisions on the ward without asking others for advice on every detail. I think I am ready to put Pleiku behind me and enjoy myself here.

Sunday, January 10, 1971. I have such a crush on John. Of all the people I've met in Qui Nhon, he's the most fun to be with. Maybe it's because he challenges me to think. And because he's from New Zealand and different. I'm glad he's a civilian. I haven't talked to a civilian in so long I forget there is a world out there.

Monday, January 11, 1971. We have several Koreans on the ward, victims of the explosion last week. I feel the same reluctance in caring for them that I felt back in May when first caring for the Viet Namese and Montagnards. I have learned how comforting it is for my own peace of mind to be able to talk to my patients. I feel uncomfortable because I can't talk to the Koreans. In any case, the Koreans are very grateful for our care. When their buddies come to visit, they bow to us as they enter the ward. Some of them have built a lovely rock garden for us on a small patch of bare dirt at the bottom of the ramp that leads to the ward.

The Koreans have a reputation for tough discipline. We feel they are the only thing between us and the Viet Cong. With the pullout and the drug problem, our guys are getting very lax. We sometimes joke that the U.S. troops are more of a hazard to us than the enemy. There is a story circulating that a few weeks ago the Koreans found a guy asleep on guard duty and had a firing squad shoot him. I don't know if that is true or not because I find such a contrast between building the garden and putting a man before a firing squad, and yet I feel there is something essentially oriental about both of those acts. Maybe John is right that we Americans don't know much about the rest of the world.

Tuesday, January 12, 1971. The possible Tet offensive is our favourite, sometimes our only conversation at meals. Everyone has an opinion or has heard a rumour or has a good friend who knows the real scoop. Our imaginations are up to such a pitch that we will be disappointed if nothing happens during Tet.

Our orders are to keep a bag packed during Tet in case we need to be evacuated from the hospital. No one believes the Army will evacuate nurses from this hospital. We are the only full-size hospital in this area and if there is a battle here, the soldiers will need us. Our patient load has been reduced to almost nothing to make room for expected casualties and we spend more time at work waiting than working. The Emergency Room staff called a meeting a couple of days ago to review mass casualty procedures with the staff in the rest of the hospital. I was surprised how a couple of months working on a ward has made me rusty. It was difficult to wrap my imagination around a big influx of casualties.

Wednesday, January 13, 1971. I have been in this country eight months and I've never had a chance to be in a Viet Namese home, eat a meal with a family, attend a play or a concert. We laugh at the plays on the Viet Namese television channel. It seems that all of the plays, as near as we can tell, are about a young farm girl sending her fiancé off to war. The only Viet Namese we meet are the patients, our mama-sans who do our laundry, or the occasional officer who tours the wards. We think all Viet Namese children have lice, all girls over fourteen are prostitutes, all adults steal, all Viet Namese food will make us sick and all of the people really work for the Viet Cong. I don't think I will learn anything else about their culture. I wonder how in spite of decades of war they have farmed, built, married, raised families, educated their children. I wonder what their art is like, their literature, their religion. I don't think I will learn the answers to those questions here.

Wednesday, January 20, 1971. Seeing *M*A*S*H* was funny, but living it was even funnier. A couple of days ago the Military Police went after a guy who had gone absent without leave. The found him in downtown Qui Nhon and there was a gunfight. They shot the guy in the chest, and he was brought into the Emergency Room barely alive. They took him to x-ray and the x-ray showed a live grenade in the middle of his chest wound!

The Chief Surgeon, Colonel B. (or Roger Ram Jet, as we now call him) jumped in front of the patient and ordered everyone out of the room. The surgeons, now in flak jackets, started arguing about who was going to do the surgery. As one of them said, "I didn't want to do it, I just didn't want to see any of the lifers get a medal for this."

The corpsmen quickly constructed a bunker out of sandbags in the parking lot and Colonel B. laid down the law, saying he was going to do the surgery alone. They wheeled the patient inside the bunker, carefully lifted him off the stretcher to the table and saw—lying there on the stretcher—the grenade. No one thought to take off the guy's clothes before they took the x-ray. The grenade was in a pocket of his jacket. Talk about some embarrassed surgeons. If we want nasty looks all we do is walk up to one of them and say, "Heard any good grenade jokes lately?"

Friday, January 22, 1971. We are all preparing for Tet. The hospital has doubled the perimeter guard and the enlisted men are pulling extra details. We have been ordered to remain on our own compound. Flak jackets and helmets are mandatory at all times. We even eat in the mess hall with them on. Every evening the guys come into the Officer's Club and check their weapons behind the bar, just like the old west. We make jokes about Tet, but we remember all too well the stories of the blood baths in 1967 and 1968.

The Viet Namese, on the other hand, are getting ready for their biggest holiday of the year, a time of birth and renewal. People have painted red and yellow South Viet Namese flags on their houses and are making decorations and treats. One of our ward workers brings us a sweet jelly-like substance surrounded by wax and leaves. We break the wax open and suck the filling out. It tastes like candy. We give our Viet Namese workers gifts and they have the week off.

Sunday, January 24, 1971. John and his friend Patrick are at the club tonight. They have been drinking since noon and are absolutely potted. Their New Zealand accents are coming out so strong I almost need an interpreter to understand them, but we have a lovely evening talking and laughing.

My extension has been approved! I'm in the Army for an extra year. Now if they will only come through with my promotion—which is five weeks overdue—and my next assignment I will be much happier with the big green machine. Soon I will be under one hundred days and I want to know where I'm going. I still hope it will be an orthopaedic ward at Ft. Bragg. I've earned it.

Monday, January 25, 1971. I finally get a phone call through to Arthur down in Dong Ba Thin today. He says he's having the same good time down there that he had in Pleiku and that life in general is going well. We can't talk very much about Tet on the phone because it's not a secure line, but we have enough of a background to use a kind of code. I want to tell him I am worried about our compound being over-run. "Remember that conversation we had about Tet?"

"That evening it rained so hard?"

"Yeah, that one."

"I remember."

"I'm worried about what we talked about."

"Don't worry. It'll never happen."

Apparently he's close to Cam Ranh Bay because he tells me to call him if I go on R & R through there and he will come out to pick me up. I said if I do that,

I'll never get to Bangkok, that I will spend the whole six days down there with him and Ron. Of course that would save me some money, but I think I'd rather go to Bangkok.

I am allowed one R & R and one leave during my year in 'Nam. I've decided to skip my leave so I will get it paid out and have more money when I go home. I can take my R & R in Japan, Okinawa, Australia, Hawaii or Bangkok. Some people put their leaves and R & R together and go back to the States, but I can't see any point in that. There are days that I know if I go back to the States, I'll never come back here. I'll go and chain myself to some fence somewhere rather than climb on that plane for here again. Besides I'm going home anyway in four months.

I've asked for R & R the second week in March so I will be in Bangkok for my birthday. In addition to it being my birthday, I want to wait for my R & R so that when I come back, I've only got about sixty days left in-country. I should be able to do the last two months practically standing on my head. I have a thousand dollars in the bank and I intend to blow it all on the biggest birthday party I've ever had. It's still six weeks away and it seems like March will never get here!

...The Army came through with my promotion:
Captain Sharon Grant, A.N.C.! ...

Tuesday, January 26, 1971. Tet starts at midnight tonight. There are a lot of fireworks, shooting, flares. This is the beginning of the year of The Boar, though I'm not sure of the significance of that. Ward 4 is filling up; there are a lot of booby traps being set off around An Khe. Fortunately, none of them have resulted in serious injuries. Today is a lot quieter than I thought Tet would be. By now I thought we would be defending our compound from the last barricade, but it's almost a normal day.

The Army came through with my promotion: Captain Sharon Grant, A.N.C.! I don't tell anyone except our Head Nurse, Mary. We just quietly disappear after lunch and go over to headquarters. The colonel pins the railroad tracks on me at 1330 and Mary takes a picture. I want to see how long it takes people to notice. On all my letters I'm just putting the new rank and waiting to see what response I get. But I do call John and tell him and he congratulates me.

❀ ᄇ ❀

Calgary, Alberta. The year of the Boar, also known as the year of the Pig. I didn't know until years later when I met a man who was interested in Chinese medicine that I was a Boar, or to be more specific, I was born in the year of the Boar. It was my year and it started off most auspiciously with my promotion.

❀ ᄇ ❀

Thursday, January 28, 1971. It feels really neat to be a captain. Of course I sign all the charts with the wrong rank and answer only when someone calls me lieutenant. I wish I could cash a check today so I can buy the bar tonight, but we are still confined to the compound and there isn't much action at the club. I want to wait until John is there so I can buy him a drink. I haven't seen him in four days and I miss him.

Friday, January 29, 1971. Ninety-nine percent of the time the ward work is just like back in the States. With our decreased patient census, some days are so slow we're bored stiff. We read books, write letters, do our nails—anything to just keep from going crazy between the time the work is done and the shift ends.

We wait for something to happen. We have a lot of time to think in this hurry-up-and-wait job. Lately, I think a lot about my role as a soldier. I guess it comes from talking to John, and from being newly promoted.

I think I am grownup here; in some ways I am. Part of that adult feeling comes from making more money right now than I ever have before or than I'll probably make for a long time after I leave here. I draw hazardous duty pay as well my regular salary and sometimes I envy the pilots who draw flight pay as well. I guess pay inequality is one part about of a soldier. Like a lot of nurses I have my degree, but the guys with only a high school education, guys who are pilots, who are actually in combat are paid more than I am. The Army offers a large re-enlistment bonus, called a re-up bonus, for the combat specialities: artillery, armour, and infantry. The patients talk a lot about whether another tour of duty would be worth the re-up bonus. If they have done their time here, they figure the next tour would be Stateside or in Germany or Japan. But there's always this nagging feeling the Army might send them back to 'Nam.

Very few of the nurses I know plan to make the military a career; those who do are men. I read somewhere that three percent of all nurses are men, but that twenty percent of the nurses in the military are men. Guys taking care of guys—somehow it's right.

There are some older women here, too, and I wonder about them. I'm twenty-three, almost twenty-four, and there are days this war exhausts me. I don't know how someone in their forties or fifties stands this pace.

Sometimes I think about making the Army my career. Lifers are supposed to be people who can't make it anywhere else. There was this lieutenant-colonel at Ft. Riley. She was close to retirement and she had her own house and took fabulous vacations. She was really good at supervising nurses and corpsmen, really good with interpersonal skills. She worked permanent nights as the Night Supervisor because she said that there were too many hassles working during the day.

We had a big inspection and she came down to the emergency room and helped us clean. She didn't just give us orders on what to do, she came down and asked, "What can I do?" One night—I seem to recall a lot of night shifts at Ft. Riley—she was down on her hands and knees scraping gum off the floor with a butter knife. I asked, "Colonel, should you really be doing that?" She said, "If Florence Nightingale could make beds, I can do this." She wasn't talking about putting sheets on beds. She was talking about sewing mattresses and stuffing them.

That really impressed me. She taught me never to ask the corpsmen to do anything that I wasn't willing to do myself. Sometimes in Pleiku we nurses carried stretchers just to show the corpsmen we could do it. It made them very uncomfortable. They would say, "Ma'am, are you sure you should be doing that?" And I would say, "I knew this Colonel at Ft. Riley who was willing to get down on her hands and knees and scrub the floors before an inspection. If she could do that, I can do this."

I don't think I'd do the same thing now, not because any kind of honest work is demeaning, but because the system makes it demeaning. There wasn't any reason for a sixty-year-old lieutenant-colonel to be down on her hands and knees;

there wasn't any reason for a twenty-three-year-old lieutenant to be carrying a stretcher too heavy for her to handle.

Right now, everything is up for grabs in my life. I think after Ft. Bragg—I keep pretending that assignment is automatic—I need to get out for a while, see what civilian life is like again. If I don't like it on the outside, I can always re-enlist, even without getting a bonus. When I came here I thought this was the greatest adventure going. But it's turning out to be pretty tame. Everything is provided; everything is required in return. I think I want to see what I can do on my own.

Assuming, of course, I live through Tet. It's probably going to turn out like the Army, to be pretty tame. It's like being all dressed up with no place to go. Hurry up and wait. We are like a high-performance racing cars, straining at the Christmas tree, waiting for the lights to blink yellow and green. We have stripped down the wards and told ourselves we must be ready for anything. We're ready to see if we can match whatever Tet is going to throw at us. The problem is that Tet isn't throwing anything at us.

❀ ꆛ ❀

Calgary, Alberta. I'd heard some absolute horror stories from the enlisted women I worked with in Kansas. In basic training they were gotten up at 0430, had to run miles, had to stand in freezing weather in underclothes, were cursed and yelled at and called "cunt" by their drill sergeants. They told us about a lot of lesbians among the enlisted women; a lot of sexual harassment from the men. They didn't let women corpsmen serve in Evac Hospitals. They said it was because corpsmen might have to be pulled to the field, but I thought it was because they thought women too dangerous sexually.

Perhaps they thought nurses came from a different class of people. More educated. Less rough. More refined. Somehow, just not quite like enlisted women.

I was as frightened of those other women as the Army was. They looked so independent. One of our corpsmen in the Emergency Room at Riley cursed like a sailor and the idea of a woman using profane language shocked me. Lesbians scared me. Black women were people from another planet. There was this whole world, full of women who thought differently, spoke differently, behaved differently, were different ages and colours and gender orientations and I wasn't sure how to handle being around them. I was afraid that something would rub off on me; that somehow I would become corrupted. I think that was one of the reasons I enjoyed myself in 'Nam. It was such a male world. I didn't have to worry about relating to other women.

When I was twenty-three, everything was serious. I had to behave. I had to live up to standards. I had to learn because I was so green. I didn't dare have any fun because I might miss something I was supposed to be learning. I had to be sober and responsible. I had to make sense of this somehow, to fit what I was doing into some kind of historical context. That line of women, from Florence Nightingale sewing mattresses to the colonel on her hands and knees to me, ran as an unbroken line. I could feel that unbroken line of women behind me, urging me to do my best, to not let them down.

❀ ⌘ ❀

1971 FEBRUARY 1971

Monday, February 1, 1971. Tonight is my promotion party so I buy the first round of drinks at the Officers' Club. Some of the helicopter pilots from the 7/17 Air Cav teach me a new card game. Cards are dealt to the people playing. First ace dealt names a drink, second ace states the size, third ace pays for it and fourth ace drinks it. The drinks won must be drunk in order. I drink, in order, a double martini, a single creme de menthe and 7-up, Johnny Walker on the rocks, a screwdriver, a flaming hooker and two whiskey and Cokes. They throw us out of the club at 2300, so we come to the room and continue the party.

Tuesday, February 2, 1971. I will offer a reward to know what went on in my room between 2300 last night and 0300 this morning. When I sober up enough to realize it is 0300 this morning, there are two milkshakes in the room and a big, black, furry dog I have never seen before. The nameplates on the door are missing. I have a terrific headache. I remember leaving the club last night, but the rest is hazy.

I have difficulty focusing on work today. We are in a holding action, more of the Army's usual hurry-up-and-wait. One ward is closed to keep it ready for casualties because there is a big push somewhere. Passenger movement in-country is canceled and there is a news blackout on military dispatches. Of course, rumours are everywhere and most of them say we are going on the offensive. If anything, we probably know less than the people back in the States who watch the six o'clock news. But I'd rather be in the dark here than watching the news at home.

Wednesday, February 3, 1971. The 101st Airborne is on the offensive north of us in I Corps. The first thing I hear this morning is that plan-loads of casualties have landed from the north. Rumours fly about how many are coming in, who got hit, how many died. The Operating Room moves patients through so fast they come to the ward with clay matted in their hair and dried blood on their hands.

By noon every bed is full. We scramble to find extra I.V. poles, more supplies, more dressings. The guy I yelled at this morning because he refused to get out of bed is now not only up, but serving the supper trays because the corpsmen are busy. The ward becomes strangely quiet. The patients turn off the TV and the tape players. Some of them just can't watch the influx of new casualties. They come by the desk and say, "I'm going to the Red Cross Rec Room. Be back later." Others stay to see if they can help. They fill water pitchers, hold cigarettes for men whose hands are bandaged, run errands. One of the patients, a staff sergeant almost twice my age, stands in the hall by the bathroom door, his back to the wall so he won't fall.

"You all right, sergeant?"

"I just watched you change the lieutenant's dressing. His leg was split from the knee up. I saw the bone."

I dig in my fatigues pocket for some money. "Why don't you go down to the snack shop and get the lieutenant a Coke. He'd probably like that."

He waves the money away. "That's okay, captain, I've got some." He comes back with all the Cokes he can carry and hands them around the room.

There is a Spec-4, badly hurt, dirty, tired, in pain. When I ask him how he is, he winces and says, "I'm okay, but can you find out about my buddy? He was right next to me when he was hit. I have to know if he's all right." I make some calls and come back in a few minutes to tell him that his buddy is dead. I try to remember to call the chaplain to come to talk with him.

The Red Cross workers come around with pens and paper so the patients can write to their families. The more seriously-wounded ones can't write; they are still too much in shock. Sometimes the Red Cross women gently prod them, "I'll write a short note for you; just to tell your wife that you're in the hospital and will write yourself in a few days. No, I won't tell her about your leg. You should tell her that yourself, in your own words. You'll know how when the time comes."

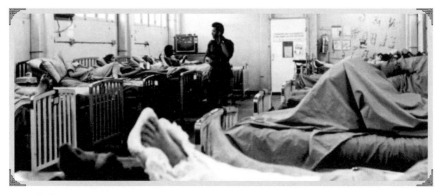

If they are ambulatory, the patients go down to the Red Cross room to make a M.A.R.S. call. Ham radio operators in the States have set up the M.A.R.S. network for relaying calls. It means a lot to the guys to be able to talk to their families; it means a lot to the families to actually hear their voices.

One man has a tracheostomy, two I.V.s and his jaws wired together. His chart says he's eighteen. When I ask him how he is, he holds up his fingers in a peace sign. I go to the supply room and cry.

Sometimes there's no time to get to know the patients. We fill up with fresh casualties, manifest them on air-evacs, send them out, admit more casualties all in the same shift. We have had several burn cases recently and they required a lot of care. I've spent a lot of time feeding and taking care of one of them. He asks to see me before he goes out on air-evac today. I kneel by the stretcher and he whispers, "I'm scared." He can't see because his face is bandaged. I want to have time to ask him what he's afraid of, to have a chance to talk to him. Instead I touch him on the arm. He grabs my hand and holds it. I lean very close to him and whisper in his ear. "Whatever you're afraid of, it will be all right. There are going to be other nurses down the line. You talk to them, okay?"

"Okay." Then they pick up his stretcher and take him away.

I work the full twelve hours with no lunch and no breaks, skip supper to catch up on treatments, thinking I will grab a sandwich later at the club. When the night nurse finally arrives, I stay an extra hour mixing I.V.s and making charts. I come home hungry and fall exhausted into bed, lying awake staring at the ceiling for a long time. I want to have done more.

Thursday, February 4, 1971 (100 days left). Shortly after I came to Qui Nhon I marked the last hundred days in this journal. It seemed like it would take an eternity to get here, now it seems to have taken only a day. I don't want to leave in three months. How can I go back to watching this war on TV? How can I leave these people, the ones I work with, the patients, my friends? How can this war, which has become so personal, go on without me? It feels like I will be walking out on a play in the middle of the second act.

Those of us with a hundred days or less left are "short-timers." We have short-timer's calendars. Some of them are drawings of a woman with her legs spread apart. The numbers start on her thighs and one day left is her vagina. My calendar is a helmet sitting on top of a pair of combat boots. The idea is I'm so short my helmet comes down to my boots. The calendar is divided into one hundred spaces, each numbered. I start today at one hundred and colour in one a day. When the picture is completely coloured, I can go home.

Friday, February 5, 1971 (99 days left). About 0200 Ed W. called from Tuy Hoa! Months without a word, then just like that, he calls. I've stopped trying to figure it out. The phone call is the best thing that has happened to me in weeks. He says that he misses me, that he wants to see me again and that he will come for a visit when he can. I know now that I'm not in love with him, but I do love him. And I'd like to go to bed with him again.

I feel like I've never found a social niche in Qui Nhon, not like in Pleiku where I could escape for a few hours with Special Forces. The only way I can describe this place is that here we are all too serious about the war. The Special Forces medics took the war as a given. It was here, we were here, so we might as well make the best of it and do the honourable thing. Maybe their idea is that war is as much a part of peace as death is of life. But here in Qui Nhon we all say how much we hate the war and we talk a lot about how lonely we are, how much we want to go home, how stupid the campaigns are.

Saturday, February 6, 1971 (98 days left). Ed calls again tonight. He is getting ready to go on R & R. My gosh, if he has been here long enough to have R & R, we both must be short! I feel guilty being in such a safe rear area when he has to fly into hot landing zones. We are too much removed from the war in Qui Nhon. No one thinks about what is happening in the field, only about how much another influx of casualties will make us work harder. I don't know what to believe any more. There are days I get more news about what is happening around here in letters from people at home than I get from the people who have been in the field.

Now that we have survived Tet, all we talk about is the U.S. pull-out. We all think there just aren't enough of us out there to protect Qui Nhon. Or maybe we believe there are too many of them. We feel like we are in danger if a big attack occurs. Guys get really nervous their last hundred days in-country. Some of the units take their men out of combat situations for the last six weeks, but the guys are still afraid of getting killed in a mortar attack or something strange like an auto accident. The Army is giving people early outs. Those people who have less than a year to serve when they go back to the States are being processed out of the Army right away. It's possible to be on patrol in the jungle on a Thursday and back home in your own living room a week later. I am so glad I have an extension. I have no idea how to behave like a civilian. It's going to be hard enough to survive the month of leave at home before my next duty station.

Sunday, February 7, 1971 (97 days left). I am beginning to believe I have been in Viet Nam long enough. Plane loads of casualties continue to arrive day after day. The work would be easier if we believed in what we are doing. I think we care about the patients, about doing a good job of caring for them, and we care about each other here at the hospital, but we don't have energy left over to care about anything else, certainly not enough to care about the war.

Monday, February 8, 1971 (96 days left). For the third night in a row one corpsman and I work a straight twelve-hour night shift without midnight chow or those long, slow hours I found so hard to fill last month. Our census has been at our full capacity for three days and from 1900 to 0700 I haven't had more than a ten-minute break. I'm scared stiff every evening when I walk in and see that every bed is full. Even with this census, there is only one nurse and one corpsman on the night shift. I ask Mary why we don't have extra people assigned to nights and she says there just isn't anyone extra to assign. The corpsman and I work hard together and somehow all of us—the patients, the corpsman and I—survive the night. I haven't been to church in months, but when we are working beyond our capacity I feel like there must be something, something I can't define, that helps me through the night.

Tuesday, February 9, 1971 (95 days left). There is another big push up in I Corps. Plane loads of casualties arrive from the north every day. The 101st is taking it on the chin again: we have so many casualties from the 101st that they have sent two patient liaisons down just to look after their men. A friend of mine, Pete C., just transferred up to the 101st. I hope he's all right. I almost write safe, but since he flies Chinooks, I know that isn't possible. Unless he comes back for a visit I guess I'll never know if he makes it through. Just one more of those people who come into my life, we have a good time together, and he leaves.

Wednesday, February 10, 1971 (94 days left). John and I are seeing less and less of each other as time passes. With the increased activity in the area he has been working as hard as I have and my wards keep me so busy that all I do is work and sleep. I miss him, but not enough to worry about it.

Thursday, February 11, 1971 (93 days left). I am trying to decide if it's selfish to be in an under-developed country with a usable skill and not use it to help the people. I've decided it is selfish and that I don't much care. The only two important things right now are my job and my sanity. My time off is strictly my own. I don't owe anything to anyone. A lot of the people at the hospital feel the same way. When we were first in-coun-try we were interested in going to the orphanages or the leprosarium or the local hospital. That seemed to wear off in a few months. This must be one of the few places in the world where we can do our jobs and don't have to bother with anything else. Our meals are cooked for us, our laundry is washed and ironed for us, there's no grocery shopping, few errands, no place to go. We really have it easy here.

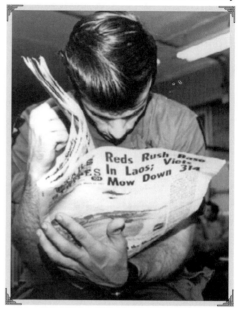

Friday, February 12, 1971 (92 days left). I meet some New Zealand offi-cers who are stationed at Bong Son. They are part of a team that operates a hospital for the civilians there. Strangely enough, they don't mind being in Viet Nam because this, they say, is where the action is right now. I wonder if that's the reason John is here. Before I came here I thought of Viet Nam as America's private war. Yet I have met New Zealanders, Australians, Koreans, Canadians and Japanese all fighting here. The general feeling around Qui Nhon is that if the Koreans weren't here in such large numbers that there would be a lot more enemy activity. The R.O.K.s are supposed to be good in a fight and the Viet Cong are supposed to be afraid of them. Perhaps this is one answer to our involvement in the war: pull out and let Orientals fight Orientals. We just provide machinery, weapons, supplies for them. War by remote control, an interesting idea. I don't think we understand the people fighting here. I don't think we will ever be able to win here because we don't understand them. The way we fight isn't the way they fight.

Sunday, February 14, 1971 (90 days left). Valentine's Day. There are riots again in the city, some within sight of the hospital. The rioters burn cars and rubber tires and the heavy black smoke drifts over the hospital. Viet Namese civilians stand outside the barbed wire that surrounds our compound and toss rocks at us. At least they aren't tossing grenades.

Everything is off-limits again. We have drawn our gas masks from supply room one more time and the supervisor tells us to barricade the doors to the ward. There are no locks or latches on the wooden doors. We push beds in front of the doors and put a two-hundred-and-seventy-five pound patient in each bed. Great lot of good that will do if the locals want to overrun us. So far they've been satisfied with burning the vehicles and one of the construction buildings.

Monday, February 15, 1971 (89 days left). The staff on our wards are really tense. Perhaps it's the added patient load or the riots, but the result is that tempers are short. I yell at corpsmen and patients. Work isn't getting done. The doctors have lodged a complaint with the Chief Nurse about the quality of the nursing care. Our Head Nurse, Mary S., calls a meeting with everyone and we spend about two hours getting the complaints out in the open.

The corpsmen think the nurses demand too much of them. Because of the riots the corpsmen have to pull extra guard duty in addition to working on the wards. Some of them are getting only three or four hours of sleep a night and they are even more exhausted than the nurses. The nurses think the corpsmen don't behave in a professional manner. We need more staff, both nurses and corpsmen, but due to the pull-out our authorized strength has been cut and the Army isn't sending replacements. Getting all of this out in the open doesn't do much to solve the problems. Today we are being extremely polite to each other, but the real, underlying anger is still there. The only things that are keeping me going are counting the number of days I had left and Ed's phone calls.

I'm such a kid about those phone calls. The communal phone is in the passageway outside our room. Anyone who is walking by the phone answers it when it rings and I feel a pleasant little shock when someone knocks on my door and says, "Sharon, it's for you." I never dated very much in university, never had boys call me. This is a completely new experience for me and I love it.

Tuesday, February 16, 1971 (88 days left). The 7/17 Air Cav isn't Special Forces, but they are a good group to pal around with. We sit around on their compound tonight eating beef stew and singing folk songs. It isn't anything big, anything expensive, but it's sharing and I like it a lot.

The important thing here is that we share whatever we have: our food, our booze, our music, our time. We even share our beds. If someone in The Swamp is on night duty and their bed vacant, chances are some stranger with no place to stay sleeps there. I'll come back to our communal room at 0730, shake a stranger's shoulder and say, "Okay, everybody out."

He gets up. We sit side-by-side on the bed, both of us half-asleep, him putting on his combat boots and me taking mine off. We exchange a litany of introduction and information that is a regular part of our lives.

"Where have you come from?"

"Where are you going?"

"How much longer do you have in-country?"

Then he leaves and I crawl into the still-warm bed and fall asleep, surrounded by the smell of a stranger still lingering on the sheets.

Wednesday, February 17, 1971 (87 days left). Ed calls tonight. He says he will try to get here soon.

"When?" I demand.

"When I get there."

So one day or night he will tap me on the shoulder and say, "I'm here." I never know, when I get up in the morning, who I'll see that day. Anyone I've ever met in the Army is likely to wander through for five minutes or an hour or a week. If there is time we have a Coke or dinner. We always exchange information. Where are the people we know? We exchange addresses, knowing we'll never write, but somehow there is a sense that having that little slip of paper is some kind of security. If we end up where they are, we'll know someone to call, just like they knew someone to call here.

So when Ed comes, I'll drop everything and see him for as long as I can. And I wish it would happen soon.

Thursday, February 18, 1971 (86 days left). One of the Red Cross women invited me to go on a boat ride with her and some of the patients today. It is a lovely day, hot, with a gentle sea and white clouds floating on the sky.

We leave from the pier and make our way through the small fishing boats where we believe the Viet Cong hide during the day. I wonder if that's true or if these are just fishermen who don't really care that we are off for a day's relaxation.

I don't know where the boat or crew came from. They look Korean. Perhaps this is another gesture of kindness towards us, like the rock garden the R.O.K.s built. In any case, the three men keep to themselves, standing on the small bridge, chatting in a language I can't understand.

There aren't any weapons on this boat, at least none visible, and I wonder what would happen if we were attacked. I can't go anywhere any more without considering that question, "What would happen if we were attacked?" I understand now why Barry would never sit with his back to a door. It's a habit I've taken up myself. I've gauged the size of the boat, found the life preservers, located the first aid kit, all of those things that I now do automatically.

The six patients are convalescents. They should be in Cam Ranh Bay, but there is so much air traffic still bringing casualties down from the north that the planes aren't available to take them there. There isn't much room there either in the Medical Holding Companies. The slightly wounded from that first influx of casualties we had a couple of week ago are all down there by now and there's no room for these men.

It's getting harder for the Red Cross workers because they have a lot more patients to work with. They provide books, a pool table, bingo, movies, puzzles, card games, sometimes boat rides. I don't know what these women are doing here. I get this superior attitude towards the Red Cross women that I'm doing real work here, but they're just decoration. Sometimes I am jealous of them because they get to do fun things while I have to work so hard. It's especially hard when they come back to the ward about lights-out with a group of laughing patients and I know they have been off somewhere having a good time while I've been slogging away with treatments and urinals.

I feel really out of place on the boat today, probably partly because I'm feeling guilty about having a good time myself today. I don't know why I should have been singled out to go on this lovely boat ride while everyone else has to work on the ward. Maybe I'm afraid the other nurses will now be jealous of me.

❁ ♫ ❁

Calgary, Alberta. It took a while to look at that entry without flinching. I hate to think I was that petty about other women, but I know that I was. It had a lot to do with my insecurity as a woman, as a competitor for the men's attention. The Red Cross women wore blue and white dresses and we wore our fatigues and combat boots. Somehow they looked more feminine and there were times when it would have been more fun to play cards than to do dressings. They did so much to help us on the wards. I guess more than anything else they were our social workers. They helped the patients sort out what they would tell their families, they linked up patients with their families, they worked on problems at home for the patients. And those things we perceived as playing—the cards, the puzzles, the movies, even the boat rides—helped the patients forget the fighting, helped them through some very long and hard days.

I enjoyed that boat ride and it took me a long time to see that the Red Cross was there to help me, too. Maybe the woman who asked me to go that day saw how hard I'd been working, knew even better than I did how desperate I was for a break. I'm glad she asked me to go with her.

❀ ❧ ❀

Friday, February 19, 1971 (85 days left). Kahuna comes in unexpectedly tonight. I'm standing at the bar in the club when he taps me on the shoulder and I whoop with delight because I'm always glad to see him. He's going north to fly Dustoff as Aircraft Commander. I have been in-country long enough now that the people I met months ago are old-timers by now. We are the ones with responsibilities. He will probably be in the middle of the big 101st push that's still going on and I think he'll do a good job.

The last hundred days are aging me faster than the two hundred and sixty-five that went before. I know the risks and the dangers. The shorter my friends and I get, the greater the chances of getting hurt. We are all feeling so shaky these last three months. Every day I colour in one more block on my calendar and it feels like tempting fate, like playing out odds that are already too long.

Saturday, February 20, 1971 (84 days left). The ammo dump blew up again last night about 0100. I got up shaking and Kris, the man Diane has been dating, stuck his head in the door. I was half-naked but stopped worrying about modesty a long time ago.

"Diane here?"

Never mind the nakedness, just keep dressing. "No, she's still out with the band." She was singing with a group that the enlisted men formed.

"There may be sappers tonight. Go to the bunker."

Like I really knew or cared where the nearest bunker was. There were rats in the bunkers and I'd rather take my chances with sappers than with rats. I put on my helmet and flak jacket—both were covered with dust—and dug under the bed for the gas mask. I sat on the sofa and waited, cold, shivering, wondering what had been hit. I felt so vulnerable. There was no built-up bed with a double mattress to climb under as there had been in Pleiku, no place to wrap myself in blankets and curl up in the fetal position until the attack passed. I sat on the sofa and waited, twiddling my thumbs as if I was waiting for a date that had stood me up. After twenty minutes I figured, "Hell, I'm going back to sleep again." I lay down still in the helmet and flack jacket and closed my eyes.

A second explosion rocked the room. "If they're going to do that every half hour, forget it. I am going to be tired enough in the morning. I need sleep." I went to sleep with my gas mask curled under my arm like a teddy bear. A little after two, Major M., the Assistant Chief Nurse, knocked on the door. "We're on Yellow Alert III. You can take the flak jacket off."

Even in my sleep-befuddled condition I wondered where they got these terms. I wondered if they had a chart posted somewhere, full of colours and levels of alert: "Yellow Alert III. Remove flak jacket."

I tried to take the flak jacket off and found my rusty zipper had stuck. It was rather embarrassing to call Major M. back and ask her if she could help me undress.

Monday, February 22, 1971 (82 days left). Terri and I finally move out of The Swamp today, the last of the six to get our own room. It has been an interesting and painful experience to watch the newbies become old timers. One of them is a psychiatric nurse in the States. She enlisted on the condition that she would do a six-month tour in 'Nam. She's terribly depressed by the drug problem and her inability to solve emotional problems that can't be handled here, that perhaps can't be handled at all. She doesn't have the power to send anyone home and she has realized that what the Army wants her to do is to make her patients sane enough to go back to the field and get killed.

Another nurse works on the medical ward. Three months ago she knew nothing about malaria, dysentery, fevers of unknown origin. Now she is an expert. She went for a while every Sunday to the leprosarium, but that stopped at Christmas. She was too overwhelmed by the poverty, the open wounds, the kids that vomited worms. She has asked for a transfer to Phu Bi so that she can take care of casualties.

The third one works in Intensive Care. Before Christmas she would come back to the room and cry. We would hold her and tell her that it means something that she is there when someone dies. Now she doesn't cry any more. The Chief Nurse is on her case all the time because she's singing with the enlisted men's band. She told the Chief Nurse where she could go and got an official reprimand on her record. As she said, "What were they going to do to me, draft me and send me to Viet Nam?"

Terri is still my roommate. We have been together since June in Pleiku and there are times when it is as hard for me to live with her as it is for her to live with me. Sometimes we are too close, have been together too long, know too many secrets about one another. I am also a little jealous of her because she has been made Head Nurse on the Orthopaedic Ward. I'd have liked that job.

Life with Terri is also hard because of her engagement to Bill V. The colonel in Pleiku promised them they would be stationed together. Then the Army sent her here and Bill to Phu Bi in the north. It has been terribly busy around Phu Bi: they catch the brunt of any of 101st pushes. She's been so worried, especially when we hear rumours that the medics up there are being pulled out of the hospital and sent to front line units. Now Bill's commander doesn't know if he will give him time off for the wedding and honeymoon. Bill has threatened to desert if he doesn't get his leave. Both Terri and I are angry at the stupidity of the Army and can't do a thing about it.

In spite of our sometimes rocky relationship, it is good to have Terri as a roommate. We have been here almost the same length of time, we speak the same language, understand things we don't have to communicate. And we have built up a store of memories over the past nine months.

It's certainly nice to have our own room again. Ever since we arrived in Qui Nhon we haven't had any privacy. On the wards we are always in full view of the patients; in The Swamp we had people coming and going at all hours. There were times when the only vacant space was the chapel. I went in there and just sat, grateful for the silence and the chance to be alone.

Our room is two doors down from The Swamp, which we assume they will finally turn back into a recreation lounge for the nurses. There aren't any windows and the large silver air-conditioning ducts run beneath the ceiling over my bed. The hooches are air conditioned to keep out the noise and dust from the runway next door, so we can sleep better during the day when we are working night shift. Anyway, there are these two blank walls, an iron-framed cot and a small bedside dresser. There's a faded blue plaid blanket on the bed. I inherited it from the previous occupant and will probably leave it for the next one.

There's a lamp suspended on the wall. I inherited it along with the bedspread. On the wall I have hung a Crown Royal bag decorated with unit pins, my Dustoff cap from the 283rd Dustoff, a plastic ornament my mama-san gave me at Christmas time, three framed pictures of Pleiku, a small Louisiana flag and a woven

Montagnard bag. My dog tags hang on a nail over the bed. On the top of the bedside dresser I have a white alarm clock, a portable radio in a black leather case, the 'Yard pot the corpsman who drew my name at Christmas gave me and two cans I've covered with contact paper. The paper is white with yellow velvet flowers in it; I ordered it from the Sears catalogue. One of the cans has pencils and pens in it, the other has a plastic lid on it. They are old coffee cans, in which my aunt sent me cookies. When the cookies are gone, I wash the cans and store film in them.

On one corner of the dresser is a small wooden box in which I keep my jewelry and watch. It's about three inches square; while I was at U.S.L. I decoupaged it with some of my favourite pictures. I wanted something to take with me to Viet Nam, something personal. So I took that little box because I liked the pictures and because it reminded me of being back in university.

Terri's half of the room contains the same furniture: a bed, dresser and metal locker. We arrange the lockers back to back, partitioning the small room into two smaller, darker spaces. We share a small refrigerator.

Terri's mother sends her wonderful care packages from their farm: homemade jam, fruit cakes and our very favourite, Colby cheese

made on the farm. We save the Colby, doling it out to visitors in very small slices, hoping to make it last until the next package arrives. If it has been a really bad day, Terri will look at me, I'll look at her and we'll say, in unison, "Get the Colby." Then, like children who are sneaking something out of the pantry, we'll hide on her side of the room and nibble away at the cheese.

Our bathroom is shared with the two nurses who live in the room next door. The bathroom has open beams under a tin ceiling and chicken wire stretches below the beams. The wire keeps the rats from falling from the rafters into our bathroom. We can sit on the toilet and watch them scurry overhead. At least it's a lot cleaner than the bathroom in Pleiku. The walls here are not decorated in early mould.

Tuesday, February 23, 1971 (81 days left). General Anna Mae Hays, the Chief of the Army Nurse Corps and the first woman general, visits us today.

She has always been one of my heroines and I can't believe I am actually getting a chance to meet her.

She turns out to be a slight person, much shorter than I expected, but with a very polite way and quite voice about her. I actually have my picture taken with her!

Some nurses come from other hospitals and we have a bit of a reception. One of them is Sue E., the girl I spent three days with at Travis Air Force Base. She is down in Tuy Hoa. I ask her if she will look up Ed for me and say hello. It makes me feel better to know someone in the hospital where he is stationed. If anything happens to him, she will be there to take care of him. It would be fun to leave the country with her, but she has a five-day drop, so she is leaving the week before I do.

Wednesday, February 24, 1971 (80 days left). Back in the world it's Girl Scout cookie sale time. I sent $10 to my old council, asking for a couple of boxes of cookies. Yesterday the sergeant called me from Supply Receiving at the air field.

"Captain, I have your Girl Scout cookies here."

"Oh good, I'll walk over after work and pick them up."

"Lady, have you got a truck?"

"No. Why?"

"I've got twenty-four cases of cookies here for you."

There's a letter with the twenty-four cases. My old scout troop collected money for the cookies and sent them to me. There is a picture of the girls mailing them and the letter says that the picture will be in the local paper.

I give the sergeant at the air field and the corpsman who drives me over in a jeep a box of cookies as payment. The corpsman says his sister sells Girl Scout cookies and he wants to pay me for the box. I have trouble convincing him they are free. I take them to the Red Cross room and asked them if they will help me deliver them. We go around this afternoon, them handing out on the different wards. The looks on the patient's

faces are wonderful. Real back-on-the-block food! The Viet Namese children don't understand the Girl Scout part, but they do understand cookies. I take pictures to send back to the council. Who knows, they might put those pictures in the paper, too.

Thursday, February 25, 1971 (79 days left). We are losing a lot of chopper crews in Laos, so many in fact that they are pulling pilots from Qui Nhon as replacements. I know at least five who have gone in the past couple of weeks. When I first came to 'Nam I would have been worried sick about them. Now they go and I don't think about them very much, except at odd moments when I hear how many aren't coming back.

There isn't a thing I can do. If Kahuna or Pete C. or Bob H. buys the farm, someone will tell me about it after it is too long over to be changed. And yet, I know what my reaction will be: a cold shock wave as if someone has thrown ice water over me, and a rising wave of nausea that will make me sick of everyone and everything around me. And pain when their name is mentioned, yet wanting and needing to talk about them. Trying to keep their memory alive, what they said, what they did, what we laughed about together. And a sudden need to pray for them even though I don't believe any more. After a while it will stop hurting and they will fade around the edges, the way Barry has started to fade around the edges. It has been that way with Barry. If it happens again, it will be the same.

Sunday, February 28, 1971 (76 days left). We continue to have plane loads of casualties from the north, nothing like the numbers we were getting three weeks ago but they are still coming.

Tonight I stand in the covered walkway outside my wards and feel the warm wind blow around me. Below, on the brightly-lit runway, I see people who have already worked twelve hours wait for an air-evac of wounded. We are tired and the adrenaline pumping through us is all that is keeping us going. It is supposed to be a big casualty load; we have heard rumours of it all day. At least we have a lot of empty beds right now. Somehow we will find the nurses and corpsmen to take care of them.

A C-130 lands; its motors deafen us as they throw up great clouds of dust around the waiting litter bearers. The back swings open like a gaping, yellow mouth. How many litters like this have I seen? Dozens? Hundreds? I stopped counting a long time ago.

In the end, the number of casualties on the plane is disappointingly small. Only three are admitted to our wards. I stay to admit one of them and suddenly am not interested any more. The big air evac has turned small and everyone goes back to the club or their hooches with a sense of anticlimax and disappointment. Waiting doesn't work well for us. We have been promised action and a chance to be useful. That's what we need, not the letdown of a half-empty plane.

I dress and go over to the Officers Club, coming out drunk about eight o'clock. I know there is no chance of going to sleep so I walk over to the 7/17 Cav by the back way, through the Military Police compound, down by the Chinook hangers and across the P.O.L. yards. It is all industrial, just like walking though the warehouse section of some big city. And yet I feel very safe. I know the route like it is my own back yard, even the short-cuts like walking through the six-foot pipes in the P.O.L. yard. Sometimes a face pops out of a lit doorway, a duty sergeant wondering what the noise is. I wave and say, "Just passing through," and they wave me on. When I arrive at the Cav's compound, they are holding a wake. They have just received word that two crews were killed in Laos. I knew men on both crews. I hate this war.

1971 MARCH 1971

Monday, March 1, 1971 (75 days left). My R & R is scheduled for this weekend, but now the planes aren't flying in-country: we think there might be another big push in the north. The Spec-4 at the air field isn't very sympathetic. "If you can't get to Da Nang, tough luck. What do you want me to do, lady? There's a war on."

All I know is that if I don't get out of Qui Nhon soon, something in me is going to snap. Okie, one of the 7/17 pilots, is just back from Bangkok. We spend the evening sitting in a corner of the Officers' Club while he tells me about places to go and how to bargain for everything from taxi rides to souvenirs. Bangkok sounds fantastic, like a dream world. I can't believe I'm going to a country without barbed wire. It will be great to be able to go wherever I want in a city.

Tuesday, March 2, 1971 (74 days left). I call Ed tonight but he is out on a mission. He calls back later. Damn, do I ever want to see him right now. He made Aircraft Commander yesterday, so he will have more responsibility. I wonder if he has changed during the past few months. He sounds the same on the phone, but I can't see how he can have gone through the past few months and not have changed.

I hear that 5th Special Forces Group officially goes home today. I guess that means the colours go home to Ft. Bragg. I still know men who are in-country. They wear different patches and call their units by different names, but the men are still here. Only about ninety people have actually gone back to North Carolina with the colours.

I also hear that the 71st Evac has gone home. I think they were from Fort Campbell, Kentucky, and that's where the colours would have gone. Again, only a few of the people are actually back to the States. They have taken the colours with them, had a parade and packed the colours away in a box. Until the next time they are needed.

Wednesday, March 3, 1971 (73 days left). Whatever flu bug is going around finally caught up with me. We are so short-staffed on the ward that I feel bad about going on sick call. The doctor has put me on quarters, so I come back to the room, sleep for twenty-four hours and feel like I can use another twenty-four hours of sleep. I'm determined to lick whatever this is by Friday. The incountry planes still aren't flying, but I am manifested on the air evac flight for Friday morning.

More of the Cav has gone north. I hope they are all right.

Thursday, March 4, 1971 (72 days left). This last day before going on R & R has to be the worst. I have so many things to do and absolutely no desire to pack or do any of the necessary chores. Somehow I've made it through the day.

Friday, March 5, 1971 (71 days left). Da Nang. Here I am in Da Nang again, nine months after I first saw it. Everything was strange and new then, but now it's just another place. Margaret and Marie have been back in the States for months. I'll probably never see them again and that makes me a little sad. Our group from basic is breaking up, going back to civilian life.

At least the billets at the R & R centre are clean and just right for want I want to do, which is sleep. I am more tired than I realized. I have slept almost sixteen hours since I arrived. It seems all I want to do lately is sleep.

Saturday, March 6, 1971 Bangkok, Thailand! and not counting the days left! I can't believe I am really here!

This going on vacation courtesy of the Army isn't like taking a civilian vacation. We have a lecture when we arrive about Thai customs, a mini-version of what we had when we arrived in Viet Nam. The sergeant gives us this list of safe places to stay and suggestions for things to do and see. Of course, everyone who has been here before or has friends who have been here have their own ideas of where to stay. Different units favour different hotels. Special Forces told me the name of the hotels where they always stay and I want to get as far away from them as possible. This is my holiday and I just want to forget the Army and everything connected with it.

The R & R Centre runs tours. I guess that's also a way to keep us safe and out of trouble here. I sign up for three of them over the next week: a river tour of the city, an all-day upcountry tour and a tour of the shrines and temples. I also lose my military identification card at the counter when I pay for the tours and, after I discover it is missing, I am terrified that I will be stopped by the military police and found to have no identification. I haven't realized before that I have no other identification: no drivers' license, no credit card, nothing except my little missing card. The specialist at the tours desk gives me a lecture when I go back to retrieve the card and tells me if I lose it again I'll be in a lot of trouble.

A group of us wait outside the R & R Centre for a bus; the bus travels to several hotels and finally brings me to the Siam Hotel. I am so excited about this city. It looks so clean and modern after Qui Nhon. There are beautiful buildings and people in the most wonderful clothes. I could have taken ten rolls of film on the way from the airport, but restrain myself because I have a whole week here and pictures from bus windows never turn out very well.

The hotel has bathtubs, real stores and king-size beds. I haven't been in a bathtub in almost a year. The first thing I do is buy shampoo, cosmetics and bubble bath in one of the hotel's stores and spend a couple of hours bathing, giving myself a facial and conditioning my hair.

Then I go for a walk around the hotel. It is all glass and teak wood walls and what look like acres of private flower gardens behind the hotel. There is a row of flagpoles on the lawn in front of the hotel and I have been told that each morning green-jacketed bell boys raise the flags of the countries from which the guests come and take them down each evening. The gardens are full of the most beautiful red and yellow flowers. I find the colours absolutely startling.

All I have seen for nine months is grey concrete, olive green clothes, pale blue pajamas, green walls and blood. I have forgotten that there are other shades of red. There are monkeys and birds in the gardens, too. Some of the men who are on R & R have met their wives over here and I watch one couple introduce their little girl, who looks about two years old, to her first monkey. Both the girl and the monkey squeal the same amount. It's the first time in months that I have heard a child laugh.

I've deposited a thousand dollars in the hotel safe and I am going to spend it all during the coming week. There are so many shops it's impossible to know where to start.

Sunday, March 7, 1971. I spend this morning walking through Bangkok, taking pictures and bargaining with street vendors. I just walk and walk and walk, down any street or alley that pleases me. My mother would die if she knew some of the places I have been this morning. I have forgotten what it's like to walk on a sidewalk, be in a crowd. My eyes are constantly roaming the situation, looking for a grenade, for a person with a rifle. There are no guns here. Even the policeman in a brilliant white shirt and shorts, standing on a box in a busy corner directing traffic with white-gloved hands, is unarmed.

The Thais have little decorated houses in their yards. Even the garden at the hotel has one. The little book we were given explains that these are for the spirits to whom the land really belongs; if the spirits are provided with a place to live then they allow people to live on the land in peace. Even apartment buildings have the same kind of little house attached to the side of the building or the balcony.

I have been told that the custom is to haggle and I have a lot of fun doing it today. I bargain for a pink glass statue and probably pay too much, but it is my first attempt at bargaining. I agree to buy papayas if the lady selling them will let me take her picture. We both giggle during this transaction. Twice I get out of cabs in the middle of heavy traffic, telling the cab driver he wants too much, and successfully flag and bargain with another cab driver.

But it isn't all peaceful, even here. I read in an English-language newspaper that there have been riots here lately, university students demonstrating against the government. I walk past the locked gates of a university plastered with posters and graffiti in a language I can't read and think of the bare, grenade-marked school in Qui Nhon, of those university students in white ao-dias who brought us presents at Christmas. I don't want my country to destroy this or any other country ever again.

Down a little side street, wedged between two brown stone buildings, I find a small white gate. Written on the gate in gold letters is L'hopital de Marie et de l'enfant Jesus. On an impulse I knock. A nun with a black habit and a European face opens the gate. In French, I ask her if I can see the hospital. At first she hesitates, then I explain I am a nurse on vacation in Bangkok and she invites me in. She has a different accent, perhaps Flemish, and my university French is completely inadequate for more than simple conversation. Mostly we just walk and look.

The walls are whitewashed and so very clean. They remind me of the walls in a convent where I once went for a retreat. I remember the smell of fresh-scrubbed wooden floors from that retreat house and I get that all mixed up with scrubbing the Emergency Room in Pleiku for the I.G., as if those two events in my life are two slides mounted in the same frame with the images overlapping. I want to tell somebody about the images so that they can help me sort them, but there is only this middle-aged Belgian nun beside me, her hands folded under her habit. I say nothing and keep walking with her down the sunlit corridor.

She asks me if I am Catholic. I lie and say yes because I can't tell her about Ed and the statue of the Virgin Mary and not believing any more. It seems to please her because she takes me down to the end of the hall and shows me a very old statue of Mary and Jesus. As best I can understand her French, the statue has been blessed by a Pope and came with the first nuns who came to Bangkok to set up a maternity hospital. There is a little kneeling bench in front of the statue. She invites me to pray with her. I am sure lightning is going to come out of the statue and strike me. But I light a candle and pray for Barry's soul because when he died I still believed. Maybe that kind of prayer can still be heard.

As we are leaving the alcove I see a mother and baby in one of the rooms. The sunlight comes through the window in broad beams and has collected on the white iron bed and sheets. Beside the bed is a small iron crib with a little piece of yellow flannel blanket in it. The baby lies beside his mother at her breast; they both sleep in a pool of warm light. I rest my head on the door frame and just want to stand there and remember what peace is like. The nun looks at me very strangely, then takes my arm to lead me away.

We have tea in a little garden in the middle of the hospital. She takes great pains to arrange her habit when she sits down. I am quite conscious of my dress. Having worn fatigues for so long, I have forgotten how to sit in a dress, a short dress, in front of a nun. I constantly change positions, tug at my skirt, try to cover my knees. She pours tea from a white china pot and there are little lemon-flavored cookies on a white plate.

She asks me if I am on vacation with anyone? I tell her I am alone. She says, "American women come to Bangkok when their husbands are on leave from Indochina. I thought perhaps you have someone in Indochina?"

"No, I'm the one on leave from Indochina."

She looks as if she has not understood what I said. I go through the sentence in my head, translating what I have said, looking for the grammatical error. I try a few other sentences, explain that I am a nurse, that I take care of the wounded. She sits very still with her tea cup resting in her hands. Finally she asks in a strained voice, "Are there many like you?"

"About four hundred."

"Mon Dieu."

In the silence between us I realize she has never thought there are women in the war. She says, "We will pray for you."

I am very uncomfortable. I look at my watch and pretend I have to hurry to catch a tour bus. I give her fifty dollars for baby clothes and thank her for the tour. Then I take a taxi to the Officers' Club, have several drinks and a marvelous dinner at Le Chalet.

I think I should be tired by now. If I were in Qui Nhon, I'd be asleep by now. But somehow I can't sleep here. The war is becoming a little remote, though I still catch myself thinking about Ed and other people back at the hospital.

Monday, March 8, 1971. Today is my twenty-fourth birthday. To celebrate I spend the morning at James Jewelers on Pcthburi Street. Everyone in the military who comes to Bangkok knows James Jewelers. I call them and they send a car to the hotel to pick me up. As soon as I walk in the door of the shop, a small man bows to me and asks me if I want tea or beer. Special Forces has warned me about the beer: it's eighteen percent alcohol, so I take tea. The Mohammed Ali fight is today and everyone in the shop crowds around the television set. There are several Americans in the store and the clerks give us the best seats in front of the television. They ply us with beer or tea during the whole fight, ask if we like boxing, and expect us to cheer with them when they think a particularly good blow has been landed. When the fight is over, I get down to some serious shopping.

The back wall of the store is about twenty feet long. It's covered, floor to ceiling, with a wooden cabinet in which there are hundreds of small drawers. I sit on a stool at the counter in front of the cabinet and tell the man what I want: jade for earrings, opals for a ring, pearls, on and on. He runs his finger down a row of small drawers until he finds the right one, spreads a black velvet cloth on the counter and dumps twenty to fifty stones on the cloth. We paw through them, sorting them as I have sorted buttons as a child, not this one, not this one, maybe this one, wrong shape, not enough clarity. If I see nothing I want, he goes to the next drawer. I could go back every day for weeks and still not see the contents of all of those magic drawers. I buy quartz figurines, jade earrings, a moonstone ring for myself, my mother, my father and my two brothers, rubies, amethysts, star-sapphires and bronze ware. I also leave the war medal that Special Forces gave me to have one made just like it in gold.

There is an American couple sitting at the counter next to me. He is an Air Force Captain stationed down south, below Saigon. He's drunk on Thai beer and looking for a diamond and sapphire ring for his wife. I am embarrassed by his loud voice, by the way he slaps the clerk on the back.

"Yes, sir, pal. I have to hand it to you gooks, you can really make jewelry. Why, the folks back home will just pop out when they see that stone. Can't find anything that showy back in the States."

I've seen enough geographic bachelors to recognize one. He probably has a girl down south of Saigon. I wonder what he will bring her from Bangkok?

I have lunch at a seafood restaurant where I select fresh shrimp as big as my fist and watch them boil in a cooker brought to my table. Then more shopping in the afternoon, and dinner with an Air Force nurse I've met at the hotel. We go to a revolving restaurant where we can watch all of Bangkok slowly rotate below us. We decide to go all the way: a before-dinner drink, appetizer, soup, fish, steak, salad, dessert, cheese and biscuits and an after-dinner coffee and liqueur. We spend over fifty dollars each on our meal, more than I've ever spent on a meal in my entire life.

Tuesday, March 9, 1971. All of this sightseeing and shopping is nice, but I'm glad to get back into some sort of routine today. This is the first of my tours, the water tour of Bangkok.

Much of the life here centres on water transportation. There are people living on houseboats, washing elephants, bathing in the river, towing large loads of bamboo behind barges. I am afraid I'm turning into one of those tourists who only sees the sights through the viewfinder of a camera and will have to wait until the pictures are developed to see where I've been.

It's like living in a geography book. It has been so nice to pretend that this is a fantasy land and there's no war in the world. I've been doing that successfully the past few days, but I can't keep it up. I look at the houseboats and see poverty. The elephants remind me of the ones that the Viet Cong use to carry weapons. One of the patients told me about blowing one up once. He said there were elephant parts all over the jungle. When I watch the people bathe in the river, I wonder about parasites, typhoid, skin rashes.

One of the small boats carrying sugar cane and rice disappears into a gate cut in a high, thick fence. I catch a glimpse of a beautiful white plantation house inside the fence. What is it like to be insulated from the world behind a fence like that? I don't think I'll ever know a feeling of security like that again.

Wednesday, March 10, 1971. It's hot today, with a blue haze lying over the countryside. This is the day for the long bus ride through the northern part of Thailand. All of us on the bus are either on R & R from 'Nam or wives or girlfriends of people on R & R. I am the only unescorted woman on the tour, which is all right. Why do I need an escort to take a bus ride? I feels underdressed in a white sundress, tennis shoes and cotton socks. My feet actually ache from not having worn combat boots for a few days.

The countryside reminds me of Louisiana. They both have the same heat, the same blue haze over rice paddies and sugar cane fields. I feel like I'm riding the milk run along highway 61 and across the Atchafalaya Basin from New Orleans to Opelousis. I fall asleep in the air-conditioned bus and wake to look out of the window, thinking that the bus driver will announce Gonzales or Krotz Springs as the next stop.

We begin our tour by visiting a Buddhist temple and from there take a boat ride down a long, cool, blue river. The river trip sets off more memories of home. My friend Wes B. from New Iberia was in 'Nam last year, down in the delta region. Before he left the States, after he came back, before I left we went fishing together off Cypremort Point. In two months, when I go home, I want to go fishing with him again. That fishing trip is what I think about most when I think about going home. I want to sit in a boat, as I do today, and feel the wind blow in my hair and smell the wet, fishy smells of home.

Thai tourists join our group on the boat ride and the boat is full of children who lean out the side of the boat and laugh as the spray from the bow hits their faces. The guide tells us we will visit a Buddhist monastery at the end of the boat ride, but he neglects to mention that the monastery is in a cave. I am terrified of being underground and if I could get out of that part of the tour, I would do it. But the tour enters at one place and comes out at a different place, so I must go with them.

I am torn between being terrified that I am underground and wondering at the idea of the monks living under ground. Some of the passages are so small I that I pass my camera bag to the person in front of me before I can go through them. I'm following a young Air Force sergeant and in a particularly narrow passage he realizes I'm scared. He spends a lot of time coaxing me along and gives me a big hug when I make it into the sunshine again.

We stop at the Kanchanaburi War Cemetery, where they buried the prisoners from the Japanese camps in World War II. It's a large cemetery with a series of arches at the entrance, rows of identical slanted tombstones and a large white memorial cross at the back. I'm surprised at how well kept it is. The grass is neatly mowed, though it could use a good raking. There are flowers and small bushes between each stone.

John says we Americans don't know how to treat our dead; he says we shouldn't ship the bodies home. I have seen the piles of dented coffins stacked on a corner of the runway in Qui Nhon, waiting for the plane. Now that I see this cemetery I think perhaps he is right. I must remember to ask John if he knows who tends it? Does the British government hire Thai workers? Do people come from Australia or New Zealand or even England to find a particular grave? Have people taken pictures, in the same way I am taking pictures, to send to relatives too old or poor to make the trip?

NX35491 Lance Corporal
D.G. Simpson
2/19 Infantry Battalion
17th December 1943   Age 27
HIS DUTY FEARLESSLY AND NOBLY DONE
EVER REMEMBERED

I'm surprised at the ages: twenty-seven is young. Many of them were in their thirties. I think about what I know about the prisoner of war camps: the disease, the starvation, the brutality, those pictures I've seen of walking skeletons. No wonder John is angry when he talks about war. Yet it seems very peaceful here in the cemetery. A long-time-ago war. I wondered if there is still anyone who remembers Lance Corporal Simpson?

I think again that John is right. We send our dead home in stainless steel coffins that have scratches and dents in them because they have been reused so often. We make a mistake sending our dead home like that. They take the bodies to California and sort them like packages, send them to little towns in Ohio or New York or Louisiana for a closed-coffin funeral. We shouldn't separate the men who served together; they should lie buried together in a cemetery like this one.

After the ceremony we go to the river Kwai itself. Our guide says that the bridge built by prisoners washed away years ago because it was only wood. There is a new iron bridge just down river from the old bridge. I stand on the bridge and look as hard as I can upriver, hoping to see at least a remnant of the older bridge, but there is nothing to see.

I've never seen the movie *Bridge on the River Kwai* and now I'm glad I haven't. Hollywood won't have gotten it right and I would only say to myself, "I've been there and that wasn't at all what it looked like." We take some pictures, then we have to get off the bridge because a train is coming. It's a small, old steam locomotive, hauling passengers in open-windowed cars, and freight. And as the train passes I suddenly realize the

terrible pressure I've been feeling In Qui Nhon has gone away. My life is going to be all right. If something as horrible as the prisoner of war camps can end, if bridges built with slave labour can be washed away and replaced with new iron bridges where little steam trains come tootling out of the jungle filled with passengers and bunches of bananas, then things will eventually right themselves in my world, too.

Thursday, March 11, 1971. We visit temple after temple today and I am stuffed with exotic architecture and lovely oriental smells of incense and flowers. The most fascinating thing I learned today is that the Thais originally had no statues or decorations on their temples, but the Chinese brought statues with them as ballast for the ships that would return to China loaded with goods and the Thais took the statues left behind and began decorating their temples with them.

The poor clerk at the military post office and I are

on a first-name basis by now. I've been there almost every day, mailing home jewelry, bronze ware, dishes.

"So what is it today?" he asks, hefting the two-foot long box onto the scale.

"A wooden cat."

"Twelve dollars, surface mail. Take about six weeks to get there."

"That's okay. Even at that rate it will get home before I do."

I've done everything I came to do and bought all my bank account can afford. Today I pick up my gold war medal at James Jewelers and have a silver mug engraved for Ed to commemorate his promotion to Aircraft Commander. As I'm going out of James Jewelers for the last time I see a grey star-sapphire and diamond ring and I just can't resist it. Buying it blows all my remaining money.

We have one final blow-out, a night on the town. Our tour group goes to a Thai restaurant and night club. We have all collected our jewelry today and exchange pieces, try on each other's rings with "oohs" and "ahs". Everyone is convinced they should have really bought what their neighbour bought. I wear a short yellow dress and frilly yellow underpants. It has been so long since I dressed up. I'm quite shaky on my new high heels. It is fun, this play dress-up.

Everything in the restaurant is elaborately decorated with huge bronze plaques of temples, gods, feasts. The stage is surrounded by a carved lattice. The band, dressed in green and gold costumes, plays Thai music. There are flowers everywhere: on the table, in the women's hair, decorating the drinks and platters of food. I have several pina coladas, collecting the pink flower that arrived with each one into a bouquet, which I slip under my watch band. The curried shrimp arrive accompanied by gold-trimmed bowls filled with fresh coconut, raisins, dates, pink-coloured bean sprouts and several kinds of nuts. After the meal Thai women in wonderful costumes and very elaborate headresses dance. The head-dresses remind me of the temples I've seen today.

One woman who wears heavy gold armour and a tall headpiece comes down into the audience so we can see how her costume is made. I am a little taken aback to see that closeup it's quite dirty and that there are gaps between the decorations. But then I think it's all right because that costume isn't made to be examined too closely, perhaps like Bangkok isn't meant to be examined too closely. I have done the tourist thing for the past week: stayed at a luxury hotel, spent money, taken

pictures, amused myself by walking around Bangkok. I don't want to know about the drugs, the prostitution, the poverty. That's with me enough every day. This place is like the woman in the golden armour, best seen from a distance.

Tonight at supper I meet an Air Force pilot who flies Jolly Green Giant helicopters on search and rescue missions out of Udorne. He says his Crew Chief made a stencil of a giant's footprint and that whenever they are able to land in safe territory to pick up pilots, the Crew Chief uses the stencil and a can of green spray paint to paint Jolly Green Giant footprints over the landing zone. I love the idea of someone coming upon green footprints in the middle of a jungle.

It's the last night for both of us on R & R and we come back to my room thoroughly drunk and fall first into a bubble bath, then into bed together. We do more giggling and holding each other than making love. I'm ready to go back to work; in fact, I feel like I can do the next two months standing on my head.

Friday, March 12, 1971. We're up at 0400 and travel to the airport while Bangkok is still shrouded in a pink early morning mist. On the way to the airport we see orange-robbed Buddhist monks gathering alms. The last thing I see before entering the airport gates is a pair of monks disappearing into the pink early morning fog.

I arrive back to Qui Nhon to find out more of the 7/17 pilots have been transferred north. Casualties are still high up there.

Saturday, March 13, 1971 (63 days left). I am not scheduled to work until tomorrow night, but I volunteer to work nights tonight because the ward is shorthanded and I'm bored stiff. The patient census is down again because there aren't as many casualties as there have been from the war in the north. No one knows if this is the end of the spring push or only a lull. There is a typhoon off the coast and the rain is heavier than it was during monsoon. I guess that has put a stop to the action and I feel sorry for anyone out in the field in this weather.

Sometimes, like tonight, when work isn't stressful, I think about extending over here for an extra six months. I feel like after ten months I'm just getting the hang of this war. I've had the sheer conceit to wonder how this war can possibly go on without me. I guess what I really wonder is how people I know will fare without me, wonder what will happen to them and if they will be all right after I leave. But I know if I want to keep my sanity, I have to go home soon.

Sunday, March 14, 1971 (62 days left). Keith D., known to us better as Montagnard Six, is over for a visit tonight. It's great to see him again. I thought he'd gone north with the contingent that left a couple of days ago, but he's still here. He's lived with the 'Yards for a long time and sometimes I think he thinks like one. We had a long talk tonight about their values and how their communities are organized. I think he'd make a great anthropologist.

Monday, March 15, 1971 (61 days left). Back to night duty; night shift seems to be the story of my life. The corpsman I have with me on this rotation is so lazy I have to cover both wards by myself for twelve hours because I can't trust him to finish anything. I know I'm supposed to work with him, bring him along, lay down the law to him if I must, but he's absolutely hopeless and I'm tired of fighting with him. It's easier to do the work myself than try to improve his performance. I don't think I have what it takes to be a supervisor.

Thank heavens we aren't busy. There haven't been any evacs from Quan Tre lately and I wonder if the casualties are being sent to other hospitals or the number is really down. If it stays down, I guess the 101st will pull its two hospital liaisons back north; I'd miss them if that happened.

We pride ourselves on our ability to second-guess the war from the kinds of casualties that we receive. Wounds from booby traps mean Charlie isn't very active in the area. He sets the traps, then moves on. On the other hand, a lot of AK-47 wounds mean he's around to shoot at our patrols. Also if we hear that chopper crews are being moved around, it means our troops are on the offensive because it takes choppers to move them.

Sometimes I think we talk too much. In the same way that we never have any blackout conditions, no one has ever told us to keep our speculations to ourselves. It's a way of behaving that I have never become accustomed to in Qui Nhon. In Pleiku we assumed everyone who worked for us had some tie-in with the Viet Cong, so we were careful about what we said. Here, no one seems to care.

Thursday, March 18, 1971 (58 days left). My permanent change of stations orders came today: Fort Bragg, North Carolina! I'm so happy I can hardly contain myself. The first person I call is Arthur. I say, "I got my orders! It's Fort Bragg!" He laughs and says, "My condolences."

I hope a lot of the people from Pleiku will be there. This will be the first duty assignment where I actually know people before I arrive. One of the nurses on our ward was stationed there before coming to 'Nam. She says Womack Army Hospital is laid out very much like the hospital at Ft. Riley. Now, if I can only get orthopaedics, things will be number one.

Friday, March 19, 1971 (57 days left). Today breaks me. I don't know why, but today I just can't face one more day here. Everything is too much. Except for the time in Thailand, I have been drinking a fifth every two days since Christmas and tonight I keep drinking until I am really drunk.

I take Ole, one of the 7/17 pilots, out in the yard behind their quarters and hear my voice, which seems like someone else's voice, say things I can't say sober: that I'm sick of my job, that I don't understand the war, that I understand the war but that none of the people I work with do, that I can't wait to leave, that I'm considering extending here for six months.

This is Ole's second tour in 'Nam. We talk for a long time about his last tour, about what flying in combat is like, why he felt had come back for a second tour. He holds me until I can't cry any more.

Sunday, March 21, 1971 (55 days left). I didn't sleep well last
night, too much booze and crying on Friday, I suppose. For the first time I dream about 'Nam.

Dream

> Harry M., Bill L., myself and some other people I don't recognize in the dream have to go back to Pleiku to oversee a ceremony to end the war. Matt, Bill and I spend a lot of time talking about "remember when". Then it's the last day of the war. Several of us are in a new building that still smells like new wood. The walls are unfinished with pencil marks and manufacturer's stamps still visible on the lumber. A radio is on, rather an all-prevailing voice, more American than Viet Namese. It says only eight of us will get out alive and there are more than eight of us here. I knock on Matt's door and tell him what the voice had said. He doesn't believe me. Bill does. He tells me to get dressed, that we must get out of there. I put on my yellow sneakers and some kind of a coverall that goes over my shoes. There are a lot of people milling around. One person carries a green field stretcher, all rolled up.

> Somehow Bill and I become separated and I'm with two other nurses. Each of us has two flat red wax discs, about the size of a quarter, only thicker. Some of the discs will let a person out safely, some won't and no one knows which is which. I meet first Matt, then Bill. Both of them give me their discs so that I will have more of a chance of getting out. I know they are going to die so that I can escape.

> Then there are three of us together on a road: an older woman, another nurse my age, and myself. I feel a tremendous sense of isolation, of being the only three people ever to travel this road, and a horrible, unseen force bears down on us.

Then the shelling starts and I wake up screaming.

The screams wake Terri. She asks me what's wrong and I say nothing. There's no sense in trying to go back to sleep. I dress and write in my journal for a while, then take a walk around the airfield and take pictures of sunrise coming up over the light observation planes. The airfield is cool, with a breeze blowing in from the sea and the clouds are lined with pink light. I walk all around the hospital compound, past the closed headquarters building, past the rows of wards, thinking how cool and quiet and pleasant this place is first thing in the morning. I'm the first one in line for breakfast this morning.

Monday, March 22, 1971 (54 days left). I've learned a lot about soldiers in the past ten months, but I still don't understand why I like the idea of being a soldier. I like soldiers like the 7/17 pilots and the Special Forces in Pleiku and I don't like soldiers like the Air Force Major in Pleiku or that loud-mouthed pilot in the jewelry shop in Bangkok. Maybe what I'm learning has more to do with people than with soldiers.

We get such a screwed-up view of soldiers from movies and television. We see too many John Wayne movies. Over here we think John Wayne is pretty silly. It's not uncommon to hear someone ask, "Who do I look like, John Wayne?" or to comment, "Right, that was a real John Wayne move." What hurts is that the people back home expect us to behave like John Wayne: honest, fair, brave, patriotic and always winning in the final reel.

It's not like that here. I wonder if it ever has been like that in a war? War is brutal and living through it makes people numb, not tough. There are times I like being a soldier. There is something in me that compels me to value honour, strength, courage, endurance. Many of us who choose to be soldiers come into the military with the belief that being in the military, especially being in a war, is the best way to express those qualities. How can we know until we've been to war that those qualities are hard to find and even harder to maintain in a war? What I like about the soldiers I do like, and I include myself in the soldiers I like, is that we have given up on war being an easy solution to finding those qualities, but we are still looking for those values.

There are people here who never ask for sympathy for what they have been through. They expect me to be realistic enough about real war not to be shocked by or condemn them for what they have seen or done. We can't help but be saddened by what has happened to us, what we have been asked to do, what we have done, but we have learned to treat war as a fact of life.

There isn't that kind of sympathy at home. We change here. Those of us who don't change well escape into alcohol or drugs or mental illness. Those of us who change well either outgrow the Army or become very good officers. It's not us reserve officers who spend two or three years on active duty who find the honour, strength, courage, endurance in the military. Maybe a person has to be in long enough to go to staff college before they can really find those qualities. Wanting to grow more is a big factor in my deciding to extend for a year in the Army. I'm not ready to be a civilian when I go back to the world. I want the extra year around people who know what this war is like, to think about war and soldering, to think about what I've done here so I can make some peace with myself.

◆ ▷◆

Calgary, Alberta. I've thought about war and soldiering and values now for over three decades. It was autumn, 1964. John F. Kennedy was dead, Robert Kennedy and Martin Luther King still alive. Civil rights marches were still tearing the South apart. Hippy was a new word. Girls with long hair tied in rawhide thongs put flowers into the gun barrels of state militia troopers. Kent State was unthinkable. Marijuana would be the downfall of civilization as we knew it.

Viet Nam was part of the nightly news, but Hai Phong harbour hadn't yet been mined. We had yet to witness, as a side dish at supper, the exhausted faces of the Marines pulling out of An Khe or a South Viet Namese man executed with one round to the head. Only a few Dow chemists knew about Dioxin. William Calley was in high school. At seventeen, with a year of high school and four years of nursing school ahead of me, I was afraid the war would be over before I could get there.

That year in high school I took Physics, Chemistry II, Senior Math Study Group, World History, Honours English, Home Ec and Phys Ed. I spent Saturday mornings in the study-hall room taking tests—L.S.A.T., P.S.A.T., National Merit—trying to get into college, trying for scholarships. The rest of the weekend I worked at St. Francis Cabrini Hospital as a volunteer. I'd just received my Future Nurses Club cap for 1,000 hours of volunteer service. I was desperate to get into nursing school because that was my ticket into the military. Being a soldier was a dream I didn't tell even my parents.

I did tell Jeanne B., my best friend. In all-night sessions, fortified with Coca-Cola and Fritoes, we talked about our futures. Even to Jeanne, even to myself I couldn't explain the fascination with the Army, with nursing. All I know is the two had always wound themselves tightly around each other in my mind and that they had something to do with honour, strength, courage, endurance.

Jeanne's bedroom wall was lined with bookshelves. One night we tried to count the books and fell asleep just past a thousand. She introduced me to science fiction. One weekend she gave me *Starship Trooper* and I stayed up until four a.m. to finish it.

The book fascinated me. In six months I would be eighteen, the age at which Jonnie, Carl, and Carmencita enlisted. It thrilled me that she was not left behind but went to train as a pilot. I was less conscious then of the significance of women separating themselves from men at the 30th bulkhead, but was thrilled by the idea that men and women did the same work. Like Jonnie, I was bothered by Carmencita's shaved head. My mental image of her, like his, included her thick, black hair. I was disturbed by his comments that women were the reason men fought. That idea seemed silly, romantic, ridiculous. Like a child at the movies, I preferred the action to the romance. And in the action I was jealous.

Going down bugholes or burning a skinny's town wasn't my idea of fun. But I was jealous of the closeness among the men in *The Roughnecks*. I was jealous of their opportunity to be pushed, goaded, tried, tested until they either went over the hump or died. I felt cut off from that kind of a trial by being a woman. That book gave me the words for what I hoped I'd find in the military: closeness, caring, challenge, trial by fire. As Recruiting Fleet Sergeant Ho said in the book, "it was my constitutional right to serve…my born right to pay service."

So now it is May, 1992. I've lost track of the dead, of who is fighting whom today. Something must be making the nightly news. Since I've given away my television set I don't really know any more. I'm forty-five, with three university degrees, a divorce, a remarriage, a word processor and forty-two handwritten journal volumes. I've written, though never published, two novels and am about to embark on a third. I live in another country and look at the United States of America with strange and jaded eyes. I'm still in nursing, with twenty years of experience to my credit, still in love with nursing.

Jeanne is married, lives in Houston. We write to each other occasionally, still able to pick up where we left off as if we've never been apart. I beg her to type her letters because her cramped, dark handwriting fills the page. So she types, single-spaced letters with tiny margins, then as an afterthought, squeezes more messages in very tiny handwriting into those margins. We talk more about our pasts and the present now than about the future.

My copy of *Starship Trooper* is brown, brittle. I have to turn the pages carefully so they won't break from the spine. About once a year, usually on a long summer afternoon, I take it, a blanket and some iced tea out in the sun and reread it.

I'm still looking for very simple things: truth, honour, courage, endurance, strength, integrity. If Viet Nam did anything, it took away the honour, courage, justice, or at least took away my ability to believe in those things when confronted with the reality of modern war. I once heard a man named Richard Gabriel, a military expert from the States, interviewed on the radio program, *Morningside*. He said, in part,

> …The nature of war has intensified so dramatically that no sane soldier can tolerate it. Now we must modify the men to fit the weapons and drugs are the way to do that. The ideal drug is one that destroys the emotions without affecting the performance. They want soldiers without fear, without compassion, who won't surrender because the fear of death is gone, who won't take prisoners because they are fighting without a conscience. In other words, socio-paths. What happens then to courage, honour, strength and endurance, which are essentially values of mind over body?…

Hearing that I realized it isn't just my imagination that we Viet Nam veterans went through a different experience than any soldiers before us. We went through the last war where it was possible to fight as a human being. We were the ones who showed the rest of the world the edge that now must to be crossed by drugs, by androids, by who knows what they'll come up with. If that's the military of the near future and, if as he said the drugs are already being tested on animals, then I'm glad I got out when I did. I spend a lot of time trying to dissect courage, honour, strength and endurance out of the military experience and put them where they belong in the human experience. It's hard because the military tradition makes such a wonderful vehicle for them. They fit.

I want a way to have the adventure without hurting other people. I still like the adventure, the excitement, the adrenalin. Sometimes being a civilian is so terribly tame. I've learned how to take on the adventure without taking on the emotional baggage of patriotism, flag-waving and war. There's an interesting concept of war in another science fiction book, *Ecotopia.* In the society in that book, people who felt they had to have combat in their lives were allowed to go to some remote area outside the city and fight very ritualistic, limited battles among themselves. My pacifist friends say all combat is wrong, that we only fool ourselves by thinking we can have clean and honourable fighting. After thirty years, I still don't know. I do know I've salvaged something good, honourable and enduring from Viet Nam.

You've never lived 'til you've almost died.

To those who fight for it,

life has a flavour the protected never know.

—Sign over a Special Forces bar, Pleiku, R.V.N.

The first time I even saw that was over that Mike Force bar where Ed P. took me for a drink. I've had it hanging in my house in one form or another ever since I came back from Viet Nam. It doesn't really have to do with war. It has to do with confronting life straight on. If I learned anything in Viet Nam it was how to do just that. Maybe that's all being a soldier is.

❀ ꝑ ❀

Tuesday, March 23, 1971 (53 days left). I heard a funny story out of Phu Bi yesterday. It seemed the hospital commander called Saigon and asked that a woman to be assigned to the hospital in Phu Bi as his executive secretary. The Lieutenant in Personnel said that was impossible because Phu Bi was too close to the DMZ and women couldn't be assigned that close to combat. The hospital commander responded with, "Then what the hell am I doing with forty nurses up here?"

The Lieutenant says, "Oh, no, sir, you must be mistaken. There aren't any women stationed in Phu Bi."

Nobody knows how many women have been stationed in Viet Nam. There is a pretty accurate count of the nurses: about four hundred at any one time, or about four thousand since the war started. In Pleiku our Laboratory Officer was

...Nobody knows how many women have been stationed in Viet Nam....

a woman and in Qui Nhon there are some Dietitians and Physical Therapists who are women. We are told when we come in-country that the only women employed in non-medical roles are Air Traffic controllers in Saigon and Long Bien, but based on the story from Phu Bi, I don't imagine anyone knows exactly how many women are here or what they're doing. There are also Red Cross workers, U.S.O. workers, secretaries for some civilian companies doing business here, bank employees and missionaries. Terri pointed out a woman correspondent to me in the club the other night.

So all together there have been maybe ten thousand women here. Ten thousand American women compared to millions of men. There is a lot more women could do here. Almost all of the noncombatant jobs could have been filled by women, but the Army says that is impossible because even noncombatants may have to fight, because Americans won't stand for women in combat zones, because the women can't live in the conditions the men endured. I think it's because they think all the women will get pregnant.

Except nurses, of course. Our sex is ignored because we have a critically-needed occupation. In basic training we learned there was almost a draft of nurses during World War II. Congress was within two days of drafting female nurses when the war in Europe ended and freed up enough nurses to go to the Pacific, so no draft was necessary. I wonder what this war would be like if helicopter pilots or munitions experts were women?

Women go through life without thinking about war. Even in high school, when the boys were sweating every test because their chance for college and deferment might depend on it, the girls had a smugness about them. "Doesn't bother me if I flunk out. I can't be drafted." The closest they got to war was worrying about their boyfriends who might have to go. I just want women to take some kind of a stand. Demonstrate or be a part of it, but give up the smugness. We owe the men that are our friends and companions more than smugness.

Ruth asks me to take her wedding picture for her home-town paper. One of the nurses has a portable sewing machine. Ruth orders material from the States and spends all of her off-duty time making her dress. The dress isn't finished by the time she has to send pictures in order to meet the paper's deadline. We pin the dress on her, using big safety pins from the orthopaedic cast cart. We decide to shoot outside because we don't have to worry about lights and shadows. She stands against the plainest background I can find, an unpainted plywood wall behind the hooch by the garbage cans.

I've just learned about dodging and burning prints and it takes me all afternoon in the lab over at the Engineer's Compound to print her face dark enough without the white dress and veil looking overexposed. But when I'm finished, the pictures look good, as if they were taken in a studio. There is a faint dodging line that I haven't gotten quite right, but it looks like a strand of frosted hair framing her face. She is pleased with the results and mails them off to the paper. That is the way women do things here. We do things we have never done before, do them without knowing how to do them, and they work. We know where the dodge lines are, but we aren't going to tell anyone.

Wednesday, March 24, 1971 (52 days left). Our Head Nurse, Mary S., goes on R & R today and I'm to be acting Head Nurse for a week. More than anything else, that gives me a feeling of real panic. Suddenly I'm responsible for two whole wards. Here I am only eighteen months out of nursing school, and I wonder what I've learned in that time. To start with, my motor skills have certainly improved. I can actually start an IV and handle all of the equipment we have and not even blink. Have my interpersonal skills improved? Perhaps, but I still struggle with those. I don't know how this week will turn out, but at least I'm ready to try.

Thursday, March 25, 1971 (51 days left). We are working twelve hours a day in a room where phones ring constantly, people are always asking questions and air evacs are either coming or going. We are more like a train station today than a hospital. This get-em-in, get-em-out philosophy takes hold of our lives. Ever since the 101st has been sending casualties south, we load up the ward one day and unload the ward the next.

By the time 1900 comes I feel like a wind-up gramophone that needs winding. Ed calls tonight; he has called often since I came back from Bangkok. Tonight he calls to thank me for the engraved mug to celebrate him being promoted to Aircraft Commander. I'm glad it arrived safely. At first I was going to mail it, but the in-country postal service is even more unreliable than the phones. When I was in the air port in Da Nang, waiting for a plane to come back to Qui Nhon, I struck up a conversation with the man sitting next to me. He'd just been transferred to Tuy Hoa and I was telling him about wanting to get this package I was carrying to a pilot there.

He said, "Give it to me. I'll deliver it."

So I handed it to him. I guess he could have walked off with it and I would have had no way of finding him again. But today he walked into the Dust-off radio room down there and asked, "Is there an Ed W. here? I've got a package for him from a lady up in Qui Nhon."

I've learned to trust people like that. It's part of the way of life here. People can either do wonderful things for one another or they can screw each other around. The trick is learning who to trust.

At least talking to Ed takes my mind off my own panic at being Acting Head Nurse. I'm carrying on about being nervous about being in charge and he says, "How do you think I feel, flying as Don's A.C.?" He and Don U. came in country at the same time, but Ed's promotion date was a little ahead of Don's, so now he's in the A.C. seat and Don is flying as his copilot.

He tells me he scared Don the other day. They had gone into a hot Landing Zone and were taking fire. Ed hurried over that part; he didn't want to worry me, but he forgot I had an imagination. Anyway, something exploded really close on his side of the aircraft and Don was certain that Ed had been killed, so he took the controls and took off. Only he found the controls hard to operate and thought that was because Ed's body had fallen across the controls and jammed them. He was trying to decide how he was going to get the ship back and what he was going to write in the letter to Ed's family when Ed said, "For God's sakes, will you give me the damn controls back." He says Don turned absolutely white and just kept saying over and over, "You're not dead. You're not dead."

He wants me to laugh at the story and I do. He also wants me to comfort him. I can hear that in his voice, especially when he talks about the explosion happening right next to him. But he's in Tuy Hoa and I'm here and I can't hold him. I miss him so much.

Friday, March 26, 1971 (50 days left). I'm surviving as Head Nurse, but I'm not enjoying it. I don't think the people who are working with me are either. I have this idea that everything has to be done by the book and I guess I'm behaving as if the wards have never functioned properly until I took over. Mary is due back in a few days and I think I can survive until then, if the corpsmen don't lynch me first.

Ole just got orders for Laos. One of his buddies comes to look for me on the ward today and tells me Ole is leaving tonight and I'd better get over to the O Club after work if I want to say goodbye. We sit for a long time in the back of the Officer's Club and just talk. There is a black light in the back of the club and it makes a snowy pattern on the drink in his hand. We talk about a lot of things, about home, about this being probably the last time we will see each other, about him going to the real war as we jokingly call it.

There was an article in Newsweek recently about pilots. It tried to explain how they could be so young and so old at the same time. He is twenty-three or twenty-four, my age, but the grey in his hair makes it hard to believe his age. When the light from the bar catches his face a certain way I know the lines around the eyes weren't there when I first met him.

I remember the first time he came to the club. I thought him loud and obstreperous, certainly someone I didn't want to get to know. Somehow along the way he grew on me and we became friends. He taught me to play liar's dice, though I never win when I play with him. We spend a lot of long nights drinking and talking. It's different here than it was in Pleiku. The Cav guys are basically decent. Many of them have been to college and they are as likely to be found reading a book as drinking a beer. They're polite, they're kind, they're roaringly funny when they get drunk. Somehow in Pleiku I felt like one of the boys. Here I feel like their friend.

Ole and I both know why he is leaving but neither one of us says it. The casualty figures for chopper pilots in Laos are up and he is going to replace one of those statistics. He believes, as a lot of pilots do, that you never talk about the possibility of crashing or you will. So we talk around everything but that.

But I give him my war medal, the brass one that Special Forces originally gave me, and he says he thinks it will be a good luck charm. It's a silly thing, really, just a piece of metal. It doesn't even have the significance of being a religious medal, but he says it will bring him luck and we both want to believe that.

He insists he is going to request a safe, paper-pushing job in his new unit and that he has seniority so he's sure to get what he asked for. His buddy ratted on him earlier today. He told me Ole asked for a combat assignment.

I snap one more picture of him and, exasperated, he takes the camera out of my hands and says, "No more." "Come on," I say, "One more: the typical American hero defending home, motherhood, apple pie and President Nixon's Indochina policy pose." We both laugh and he hands the camera back to me. So they finally close down the bar and throw us out. We stand in the rain waiting for his ride to come. We make the time last as long as we can. Then his ride comes. We hug and he goes off to do what he has to do. And I go home to bed and pray for him before I fall asleep.

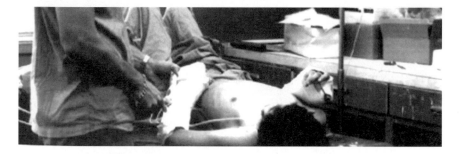

1971 APRIL 1971

Thursday, April 1, 1971 (44 days left). I am over at the O Club this afternoon having a Coke with two officers I know sightly. They are talking about being patients in military hospitals. Both have been to Viet Nam before and both have been wounded and med-evaced. For almost a year I have been so closely connected with fresh casualties that I have lost track of what happened to them after they leave us. These men talk about the whole process, what it feels like to be carried into an Emergency Room, how one of them went into shock on his way to Surgery, about being flown back to the States, about the long process of getting well. They say they have forgotten a lot of the pain and remember more of the funny things. Sometimes they remember a particular nurse or corpsman who took care of them, a face or a name or the way the person touched them.

It's been a long time since I've thought about all the men we save, all the ones who go home to get well. The men that I took care of months ago when I first arrived in Pleiku are home now, most of them well and out of the Army. I wish I'd kept some kind of a record, names or notes so I would know how many successes we've had.

Saturday, April 3, 1971 (42 days left). What a horrible day! Casualties have come in since 0900; it's now almost 2200 and no relief in sight. The doctors have been in surgery for over ten hours and all of us are walking around in a fog. My feet weigh a ton and all my neck muscles are as tight as piano wires. I'm writing this on a fifteen break and as soon as that's over, I'm going back to the ward. I have to because there just isn't anyone else who can work and the work has to be done. Dexadrine and the booze I drank last night are using up all my reserves. I feel like I am skating on a very thin edge. It's hard to stop my hands from shaking. Time to go back to the ward.

Sunday, April 4, 1971 (41 days left). The casualty load yesterday has me physically and mentally exhausted. I don't have any confidence in my ability to make even simple decisions. Tony and one corpsman had all of the beds filled by 2300 last night. Not only did they take care of all those patients but did

192

all that was necessary to manifest them out on an early morning air-evac. I don't know how. I admire them for having been able to do it.

Monday, April 5, 1971 (40 days left). We work terrified that every time a chopper lands it's the start of another mass casualty. I hurry through all my work just in case the push starts again, then have to find something to do the rest of the shift to keep busy.

This time they aren't casualties from the north, but our own 173rd Infantry. Our feeling is that the Herd has been hit because it has been on stand-down too long. Carelessness is the biggest problem being here during the withdrawal phase. There are too many troops still in-country and not enough for them to do. Sappers walked right into some of the 173rd base camps and blew them away. That's just plain stupidity on our part.

Tuesday, April 6, 1971 (39 days left). The General from the 173rd comes to visit his men today. He's about six foot six. I come up to about his elbow. The guys think we look quite funny as we make rounds together.

Ed calls tonight. He's been promoted to Chief Warrant Officer Two. I am so proud of him, even though I know the promotion means more work. He sounds exhausted. His calls are about the only thing keeping me going this stretch of nights. Sometimes as I'm doing the cleaning or just trying to stay awake I think about him.

Wednesday, April 7, 1971 (38 days left). One of Ed's buddies was badly injured recently and Ed had to fly him to the hospital at Tua Hoa. Going to see his friend in the hospital upset him more than anything he has done in the past ten months. We talk for a long time tonight, or rather he talks and I listen. I've been working at this long enough to not be scared by the tubes, bottles and equipment that are attached to the patients. But as much as he has flown Dust-off, it's all new to him, especially when a friend is involved.

I know it sounds cruel, but maybe he can understand a little better now why I get so upset every time I think something might happen to him. If he's hurt, I can't care for him because we are too close. That, at least is one of the advantages of him being at another hospital. I don't have to face every Dust-off that comes in, wondering if he will be on it.

Thursday, April 8, 1971 (37 days left). Terri and I decide we must do two things before we go home: stop drinking and clean up our language. We dump all the booze we have—three cans of beer and half a bottle of Crown Royal—down the bathroom sink. Then we take everything out of the fridge: a small piece of the last round of Colby, some stale Ritz crackers, a jar of olives, some pickled onions and a jar of grape jelly. We eat it to celebrate Terri's wedding.

She and Bill were married in Hawaii. The day they came back incountry, she developed appendicitis and they were stuck in Saigon for three weeks. Not that they minded. They thought surely the Army would station them together once they were married, but no such luck. The Army says they have too little time here to be transferred now, so he is back in I Corps and she is back here.

Bill wants to go to nursing school in the fall to get his R.N. Terri figures that with his G.I. bill benefits and her working, they can just make it. After he finishes school, they want to move out west.

At least they have plans. I don't know what I am going to do, except sleep through the first two weeks of leave, them go down to Cypremort Point for a week and just sit on the beach. And go shopping for new clothes. I don't even know what the fashions are any more. Maybe I'll buy some furniture and a new car.

❀ ⴖ❀

Calgary, Alberta. It took a long time to have any kind of plans. I had put a year of my life into Viet Nam. I thought it would take another year, the year I planned to spend at Fort Bragg, to come to some kind of a resolution about it. Instead it took almost ten years. I married another veteran, lived with him five years, then he disappeared. He finally turned up a year later living with another woman on the other side of town. In April of 1979, when I was still looking for him, I wrote in a journal:

> …I guess I think Viet Nam is over. There are few people in my life who were there, people who were a part of it. It still exists in my mind. I can pull it out and look at the memory, but what good does that do? All I know is I want help.…

I didn't know, even in 1979, what I wanted help to do. Later that year, seeing the movie *Coming Home* began to break the shell I had built. In February of 1980 one particular episode of *M*A*S*H* had a dream sequence. Margaret wore a wedding dress. She and her groom were rolling on a brass bed in the middle of a field of flowers. He changed from a groom in a tux to a soldier in bloody fatigues. He got up and followed a line of soldiers through the field, leaving Margaret on the bed in a bloody wedding dress. In all the years of watching that show, that was the only episode that broke me.

Sometimes the patients were stacked like wood and we went home covered with blood. They came in; they went out. We never knew from where or to where. The war was just one room. It had bright blue walls. There were flags of the different states hung from the refrigerator and Kool-aid in the refrigerator next to the blood. We'd strip the patients naked. There might be fifty people standing there, but we'd strip them naked and leave them that way. . .

On and on, the images I had held inside broke over me like waves. I went back and looked at my Viet Nam diary. I looked at my childhood, how growing up Southern had given me an early love of violence and the military. I began to write, using characters who had been in Viet Nam. In addition to Elizabeth Pepperhawk, there was Ben Nizinsik, a veteran from Pennsylvania, who had been crippled by the war. By writing him as happy, successful, adjusted I wrote away the guilt of sending crippled men home. A second woman character appeared: Joanna Prescott. She was sitting by a pond in Kansas, crying. It was April 29, 1975, the day Saigon fell, and she cried the way I cried that day, crying for what we had lost. By writing her I began to look at my own pain.

I read a book by Vera Brittain, a woman who had been a nurse during World War I, and learned my experiences weren't unique to Viet Nam. We would have understood each other like sisters. I read about other women veterans and joined the Viet Nam Veterans of America. In October 1981, ten and a half years after leaving Viet Nam, while watching a performance of *The Hostage*, a play by Brendan Behan about the Irish Civil War, the dam broke: again from a journal:

…Then the climax of the play comes with a simulated attack on the house. Loud noises. Lights go out. Gunfire. People scream and fumble on stage in the dark. I cry, shaking, sobbing, not knowing why and not being able to stop. I run from the theatre still crying. Bob, another Viet Nam veteran, opens the door to his apartment. He holds me and we sit on an orange couch. I keep saying, "I don't know why I'm crying. I can't stop. I don't know where I'm going." I know I am not making sense and I can't make any other words. I wish the crying could go on for hours, maybe it would clean me out. Already I have stopped, my cheeks red and hot. My eyes burn. Bob says to me, "You can't keep coming to me like this every time some memory about the war bothers you. I'm on shaky enough ground myself right now. You have to work on getting yourself well." I know he is right, wonder how to do it.

After I leave Bob's apartment, I go to a house where I am house-sitting for friends. There is a loud ticking clock and their dog's toenails click as he comes down hard wooden stairs. I go to bed in a white iron bed with a thick and lumpy mattress, sinking into the softness. The dog rambles in the house, up and down stairs, looking for people who aren't there. The house is cold. Finally the dog settles beside the bed and I reach to pet matted fur. For the first time the shell about Viet Nam is truly, finally, really broken. I can begin to face up to what I was then and what I am now. I can finally come home.…

Our Army went to Viet Nam to kill people. There were sidelights, benefits or problems, depending on the perspective. We went because we were drafted. We went for adventure. We went because of honour or national pride or because our fathers and mothers belonged to the American Legion. They had done their patriotic duty and now it was our turn. We went because there were no jobs. We went to avoid the disgrace or trouble of running to Canada. We went for the money and drugs. There were millions of us and we went for millions of reasons.

For five out of six of us there was no combat. We ran the Post Exchange and the clubs, worked for A.F.V.N. Radio, typed and filed, answered the phone, issued supplies, cooked meals, drove trucks, tended the wounded. We were called R.E.M.F.s by the men in the field. It meant Rear Echelon Mother Fuckers. It meant we slept in beds, worked in air-conditioned offices, went to the clubs at night, had a weekly movie. It meant most of all that we did not kill.

For those of us working in hospitals being called a R.E.M.F. hurt. We joked about it with the patients, allowing them to call us that. What did we know of fire fights, hot landing zones, snipers, napalm, trees defoliated by Agent Orange, mud, rice paddies filled with leeches, ambushes and chi-com grenades?

I had stood ankle-deep in purple potassium permangenate solution, pouring gallons of it on white phosphorus burns, trying to keep the W.P. from burning to the bone.

I had gone to tag 'em and bag 'em in the body shed, pulled the tags from a man with no face, read the name, and realized we'd had coffee together the day before.

I had spent long nights sitting beside beds while guys smoked and talked in the dark about all those things R.E.M.F.s didn't know about.

I had nursed two men through minor injuries and sent them back to the field only to hear two weeks later they were on the orthopaedic ward with their legs blown off.

There was no bad guy in the field killing and good girl in the hospital saving lives. I was a soldier; I supported soldiers. The hypocrisy was the most painful thing. If we should have been in Viet Nam, we should have fought the Viet Cong on their own terms, fought to win. We were not John Wayne; we could not be soldiers and good guys at the same time. If we should not have been in Viet Nam, we should have left. Period. Right away. Just lay down the weapons and walk away.

In an ideal world there would be no war or at the very least it would be left to us volunteers. Involve no civilians, no draftees, no conscientious objectors, no news coverage. We would go off to some uninhabited corner and fight. At least that way we would not infect the next generation. We would not produce G.I. Joe dolls, A-team Halloween costumes, books on war, survivalist camps. As soldiers we are going to destroy the world, whether street by street as in Beruit or all at once in nuclear war. What we want most is to be out of a job. Hard-core unemployed. No soldiers needed today. Applications not being taken. As long as our countries ask us to go—for power, territory, religion, ideal, patriotism—for whatever reason, we are going to go. Those of us who consider ourselves good soldiers are going to do the best job we know how to do.

The ambivalence never leaves. There are days I wouldn't go to war again for anything. There are days, like when I see casualties being carried from a bombed building in Beruit, I would give anything to go again. There is no final word, no complete epilogue on Viet Nam. Last year I asked another veteran what the difference was between those of us who went and those who didn't. He said, "Those of us who went to Viet Nam never stopped fighting."

I don't think we ever will.

❀ ⌗ ❀

Friday, April 9, 1971 (36 days left). Good Friday. I haven't been to mass since Lent began. Somehow there is no differentiation of the days over here and one week slips into another and a whole week has gone by and now Lent has gone by without realizing it.

> Monday was a pink-orange malaria pill.
> TuesWedThursFriSatSunday was one day.
> Monday was a pink-orange malaria pill.
> One communion replacing another.

Maybe I'll get back in the habit of going to Mass once I'm back in the States. Somehow here faith is more personal. There are times on the ward I feel like God is standing right beside me, that he isn't just in the chapel.

This is not a good day. I can't remember when I've felt this sick. Several times during the shift I've been in the bathroom, on the verge of throwing up. The corpsman wants to know what's wrong, suggests maybe I go down to the Emergency Room to see the doctor. I don't tell him that what's wrong is that I'm drying out from booze. Yesterday, after we dumped the last of our stash down the sink, was the first day since I came back from Bangkok that I haven't either been drinking or hung over.

I lay down yesterday afternoon and dreamed

Dream

> I was frying a skeleton on a hot griddle, preparing a meal
> of bones for someone. It was a human skeleton, almost
> certainly a man. The griddle was very hot and the rib
> bones sizzled like meat just touched to a hot surface.

I woke up sweating and vomited all afternoon. I've been a lot of things in the past eleven months—exhausted, terrified, drunk, running on pills and booze—but never as scared as I was when I woke up from that dream. I guess the secret is to just keep moving. This isn't anyone's fault but my own. I knew I would have to stop drinking eventually and all of the dreams and the nausea are just part of it.

Saturday, April 10, 1971 (35 days left). My worst fears come true tonight: a mass casualty arrives when I am on nights. At 1900 we have 55 patients and by 0200 there is only one empty bed. The whole

night is a blur of muddy, bloody bodies; I.V.s; dressings; drinks of water; morphine injections. It isn't just our ward; the whole hospital is overflowing and they have even open the closed wards.

There is only time to take care of the bodies, no time for comforting or talking. We aren't getting any replacement staff and the hospital has about three-quarters of the staff it's allotted on paper. We pull extra shifts, work overtime, come in on our days off. I don't trust my judgment any more. If the increased patient load keeps up and we don't get some relief I don't know what's going to happen. Everyone is exhausted, running out of adrenalin and using other things to keep going.

It's about dawn when Intensive Care calls.

"This is I.C.U. Have you any empty beds?"

"One."

"We should really keep this guy down, but we're got more than we can handle. Gunshot wound of the abdomen. Filthy dirty. We haven't have time to bathe him. Watch his blood pressure. He might still bleed out."

I grab the pen out of the pocket on my sleeve and begin to make notes. "Anything else?"

"His name is Ed W."

> Ed was my first lover.
> When he made Aircraft Commander
> I brought him a silver cup from Bangkok.
>
> He drank Black Russians.
> His mustache tickled of Kalaua and JP-4.
> I would grip his damp curls.

I scream into the phone:

"Tell me his rank, tell me his rank."

The nurse is furious. She argues his rank doesn't make a damn bit of difference. I'm crying and can't answer her. She goes for the chart and I hear the metal chart back slam on her desk.

"He's a sergeant. Are you satisfied?"

"Oh, yes, yes! Send him right up."

They bring a tall man with black hair and no mustache. I help move him into the bed and as I'm putting up the side rails, for the first time I break down and cry in front of a patient.

Monday, April 12, 1971 (33 days left). Ed calls to say he might get to come tomorrow. I am still shaken by what happened Saturday night and I say, "It was the funniest thing. We got a patient with the same name as yours Saturday night." I want to tell him everything, how I felt, how I cried, but there are no words. He says, "Just hang on. I'll be there as soon as I can."

Tuesday, April 13, 1971 (32 days left). Ed finally arrives and once again we make love, long and slow, in my room. He asks me why I never came to the Dust-off going away party in Pleiku. I tell him how unsure I felt of myself, how jealous I was when he dated other women.

He says, "I missed you for a long time after that. You hurt me when you didn't come. I thought you stayed away because you were mad at me. I couldn't figure out what I had done wrong. It took me a long time to get up the courage to call you again."

Courage? He flies into hot landing zones and it takes courage to call me? I guess that's a side of him I never thought about before. He's actually here, whole, alive. He looks tired, but we all look that way. In two weeks he will stop flying and spend his last month in-country on the ground. I have some inner sense we are both going to survive this war. We've never said that our relationship is just for over here, but that's how I feel today. The hours he is here pass like minutes. I don't ask him for his address in the States. When he walks out of my room today it feels like he is walking out of my life a second time, this time for good. Maybe this relationship is just one of the things I am trying to close down so I can get the hell out of this place.

❀ ♫ ❀

Calgary, Alberta. I never did see Ed again. Of all the people I knew in Viet Nam, he's the one I wonder about the most. There are times when I'd love to talk to him again, just to know that we were both all right, that we both had survived. I don't dream about him; I wonder if he ever dreams of me?

I dream about Viet Nam when I'm tired or under pressure or something especially nasty has been on the newscast. The dreams rarely take place in Viet Nam itself; they are other countries, other places, some where I have lived and some that I only imagine. They are dreams of rescue—often the rescue of children, of having done a good job, of having left something important behind.

Dream

I am somewhere in South America, probably Mexico. There is a revolution and the group of people I am with are helping children to escape. The soldiers come into the village and we pretend to be part of the village in order to not be caught. We finally manage to get out of the village but at the cost of leaving everything we have.

Later we are back where we live. We are all involved in a school of some kind. One of the people I was in South

America with calls me as I walk through the hall by his classroom door. He says, "I just got word. Max is out safely." Max is the last person in our group down there. "He says it's really bad down there now."

And I wonder how it could possibly get any worse than when we were there. I begin to cry, really deep, wracking sobs. There are people in the hall who were in South America with me and they think, "One of us had to break sooner or later." Then I realize I am standing at the door of a classroom and the students won't understand, so I stop crying and say I am all right.

A Chinese girl, who is my friend, asked me to take a picture of her and her boyfriend. I say, "I can't. I left my camera, my jewelry, my needlepoint, everything there."

She says, "Not the needlepoint!" She has a picture, taken before I went to South America, of me in a small room, surrounded by very colourful needle-point pictures and crocheted afghans. I think I must be mistaken because I'd never have been so stupid as to take my needlework with me. I go back to my room and there are only bare walls, with little faint squares where the pictures have been. Then I know I've been where there was great danger, I've escaped to safety and I'll never see the beautiful work I've done again.

❀ ☖ ❀

Wednesday, April 14, 1971 (31 days left). Ed's buddy, the one that was wounded a couple of weeks ago, is flown to our Intensive Care Unit because his kidneys have stopped working. Diane takes care of him. She says she doesn't know if he has much of a chance. They keep him here for a few hours, then fly him to Saigon on emergency med-evac because the 3rd Field has a dialysis machine. They are going to put him on it to see if his kidneys will start again on their own. I try to think if I know anyone at the 3rd Field so I can ask her to look in on him. But the only person I knew who was there

was Sharon J. and she has been back in the States a long time. I tell Ed that
we are doing everything we can.We pass patients along, like links in a long,
great chain.

Sometimes to friends, sometimes to strangers.

Tuy Hoa to Qui Nhon to Saigon.
"Am I going to die?"
"Not on my shift. Not in my hospital.
 Hell, I don't have time to
 make out the paperwork if you die."

He laughs and shoots Diane with the
syringe of water he's conned from
another nurse.

Saigon to Japan to home.
 We are water
 trickling into a fissure in a shale cliff.
 We freeze, expand, melt, run further down
 and crack the rock a little more.

Saturday, April 17, 1971 (28 days left). Sometimes I goof! The ward is
just a zoo today, as it has been for days. There is a patient scheduled for med-
evac, but his departure is postponed once because his blood count is too low.
Because of the changes in pressure and oxygen during flight, a patient has to
have a good hematocrit before the Air Force will take him.

I spend the whole day typing him for blood, starting his IV, running the blood,
getting repeat hematocrits and giving him more blood. By 1800 his hematocrit is
just at the level the Air Force requires. I am sure he is ready to go out on the plane
tomorrow. Then I discover that with all the running around I've done, I have
forgotten to do only one thing: put the patient's name on the list for the med-
evac! I am so embarrassed.

Sunday, April 18, 1971 (27 days left). Lanie G. says there is going to
be a big operation around here soon with Koreans doing most of it, but
Americans flying them in and out. That means the Cav is going to be where it's
really hot. They have been on stand down for a long time, since things cooled off
in Laos, and they are anxious for some action. I guess this operation makes them
happy, but I can't say it thrills me. It means our workload is going to go up and
perhaps some of the people I knew won't be coming back.

Monday, April 19, 1971 (26 days left). Even with the recent push of casualties, we are beginning to close the 67th Evacuation Hospital. I go to the pharmacy today and come back to find Ward 2 has been closed and the few remaining patients moved into Ward 4. I don't like the closing any better than I did in Pleiku. We all feel insecure. We have gotten into such a routine and all of a sudden the Army has taken that away from us. We look for rituals, little ways of doing things that give us security.

Tuesday, April 20, 1971 (25 days left). Our wards combine with Wards 6 and 8 today and there's going to be trouble over that. We are two distinct units that have been functioning independently and it will take time for us to mesh. I suppose our security has been shaken and each ward wants its own policies to come out on top. Tempers are running high and I hope the patients, who are caught in the middle, don't suffer. We are getting so caught up in personal interests we're losing perspective. Our two Head Nurses call us together for a meeting today and tell us we will find a way to get along. That's the Army, just order people to get along and expect them to find a way to do it.

The crunch for me came yesterday when they closed my ward without warning while I was away at the pharmacy. It's funny, I've always thought of Ward 2 as more mine than Ward 4 because when I started here there were just G.I.s on Ward 2 and a combination of G.I.s and Viet Namese on Ward 4 and I like taking care of the G.I.s. I also liked Ward 2 more because the patients there required more care, so it was more of a challenge. Anyway, I went to the pharmacy and came back and there's a lock on the ward door and a note pinned to the door: "Sharon—We closed the Ward. Come to Ward 4." It's as if something in me snapped, as if I am too close to going home to give any loyalty to the new arrangement. Whatever is worked out among the combined staff will have to be done without me.

Wednesday, April 21, 1971 (24 days left). My short-timer's calendar is almost full. I have brought tickets to New Orleans and written my family with the date and time of the flight so they can meet me at the airport. I think, what if they don't come to meet me? I've been so protected here, always having details like meals and laundry taken care of for me. I don't know that I would know what to do in a large airport by myself. This is silly. If they don't come to get me, I'll find my way home. There must be a bus or something that goes across the lake.

Going home seems so unreal. I just can't be leaving. I look at myself, at the way I dress, at how much I have been drinking, at the language I use, and I don't know how my family will react. They'll still expect me to be that lady they tried to raise me to be. I don't know who my family thinks is coming home, but it isn't the same woman they saw off at the airport a year ago.

ॐ ✿ ৳ ✿

Calgary, Alberta. Over time, the wards closing down was a good thing for me. It helped me close out my loyalties and start looking towards home. There was one thing that was never closed out. We had a patient whose last name was Ranger. He was also a Ranger and insisted we called him Ranger Ranger. He had been on our ward with minor wounds; he was a thoroughly charming man, in love with being a good soldier. He wanted to make a career of the military. Our Head Nurse Mary and he were quite taken with each other.

About three weeks after I came home, I received a letter from one of the other nurses. Ranger's jeep had gone over a mine and he had lost a leg. I felt so sorry not to be there to take care of him. I wondered how Mary was and if they would have a future together. I never found out.

Dream:

There is a large, pale green marsh, rather like a rice paddy, with tender grass growing in the water. Suspended over it is a long flat board with an undercarriage partly like a biplane's wings, only the second wing is twisted in a very pretty way. The wood is light brown and very smooth. To the right is a big field of rich, brown bottom dirt. Not planted yet. It smells wonderful, like newly ploughed earth. A big, brown horse runs loose in the rice paddy land. This wooden thing is suspended somehow, so that it swings easily like a giant summer porch swing. There is a little walkway, wooden, across the middle of the paddy land. I am sitting at the edge of the paddy, on soft, wet grass, pushing the swing. When it goes out and back it clips the top of the grasses, not hurting them, but just making a swishing sound over the tops. It has its own rhythm, which is very pleasant. It is as if these words can be sung to the rhythm:

So I come home early from roots in the jungle
To tell other women not to pass it along.

All the colours are grey and grey-greens. The feeling is peaceful and not associated with anything. Once, towards the end of the dream, I push the swing off. It goes into a gray-green mist and I realize I have lost track of the rhythm. I am afraid it will hit the horse. I am a little afraid, but I fall into chanting the lines and right on the beat it comes out of the mist, misses the horse and I catch it.

Not all of the dreams about Viet Nam are bad ones. Sometimes, like this one, they serve as markers for how far I've come since *I came home early from roots in the jungle.* In that long, slow journey from those roots I lost the nonsense about being a lady. I've been too many other things: woman, nurse, teacher, friend, poet, writer, daughter, wife, lover, wife again to worry about being a lady.

ॐ ❀ ᚠ ❀

Thursday, April 22, 1971 (23 days left). There is a moment today, as I stand at the medicine cabinet counting pills, that going home finally sinks in. I'm fucking going home! I have to clean up my language. Not start drinking again. Stop sleeping nude because of the heat. What am I going to pack? There is no sense in taking things home only to throw them away. I think I'll leave most of my things here. Go home, start over. That's probably be the best.

Sunday, April 25, 1971 (20 days left). I am on duty tonight when the Viet Cong blow up the ammo dump again. It's not one big explosion as in January, but a series of explosions. The first two are small, hardly enough to bother us. By the time the second one explodes the corpsman and I are pulling patients under the beds and making sure everyone is all right. The electricity in the wards is out and we work by flashlight. One of our new corpsmen shows up in flak jacket and helmet, carrying his rifle. He says, "Ma'am, I'm supposed to be on the perimeter, but I just can't go. I just can't go." He is seventeen years old. I am an officer. The right thing to do is to order him to go to the perimeter. Instead I say, "I need you here. We need help to get all the patients under the beds." Then I put him to work moving the Viet Namese patients.

In the midst of all the confusion, noise, and people milling around, Phil, the liaison sergeant from the 101st, comes by the ward on his way to the perimeter.

"Hi, short round. You okay?"

"Yeah, just a little scared, but I can handle it."

"Good girl. I have to go to the perimeter."

"What's going on out there?"

"I don't know, but it may be serious. Stay ready for anything."

"You take care of yourself."

"I always do, short round."

He hasn't been gone more than a couple of minutes when the whole sky outside, on both sides of the ward, turns bright orange. One of the patients yells, "Get down!" I think this is it: the hospital has finally received a direct hit. Twenty fucking days left and right now, in this place, I am going to die. I dive for cover under the desk.

The shock wave breaks windows. Glass scatters over the beds and the door comes off its hinges, but I am still alive. My luck has held. The ambulatory patients want to go outside to see what has happened. I threaten them with court martial if they move and assign a Lieutenant in a bed by the door the task of taking names of anyone who puts one foot outside.

The Viet Namese patients are terrified, screaming, crying. We wait, make rounds, check the I.V.s, light cigarettes for patients, whisper into ears, "It's going to be okay. You're safe here." When we have waited long enough that we think no more explosions are likely to happen, we sweep up the glass and put everyone back in their beds. I listen for rifle fire, wait for Phil to come back and, when he doesn't I begin to worry that something has happened to him. He left the ward only a minute before the big explosion and was probably outside when it happened. I am tempted to call the Emergency Room and ask casually, "Did we take any casualties?" but the staff down there would think it very odd. Instead I wait.

The ward is quiet once more, but a lot of men are awake for a long time, their cigarettes red dots in the darkness. I'm not going to talk to them tonight; we have all been through too much to talk. When the Supervisor comes through an hour later I am sitting with my feet on the desk, reading a mystery. I ask her if the hospital took any casualties. She looks at me as if I know something I shouldn't and simply says, "No."

After she leaves, I realize the reason Phil hasn't come back is that the hospital is probably keeping extra guards on the perimeter tonight and he will probably be there until morning. I'm glad Phil came by. I guess he cares about me. We've always worked well together and he has been hanging around the ward a lot. I wonder if it's been for another reason besides work?

I find at breakfast why the night supervisor looked at me so strangely when I asked her if the hospital had any casualties. Kris, the man Diane dated earlier this year, was on perimeter duty when the explosions happened. He went crazy, said he had a vision of where the attacks were coming from and that God had appointed him to stop it. He grabbed grenades and tried to run through the barbed wire into Qui Nhon. His buddies knocked him out to stop him. He was placed in the psychiatric ward, sedated and restrained.

Tuesday, April 27, 1971 (18 days left). We haven't had any repeats of Sunday night's blast. Half our windows are still out, covered with plywood and tape, but that doesn't seal them completely. Mosquitoes are eating us alive tonight. It's very dark in the ward and I realize how much I've come to depend on the street light just outside the window for enough light to make rounds. Tonight I make them with just the small circle of light from a flashlight to guide me.

After we have gotten most of the work done and come back from midnight chow, I am sitting with my feet on the desk, reading a book. The corpsman says, "I don't want to bother you, Captain, but there's a large rat under the medicine cabinet." I very quietly close my book, get up, go out the door and don't stop until I reach the Emergency Room, from which I call the corpsman and tell him I'm not coming back to the ward until he gets rid of the rat. I can stand mortar attacks and Viet Cong sappers, but not rats.

Wednesday, April 28, 1971 (17 days left). This is the second time this month that I feel really foolish. We've been pretty unsettled here, with the wards combining, then the ammo dump blowing up—to say nothing of the rat—so maybe I haven't been as observant as I should have been. I should have discovered what was happening earlier.

The patients who are ambulatory spend a lot of time down in the Red Cross room or sitting out on the balconies smoking and talking. We're usually so busy with the really serious patients that we don't notice who comes and goes. There has been this one patient who I haven't seen for the past two nights. He isn't on the ward during the early part of the evening and by the time I get back from settling the other ward, he's asleep in bed with the covers pulled up over him.

At least that's what I think has been happening. I notice on his chart that he hasn't had his temperature taken the past few evenings and that the nurses during the day have charted that he has been in the Red Cross rec room all day. I think I should check him over, just for form sake. So tonight when I come back from settling the other ward I go over and put my hand on what I think is his shoulder. Only it isn't. It's a pile of several pillows arranged to look like a body under the covers and his buddy in the next bed looks very uncomfortable.

I call the sergeant on duty and tell him we have a missing patient. By the time he arrives it's almost midnight and the whole ward is awake. His buddy finally admits that the patient went absent without leave about three days ago and he's been covering up for him: signing him out to the Red Cross every day, arranging the pillows in the bed every evening.

What a joke on us. I'd feel even worse if it had been played just on me, but there are at least two day shifts that didn't figure out what was going on either.

Kris is still in the psychiatric ward. The nurses can't let any of us in to see him, doctor's orders. They are going to send him back to the States. I can't believe it happened so fast. He was laughing and joking with us the afternoon before the explosions. He was so calm then. Did I miss something? Should I have seen something in his behaviour that would have told us he was about to break?

❀ 📖 ❀

Calgary, Alberta. About six months later I was walking down the hall at Womack Army Hospital and Kris passed me. We walked past each other, nodded and said, "Hi, Kris." "Hi, Sharon." as if we'd seen each other regularly. We walked a couple of steps past each other, realized at the same instant that the last time we'd seen each other had been months before half-way around the world, turned and leapt into each others arms for a hug. He was doing well, had had several months of counseling, and was just about to be discharged from the Army. I asked him about his vision. His voice became very low and quiet. "I had it. I know I did. I just don't talk about it any more."

❀ 📖 ❀

Friday, April 30, 1971 (14 days left). John has gone away. I haven't seen him in months, don't even know if he is still in town, which is a shame. We drifted apart, found other interests and stopped seeing each other. I am still curious about many of the things we talked about. His New Zealand military background is very different from my American background. I don't know what the differences are, but I have been certain there are differences between the British tradition and the American tradition ever since I saw those graves in Thailand. John knows about the art of war, I've only had experience in the practice of war. His war was long enough ago that he has some perspective on what he did and what the war was all about. I'm too close right now for that kind of perspective.

❀ 📖 ❀

Calgary, Alberta. I have continued to be curious about the difference between the British military experience and the American one. Recently I read a book about the depiction of the soldier in Victorian English art. At one point the author writes

> "The army partook of the aura of glory created around the notion of empire by press and politicians. Popular illustrated journals particularly represented solders as bold conquerors, subduing 'savages' for their own and England's good. The middle-class construction of 'Tommy Atkins' was thus extended into the role of imperial warrior.

In the post-Crimean era the common soldier was regarded as honest, Christian, instinctively moral, however ignorant and rough." (Hichberger, Joan.W.M. *Images of the Army: The Military in British Art,* 1815-1914. Manchester: Manchester Press, 1988, p.78.)

That quote was in a chapter about Elizabeth Thompson, Lady Butler, who painted military pictures in the last half of the eighteenth century. Her sister was the poet Alice Meynell, a woman strongly anti-imperialist in her views. She comments on her sister's style of painting:

"Art has rightly nothing to do with the history of war, it should be concerned only with its anecdotes. Art should go into the byways of battle. It must love the soldier and love him individually, not in battalions." (Alice Meynell, *Magazine of Art*, 1879, p. 209 quoted in Hichberger, p. 83.)

What I learned in Viet Nam was to love the soldier, what remained to fascinate me was the idea of the soldier as an individual. What I did in Viet Nam was to go into the byways of battle. I finally understood that that's what John knew that I didn't. He never talked about tactics or strategy. He remembered individual soldiers that served with him. I hoped, as my tour came to an end in Viet Nam, that I would grow up to remember as John remembered. I did.

❀ ⚐ ❀

1971 MAY 1971

Saturday, May 1, 1971 (14 days left). I am taken out for a farewell dinner tonight at the Seaman's Club. I don't know why the Navy always seems to have better food that the Army. Maybe it's just the pleasure of eating somewhere else than in our mess hall. In any case, the shrimp and rice is delicious. Our host, Dr. G., is at his wittiest and keeps everyone rolling with stories about when he was an intern. The non-medical people at the table can't believe the stories, which completely shatter any faith they have in the medical profession.

Dr. G. is a lovely, kind man. He wants to be a pediatrician when he goes back to the States and he's building up quite a pediatric practice here. Somehow the missionaries always know when he is in the Emergency Room and they bring the children to him. He's so gentle with kids.

Tuesday, May 4, 1971 (11 days left). Tonight the whole hospital is really quiet. I am so bored on the ward that I take my break with Phil in the Emergency Room, just looking for a little excitement. The Emergency Room don't have any patients either, so Dr. G. decides to have some fun. He bandages Phil up so his head and face are covered and pours Tetracycline syrup over the bandages. Tetracycline is a thick red liquid that looks like dried blood. Then he calls Intensive Care, which has one non-critical patient; the staff there are also trying to decide how to pass the time.

Dr. G. says, "This is Emergency Room. We have an expectant patient here, severe head injury, no neuro signs. He can't last more than an hour. Just put him in the back of the room, put a screen around him and let me know when he dies and I'll come and pronounce him."

We wheel in Phil in on a stretcher and put him in the back of the Intensive Care. Then we go back to the Emergency Room, laughing our heads off. Phil has been told to wait until most of the nurses go to midnight chow and the remaining nurse is busy with the real patient, then sneak out. Emergency Room gets this frantic call about fifteen minutes after midnight.

"This is I.C.U. That patient with the head injury is gone."

"Okay, I'll come and pronounce him."

"No, he's gone. GONE. As in not here. He walked out."

"That's impossible. How could a comatose patient walk out? What are you people doing over there?" Meanwhile, Dr. G. is killing himself laughing. He lets the nurses squirm about half an hour before telling them about the joke.

Wednesday, May 5, 1971 (10 days left). Phil and I decide to play our own practical joke today. There is a fake set of orders, called The Military Way to Die that makes the rounds every couple of years. I saw it first at Ft. Riley and someone has a copy here. It says things like anyone wanting to die on duty has to request permission a month in advance and that anyone not dying at attention will be fined. Phil and I manage to get the keys to the Chief Nurse's office and use the typewriter in there to retype it so the thing looks just like other orders that come from Administration, then we post it on the main bulletin board. Everyone is required to sign a sheet indicating they have read what's on the bulletin board. There is half a page of signatures before the Chief Nurse actually reads what is on the board and takes it down. Boy, is she mad.

I don't know what's gotten into me. I never used to play practical jokes like this.

Friday, May 7, 1971 (8 days left). It is raining hard tonight, the hardest I have seen it rain since the typhoon was off the coast in March. I sit in the shadows of the overhanging roofs behind a closed ward and cry as hard as it is raining. I don't want to leave. I don't want to give up what I have here and, at the same time, I know I have to leave or go crazy.

Saturday, May 8, 1971 (7 days left). I haven't had time to write much lately because I've been too busy falling in love. This is so crazy, so sudden that I hardly know where to start.

Phil and I have known each other for several months, but we seem to have noticed each other for the first time a couple of weeks ago when the ammo dump was blown up. Somehow we just latched on to each other after that night and we've hardly let go of each other since.

Can I be in love? I think I'been in love before but never like this. Before I always had a sense of urgency, as if the whole relationship was so intense I had to be with the other person or at least think about them all of the time. It's different with Phil. I love every minute we are together, but I feel as if there will be a lot of time for us in the future.

We both know there is no use making any definite plans until he comes home next February. And yet, we catch ourselves talking about dishes and furniture and details of how our life together will be. His R & R isn't until November. He wants to come back to the States to see me then, but I tell him he should go some place like Thailand that he might never get a chance to see again.

Terri thinks we are a scream together. I have put up with so much of her talk about what at the time seemed to me all of the insignificant things she and Bill find to discuss. Now she says it's a fair turn-around that I talk about every detail of what Phil said, what we did today.

We are making so many plans without knowing if they will come to pass or not. He wants me to marry him and I don't know what to do. Maybe we should just start with a long engagement. At least that will give us time to learn about one another. I can't believe this is happening with just a week left in Viet Nam! What rotten timing. Why didn't it happen months ago, so we could have had more time together? There is so much we have to learn about one another. How are we going to manage with him here and me at Ft. Bragg? This is a whole new world for me.

Sunday, May 9, 1971 (6 days left). My last day of work and the Army certainly doesn't get its money's worth out of me today. All I do is day dream.

Phil has to go north today to get paid and I feel as if a pail of ice water has been thrown on me when he tells me. I want him to stay here, at least until I leave. But he can't and we say goodbye at the airport. He says he will try to get back before I leave, but neither of us believes it will work our that way.

Monday, May 10, 1971 (5 days left). Once again I go through the Army ritual called out processing. I have a typed, two-page list of places to go. At each place some clerk signs my sheet. Yes, I have closed out my bank account. No, I have no books out of the USO library. Yes, my shot record is up to date. Yes, I have turned in my flak jacket, helmet and gas mask. No, I don't have an outstanding bill at the Officer's Club. One by one the ties that hold me here are cut. I have a lot of regrets: things I wanted to do better, things I think I did poorly. But it is over, finally over! I feel ready to go home.

Tuesday, May 11, 1971 (4 days left). I am at loose ends, walking from place to place, clearing, no longer having a place here, having no other place to go. The Colonel gives me a Bronze Star today. It is no big deal. It isn't like the Bronze Star for Valour. This one is for service and all of the nurses and doctors get one. Still, it is rather nice. If I hadn't gotten one, I'd have felt like a child who comes home from a party without a favour.

Citation
United States Army Viet Nam

BY DIRECTION OF THE PRESIDENT
THE BRONZE STAR MEDAL
IS PRESENTED TO
CAPTAIN SHARON M. GRANT, ARMY NURSE CORPS, U.S.A.

Who distinguished herself by meritorious service in connection with military operations against a hostile force in the Republic of Viet Nam. During the period May 1970 to May 1971. She consistently demonstrated exemplary professionalism and initiative in obtaining outstanding results. Her rapid assessment and solution of the problems inherent in a combat environment greatly enhanced the allied effectiveness against a determined and aggressive enemy. Energetically applying her sound judgment and extensive knowledge, she has contributed materially to the successful accomplishment of the United States mission in the Republic of Viet Nam. Her loyalty, diligence and devotion to duty were in keeping with the highest traditions of the military service and reflect great credit upon herself and the United States Army.

It doesn't mean anything. Everyone gets one something like that. But I'm proud of what I've been able to be here. No medal can equal that.

Wednesday, May 12, 1971. (3 days left). Bill and Terri see me off at the airport today. I make her promise to look after Phil.

In my oldest pair of fatigues and dirty boonie hat, I travel all day from Qui Nhon to Cam Ran Bay. Ron S. and Ed P., Special Forces I knew in Pleiku, are stationed near Cam Ran Bay. I hitchhike out to see them. They are surprised and we just grab each other in a three-way hug. I have supper with them and then, at about 2200 hours, they take me to the out-processing station.

They form an honour guard. Ed is on one side of me, Ron on the other, both in jungle fatigues and Green Berets. One carries a CAR-15 Semi-automatic and the other a Thompson sub-machine gun. They march me into the sergeant and present me to him.

Ron says, "This woman is one of us. You take good care of her or all Special Forces will be down your neck."

Then they salute and I return the salute. They turned sharply and march out the door.

I think we have surprised even the out-processing sergeant, who has probably seen just about everything.

❀ ❦ ❀

Calgary, Alberta. Phil and I never married. We quickly discovered that once we were in different places, we had different interests. Letters didn't work in the same way being in the same place had worked. We broke off our engagement shortly after I came back to the States. In the hindsight of twenty years our intense passion is funny. We were both desperate for someone. What we were going through was a reaction to almost having been blown up when the ammo dump exploded. We learned later that there were sappers on the perimeter that night and that they were planning to attack the air base by coming in the wire at the hospital because they thought it was the weakest part of the perimeter. We each had a sense that the other was in danger that night and we wanted to protect one another. Thank goodness we did fall into each other's arms when I had only a week left in Qui Nhon. Otherwise, we might have made a serious mistake by getting married.

Bill and Terri, on the other hand, did last. They have now been married almost a quarter of a century. We still write and phone one another and, in July 1991, they came from Florida to Alberta to attend my wedding.

❀ ❦ ❀

Thursday, May 13, 1971. (2 days left). I hate military bureaucracy! It is so hot in Cam Ran Bay: with the heat coming off the white sand, it must be 110 degrees F. in the shade. All I want to do is sit in the air-conditioned Officer's Club and drink iced tea. Then some sergeant at the airfield says I can't go home until I have the correct insignia. I don't have silver Captain's bars because the only thing I've worn since my promotion is my fatigues, which have the bars embroidered on small patches.

So I go over to the Post Exchange to buy bars. They are out of them and the next shipment isn't due for a week or two! Two weeks! I'll die in the heat by then. Plus my family is expecting to meet me in New Orleans in a couple of days. I explain all of this to the sergeant, who is remarkably uninterested. So I do what I have to do. One of the guys in Pleiku taught me to finger insignia: distract a person by looking straight into their eyes and talking to them, while lifting their collar badge. It's the way I obtained most of the unit crests on my boonie hat. I always show the crest to the guy after I've lifted it, in case it has some special meaning for him. He usually laughs and tells me to keep it. So I go over to the Officers' Club and steal three sets of Captain's bars off different officers. Then I go back to the sergeant with shiny silver bars on my shoulders. I'm manifested on a plane for 2100 hours tomorrow.

Friday, May 14, 1971. (DEROS: Date Estimated Return from Overseas Service) I pack everything I can into my one duffel bag and leave my fatigues and combat boots in a corner of my room at the Transient Officer's quarters. The Army can do what it wants with them. If they want me to go to another war, they will just have to issue me more clothing. It's pretty decrepit by now, full of stains and tears. I do regret leaving the combat boots behind. They have worked themselves around to being really comfortable. But I want to limit myself to one duffel bag and they just won't fit.

It's dark when we leave and there is a hot breeze blowing from the sea. The freedom bird takes off the runway at 2130. Alice D., a nurse who worked in surgery in Pleiku, is on the plane with me along with a hundred and fifty men. All the way down the runway I think, "Please, God, don't let the plane crash on take-off." I am so close to going home. When the plane is airborne, all of us on the plane cheer, and most of us cry. The stewardesses serve champagne.

It is a long night flight. We have one stopover in Tokyo at about three in the morning. The airport is filled with wives and children and the children are cranky from lack of sleep. I buy some chopsticks and one final piece of camera equipment at the duty-free shop there. As we are taking off, I see the sun rise over Tokyo.

The flight takes twenty-two hours. Because of crossing the international dateline our watches show us arriving in Seattle only a half hour after we left Viet Nam. It is a dark, cold night and I shiver in my light summer uniform. Next to the terminal is a huge American flag, spot lit against the night. I want to kiss American soil because I'm so happy to be home, but I restrain myself.

Then we are inside the terminal. Everything is closed, even the U.S.O. room. For the first time in a year, I am on my own. Some of the people on the plane have relatives or friends who live close enough to meet them. We stand in a swirl of tears, flowers, people crying and hugging.

Alice has to hurry to make connections to her plane home. I hug her one last time and she is gone. My plane doesn't leave until tomorrow morning and I am trying to decide what to do, figure how much money I have left after buying the camera equipment in Japan. I assumed I could get money changed when I got here and I don't have much with me. No one is there to tell me where my baggage is, how to get a cab, where hotels are, where I can get something to eat, when to catch my plane home. I am completely on my own.

I finally find my duffel bag, circling by itself on the carrier. There is a Spec-4 there who has just retrieved his bag and is looking at a map of Seattle posted on the wall.

"Do you know Seattle?" He asks. "I'm trying to figure how to get to the YMCA."

"Are you waiting for a plane, too?"

"Not 'til tomorrow."

"Me, too. I didn't really bring enough money with me for a hotel."

"Neither did I."

"Where are you coming from?"

"Qui Nhon. How about you?"

"The delta. Are you staying in?"

"Yes. I'm going to Ft. Bragg."

"I'm getting out."

"Look, if you don't think this is an improper offer, we can share a hotel room. Each pay half, you know."

So we introduce ourselves and go off to find a cab and a hotel room, one with twin beds. The next morning he goes his way and I go mine. By late evening I am back at the airport in New Orleans and my family is there to meet me.

❀ ꇐ ❀

Calgary, Alberta.   *Dream*

The light is golden yellow, billowing out of clouds in the background, almost too bright. Almost, just on the edge of destroying the picture's beauty and making it garish. The man's face is faintly representative of the traditional Christ figure, he has a long brown flowing hair and beard. His eyes are closed, his head relaxed in perfect balance, his features serene. His arms are out at shoulder height, extended, with fine muscle detail. He holds his hand sculptured into a ballet position.

He is naked. All of his muscles are finely drawn; he could be a perfect anatomy representation. There are fine golden hairs on his

legs. There is a row of fine, white feathers flowing from his arms
and across his shoulders, like the feather sticks some Indians use
for dances, only these come from his body. His right foot is on a
balance beam, the kind used in gyms, light-coloured wood, and the
wood highlights the golden light behind him. His feet are posi-
tioned so that his leg muscles are clearly defined. I cannot see his
balls because the position of his left leg hides them, but I know that
he is a strong man. He is perfectly relaxed. He enjoys his practice
on the beam. There is no one else around, perhaps not even a hint
of another creature. He is simply alone in the clouds, practicing in
the light. He has no name; he is the warrior-god.

When I had this dream I was in university and had been studying archetypes,
especially on the archetype of the goddess who heals the wounded god. I had
another dream, shortly after this one, of standing beside a stone altar where the
wounded warrior-god lay. I had a knife in my hand and all I had to do to kill him
once and for all time was to plunge my knife into his chest. The warrior would
never rise again. I could stop the cycle. I didn't do it. I realized he was part of me
and that if I killed him, I would kill myself. There are things I did in Viet Nam
and afterwards that were connected with Viet Nam that I don't like about myself.
But they are part of me. If I kill them, I kill myself.

War creates a beauty almost too bright to endure. When I desired that beauty
I lived on the edge of destroying myself. When war was beautiful everything in
life seemed perfectly balanced, the true soldier was serene in the midst of chaos.
I danced to the war's rhythm. Parts of the dance were spiritual, mystic, binding
me in close connections to other soldiers. But unlike the warrior-god who was
perfectly relaxed while practicing war alone in the clouds, I found war an all-too-
human condition. The distance between beauty and horror was too narrow, the
beam I balanced on too slippery.

War kills; those who continued to practice war die. Even in Viet Nam I under-
stood this: "There is a legend that if you stay long enough in Special Forces you
acquire four things: a gold Rolex watch, a star-sapphire ring, a case of the clap
and a divorce. Some are already alcoholics. Some are burned out on adrenalin.
Some have a wife from a second or third or fourth marriage back in the States. It
seems that the smart ones, the lucky ones, get out of the business of killing and
go back to other careers, families, homes." I was not a god, practicing my art
alone in the clouds; I wasn't a goddess who stood beside the wounded god. I was
a human, who took a chance on not slipping into horror in order to be able to
experience perfect balance on the beam. Those of us who were fortunate walked
e length of the beam and then got off.

❀ ⌶ ❀

Acknowledgements

There are many people to thank for this book: Nelljean McConeghy for showing me I could write poetry, Jeff Rackham for teaching me about writing and about archetypes, Bob for opening his door and his heart to me during the rough periods, Lynda Van Devanter and Joan Furey for first publishing the poems, Candas Jane Dorsey for editing and continued support, Larry Pratt and the people at The Books Collective for publishing this work.

A special thanks to the Canada Council. Without their Explorations Grant I would never have been able to print almost a thousand photographs that I took while I was in Viet Nam.

Finally, and most especially, thanks to my husband, Ken, for all the support and practical help he provided.